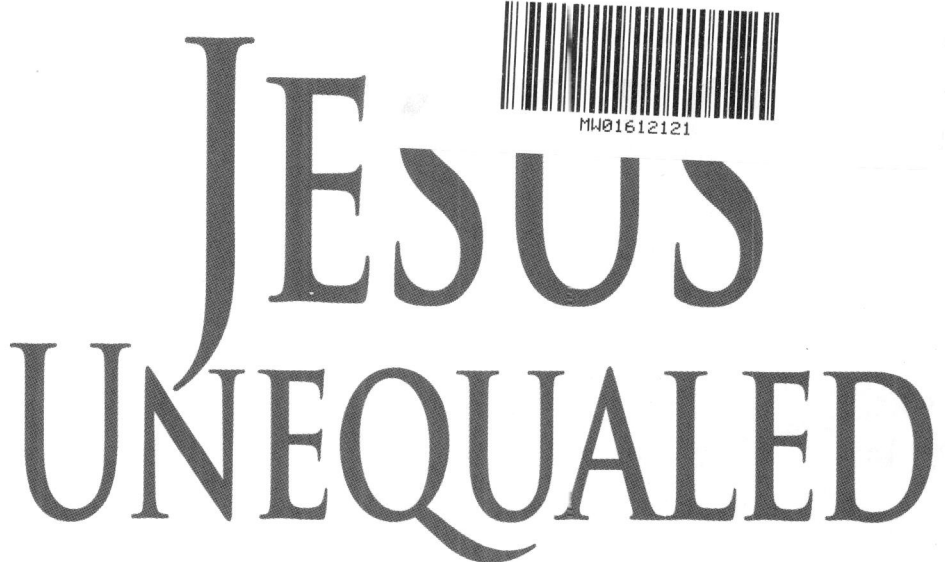

JESUS UNEQUALED

An Exposition of Colossians

"Christ is all and in all"
—Colossians 3:11

G. Steve Kinnard

Jesus Unequaled

An Exposition of Colossians

© 2013 by G. Steve Kinnard

Printed in the United States of America

ISBN: 978-1-939086-58-7

Unless otherwise indicated, all Scripture references are from the *Holy Bible*, New International Version, copyright 1973, 1978, 1984 by the International Bible Society. Used by permission of Zondervan Bible Publishers.

Book interior design: Toney C. Mulhollan
Cover design: Toney C. Mulhollan

About the author: Dr. G. Steve Kinnard has served the New York City Church of Christ as an evangelist and teacher for thirty years. He has written over a dozen books including *Like a Tree Planted by Streams of Water*, *The Way of the Heart* and *King Jesus*. He received his undergraduate degree at Freed-Hardeman College and his Master of Divinity with Languages from Southeastern Baptist Theological Seminary. He completed his Doctor of Ministry degree at Drew University. He serves as  adjunct professor of Bible at Lincoln Christian University. Steve and his wife, Leigh, live in Rockland County, New York.

 ILLUMINATION PUBLISHERS

www.ipibooks.com
6010 Pinecreek Ridge Court
Spring, Texas 77379-2513, USA

Table of Contents

Dedication

To our son

Daniel Steven Kinnard

A Mighty Warrior

Who like Arthur of old
Pulled the sword from the stone
And now wields God's sword
To change the world

Preface

Why read a commentary? Hopefully, the commentator has spent more hours than you have exploring the work you wish to understand and can give you enlightenment as to the meaning of the text.

The commentator has two tasks. The first is to understand what the text meant to the original audience. To achieve this goal, the researcher must delve into the original language of the text and the historical setting of the original audience. Once this is accomplished, the writer can move on to the second task.

The commentator's second task is to make the text meaningful to his or her present-day audience. Too many commentaries accomplish the first task, but fail in the second. It is the goal of this commentary to accomplish both. We will explore the meaning of the text in its original setting—mid-first-century Colossae. But we will also ask what the text means to us today.

Why this particular commentary on Colossians? There are many excellent commentaries on this letter of Paul (see the Bibliography at the end of this book for a list). I've read many of them from cover to cover in preparation for this book. So why read this commentary over or alongside one of the others? Perhaps because of my perspective? I come from the Restoration Movement begun by Barton W. Stone and Alexander Campbell in the early nineteenth century in the United States. I also am part of the Discipling Movement (which began in the late 1960s in the US) within the Restoration Movement. Therefore, as I approach the second task of the commentator, I'm going to ask what the book of Colossians has to say to the current state of the Restoration Movement and to Discipling churches within that movement. That's what I bring to this commentary that other commentators don't. Hopefully you will find my unique perspective beneficial and enlightening.

I use my own translation of the Greek text of Colossians throughout this commentary. My translation is quoted after the Greek text for each section of the commentary. Quotations from the Greek New Testament are from *The Greek New Testament*, Fourth Revised Edition.[1] For comparison, the *The Holy Bible,* New International Version 1984 Edition[2] is included (NIV, 1984). All quotations outside of Colossians are from the NIV, unless otherwise noted.

Introductory Material

How to Study Colossians

Before we dive into the book of Colossians, let's begin with a few helpful hints on how to study a book of the Bible.

1. Pray.

Begin the study with prayer. Ask God to lead you to his truth through the study. Ask him to show you the exact themes he wants you to explore and to show you the ways your character can change to become more like Jesus through the study.

2. Read. Read. Read.

Read the book several times. This is easier for a shorter book like Colossians than it is for a longer book like Romans. I personally would read Colossians ten or twenty times before I ever opened a commentary on the book. Read it from several different translations. Each translation will give you a different way of hearing the book. As you read different translations, new ideas will jump off the page that you didn't see in other translations. You can also listen to the text being read on an audio device while you are driving to work or riding the bus.

3. Read the book out loud.

The books of the Bible were written to be read out loud and to be shared with an audience (many of whom could not read and therefore needed the book or letter to be read to them). Paul specifically directs that the letter of Colossians be read out loud to the church. In Colossians 4:16 he writes, *"After this letter has been read to you, see that it is also read in the church of the Laodiceans and that you in turn read the letter from Laodicea."* In reading the book out loud you will see the text with your eyes, sound out the text with your voice, and hear the text with your ears.

Read the letter out loud at your church service. In 1 Timothy 4:13 Paul directs Timothy, *"Until I come, devote yourself to the public reading of Scripture, to preaching and to teaching."* The public reading of Scripture has become the forgotten element of worship. Are we devoted to the public reading of Scripture? Since we are people of the Book who wish to restore New Testament Christianity, let's restore this element to our worship.

Imagine yourself as a believer in the church in Colossae when this letter was first received. Imagine that you were selected to read this letter to the church in Colossae for the first time. Now read the letter with the same reverence that you would if you were there in the first century.

4. Outline the book.

Write your own outline of the book. Understand its major flow. Notice how Paul in his letters begins with a theological exposition and then ends with practical application.

For a short book like Colossians, it is an easy exercise to outline the book. Don't skip this important step. Your ultimate goal is to know what major themes are discussed in each chapter.

5. Pick out verses you wish to memorize.

As you are reading the text, find the verses that you wish to memorize and begin to memorize them. Putting verses to memory will help you understand the flow of the book. It will also help you appreciate it in a greater way.

6. Get background information.

After you have spent time with the text alone, begin to explore other books that can help clarify the text for you. To understand the book of Colossians, you need to understand the early church in Colossae. Introductions to the New Testament can help here. Also a good study Bible is a great tool that will provide background material to the text.

What are you looking for here? You want to be able to answer these questions:

- Who wrote the book?
- To whom was the book written?
- From where was it written?
- When was it written?
- Why? What was the occasion on which it was written?
- Why? What is the purpose of the book?
- What is the major theme (or what are the major themes) of the book?
- In other words—The Five W's: Who? What? When? Where? Why?

7. Go through the book verse by verse.

Now you are ready for a verse-by-verse exposition of the text. Take a short section of the book and look at it closely. For example, Colossians 1:1–2 is the opening. Begin by looking at this passage phrase by phrase and then word by word. Understand the flow of the passage and see what is meant in each verse, phrase, and word. Do this on your own first. See if you can determine what Paul was saying to the original audience. After you have spent time with the passage alone, then go to other books and authors for help.

This is where a good commentary comes in. A commentary not only clarifies the text phrase by phrase and word by word, but a good one can teach you how to study the Bible because you are watching the commentator study the text as you read his or her work.

8. Get practical with the study.

Each study should end by you asking yourself: What am I going to change today as a result of this study? If you don't go there, then what is point of the study? End with a goal of what you want to do as a result of the study. Pray for God to help you with that goal. The study should begin and end with prayer.

> **Practical Exercise:** Read through Colossians several times. Use various translations. At least once, read the letter out loud.

Why Colossians?

Why engage in this study of Colossians? Interestingly, although this is a short and often overlooked book in the New Testament, NT scholar William Barclay, who wrote a commentary on every book in the New Testament, said of Colossians, "There is no more difficult book in the New Testament."[3] Well, that piques my interest. I enjoy a challenge. So if this book is a "difficult book," then that's one reason for studying it. But, admittedly, it's probably not the best reason for studying Colossians.

Perhaps we should study it because it is a book that isn't studied that often. Ernest D. Martin in his commentary of Colossians states:

> For many people, memorizing the names of the New Testament books involved the rote mastery of the sequence: Galatians, Ephesians, Philippians, Colossians. Colossians is the shortest of the four and for many persons the least familiar. However, one quickly discovers that Colossians is high-voltage material.[4]

Okay, it's not studied that often. But do we really want to take the time to study the book just because it isn't studied often? Perhaps Martin's last comment is a more compelling reason to study Colossians: "Colossians is high-voltage material."

I believe the best reason for studying Colossians is this: Its major theme is the supremacy of Christ, and we need to focus on Jesus in order to make sure we don't focus elsewhere. Douglas Moo writes:

> The christological teaching of Colossians...certainly does move beyond what we find in the other Pauline letters. In none of the other letters is the cosmic significance of Christ so clearly or consistently portrayed. He is the "image of the invisible God" (1:15), the one through whom God created all things (1:16), and the one through whom he has reconciled all things (1:20). He is the head of every spiritual power (2:10; cf. 2:15; 1:16, 20). "All the fullness"—the fullness of God himself—has come to dwell in him (1:19; 2:9).... To be sure, the universal supremacy of Christ is not so clearly taught in any other letter of Paul.[5]

If Moo is correct and no other letter of Paul teaches the universal supremacy of Christ as clearly as does Colossians, then that alone is reason to dive into this letter. By reading it, we can fall more deeply in love with Christ.

But, as my good friend, Mike Taliaferro, is known to quip, "That's not all; there's more besides." Colossians contains many other important themes that deserve our attention. Richard R. Melick in his commentary on Colossians writes:

> This little epistle contains distinctive teachings about the person and work of Christ, about Christian living and relationships, and about Paul's conception of his ministry. Studying the epistle is an adventure in Christian theology. It reveals Pauline thought and authentic Christian living. The pages of the text are alive with relevance and challenge the reader to a more reflective and informed faith.[6]

See, "there is more besides." So let's approach this study of Colossians with great enthusiasm understanding there is much that can be gained from a study of this "difficult book."

What do we readily know of Colossians?

- Written by Paul
- One of four prison epistles
- Four chapters long
- Talks about the supremacy of Christ
- Speaks against false doctrine
- Has a nice section on the family in chapter 3
- Begins with theological teaching and ends with practical instruction

Hopefully, after studying through the book of Colossians, we will know more interesting facts and ideas about the book.

Now, let's explore the background of Colossians by answering some basic questions: Who? To whom? From where? When? Why?

Then we will move on to discuss some of the major and minor themes covered by Paul in his letter.

Background Material

Who? Paul.

The apostle Paul wrote the letter to the Colossians, to a church that he probably never visited (2:1). This was a church that was begun by his fellow servant in the ministry, Epaphras. I will write about the occasion for writing the letter later.

More than a few scholars doubt Paul's authorship of the book, but to throw doubt on the Pauline authorship is a recent development in scholarship. New Testament scholar Donald Guthrie writes, "There is no shred of evidence that the Pauline authorship of the whole or any part of this epistle was ever disputed until the nineteenth century."[7]

Some scholars posit that the style of writing and the theology of the letter don't suit Paul. Some say the heresy attacked in the book is second-century gnosticism (thus too late for Paul's authorship). But these reasons for doubting Pauline authorship are mere conjecture and don't hold weight. Paul's style and vocabulary shift from letter to letter depending on his audience. Plus, if Paul used a different amanuensis (scribe) for various letters, then that would account for changes in style.

Style arguments are always highly subjective. Authors change style all the time. Just look at the different styles of the writings of one of the greatest authors of the twentieth century, J.R.R. Tolkien. Tolkien used three different styles in his three major works: *The Hobbit, The Lord of the Rings,* and *The Silmarrillion.* All three works are vastly different stylistically. *The Hobbit* is a children's book and reflects the style of children's literature. *The Lord of the Rings* is an epic narrative written for adults, and its style reflects high fantasy writing at its best. *The Silmarrillion* is a book of mythic tales about the creation and early history of Middle Earth. It reflects the style of mythic literature. Three distinct works with three distinct styles from one author. There is no reason to reject the Pauline authorship of Colossians based on stylistic difference from his earlier works.

What about the theological differences? Arguments based on theological differences are usually built on silence (on what Paul didn't say that the scholar believes Paul should have said). These types of arguments are built on straw. For example, those who say the heresy the letter opposes is second-century gnosticism are attacking the authorship of Paul based on supposition that can't be proven. In fact, most scholars state that the heresy attacked by the letter clearly isn't second-century gnosticism, but an earlier heresy that had some kinship with gnosticism (for example, ascetic practices). The exact content of this heresy will be discussed later.

There is no valid reason to doubt Pauline authorship of the book. The letter was received into the canon as Pauline, accepted into the early church as Pauline, and purports to be Pauline. The book ends with Paul stating, *"I, Paul, write this greeting in my own hand"* (4:18). Enough said.[8] The book was written by Paul.

To Whom? Colossae.[9]

> Colossae was the least important church to which any epistle of St. Paul was addressed.[10]
>
> —J.B. Lightfoot, NT scholar

Map of Asia Minor. Notice the Tri-City Area of Hierapolis, Laodicea, and Colossae.[11]

Colossae was part of a tri-city region in the Lycus Valley, which is located in south central Turkey today. The other two cities in this region were Laodicea and Hierapolis. Laodicea was mentioned as one of the seven churches of Asia Minor in Revelation 3. It had the dubious distinction of being the "lukewarm" church.

Colossae was located 100 miles (161 kilometers) east of Ephesus and 135 miles (218 kilometers) west of Pisidian Antioch. This location on the east-west corridor of central Asia Minor led to Colossae becoming a thriving community as early as 485. In 480, Herodotus called it a "great city of Phrygia." In 401 BC Xenophon calls Colossae, "a city inhabited and prosperous and great."

A mixture of Jews and Greeks made up the population of Colossae in the first century (some 11,000 Jews by AD 62). Concerning the people of Colossae, Melick writes:

> The cities had a mixed population. The natives were Phrygian. Because of the military and commercial heritage of the valley, however, Greeks may have settled in the area during the Greek period of dominance. To this were added Jews of the Diaspora, Romans involved in politics, and various ethnic groups drawn by commercial interests. The exact population mixture of Colossae during this time is unknown. From the epistle, both Jews and Gentiles lived there and became part of the church.[12]

This mixture of people in the city and the location of Colossae on a well-travelled highway led to an amalgam of religious and philosophical beliefs existing in the city. In his commentary on Colossians, Douglas J. Moo writes:

> The diversity of population and exposure to the latest ideas via travelers on its major highway meant that Colossae was a place where many different religious and philosophical viewpoints thrived and probably mixed together. This diversity helps explain the apparently syncretistic religious movement that was affecting the Colossian Christians and that gave rise to the letter. At the same time, as we will see below, this diversity makes it notoriously difficult to pin down the exact contours of this movement.[13]

The Lycus Valley was made of dark volcanic soil, which provided good fields for sheep to graze. Thus a nice wool industry grew around Colossae. The city was known for a deep-red-colored wool called Colossian wool. William Hendriksen writes:

> Hence, on the rich meadows of the Lycus Valley grazed great flocks of sheep, bringing riches to the manufacturers of garments. This was all the more true because the waters of this valley were impregnated with chalky deposits. Now although these chalk-formations rendered parts of *the soil* barren, *the chalky waters* were just right for the purpose of dyeing cloth. This was an additional reason why the garment-industry flourished here.[14]

In the first century, Colossae was a city on the decline. About twenty years before Paul, Strabo noted that the city of Colossae was a "small town." Colossae was one of the less impressive cities of the first century to receive a letter from Paul. Martin writes:

> In pre-Christian times Colossae was the most prominent of the three Lycus Valley cities. Colossae is listed in the annals of Herodotus and Xenophon (both in the fifth century B.C.) as being a large, prosperous city. However, in Roman and Greek times Laodicea and Hierapolis surpassed Colossae in size and significance. Colossae may have been one of the least of the cities in which a church received a letter from Paul.[15]

If you are from New York City, then Colossae would have been like Boston or Philadelphia, not a very important city at all (I'm just kidding. Okay, I'm a little bit serious).

And it is very likely that Colossae didn't have very long to contemplate the letter that Paul sent to the church there. Martin writes:

> A major quake in A.D. 60–61 is known to have destroyed Laodicea. Less explicit evidence implies that Colossae and Hierapolis were also devastated at the same time. Laodicea and Hierapolis were soon rebuilt, but Colossae apparently was left in ruins, since later historical records do not mention it.[16]

The present day site of Colossae is uninhabited and unexcavated. Paul's letter must have made an impact on the church in Colossae, but the disciples never knew that their lives would soon be devastated by a major earthquake that would destroy their city within months after receiving Paul's correspondence. We never know what the future holds for us. Therefore, we must live every day to the fullest.

Paul was in prison when he wrote the letter to the Colossians. It was a letter written to a small church in an undistinguished town. Why did Paul take the time to write to a church he did not plant, a group he never visited, in a town that, to be honest, wasn't all that important? Two reasons: (1) For Paul, each local church was God's church filled with God's people and because of that was important. God called Paul to be an apostle to the Gentiles; therefore, in a special way, all the Gentile churches were under Paul's care. (2) Epaphras' report about the church in Colossae moved Paul's heart, so Paul sent the letter to encourage the church. This demonstrates the importance of relationships.

Paul wasn't as concerned about the distinction or size of a church as we sometimes are today. The church at Colossae was not a "pillar church." In that region of the world the pillar churches would have been Ephesus or Pisidian Antioch or Laodicea. "Pillar church" wasn't a part of Paul's vocabulary. He cared about every church. Here he sends a letter to a smaller church in an undistinguished city that was on the decline and didn't survive very long after receiving the letter. But the letter remains to show us Paul's love for the church universal.

Epaphras, not Paul, is given credit for bringing the gospel to Colossae (Colossians 1:7). Most likely, Paul never visited the church, but he knew many people in the congregation there. How do we take the reference in 2:1 where Paul mentions people who had not seen him "face to face" (NRSV)? This could mean new Christians who came into the church after Paul's visit (a visit never recorded in Acts). Or it could mean that Paul never visited the church in Colossians. I am of the second opinion.

Here is a very possible scenario: Paul was in Ephesus for three years (AD 53–56). Around that time, Epaphras, a native of Colossae, became a fellow servant of Paul. Epaphras then introduced the gospel to Colossae and to the tri-city area in the Lycus Valley. Peter T. O'Brien writes:

> And it is to be inferred from the references to Epaphras in the letter (1:7, 8; 4:12, 13) that the congregations founded in these three cities were the fruit of his evangelistic endeavor. He was a native of Colossae (at 4:12 he is described as "one of you") through whom the Colossians had learned the truth of the gospel (1:7).[17]

Martin writes:

> All this means that when this letter was written, the church at Colossae was probably not more than about eight years old, and perhaps younger. If, as the evidence suggests, life in Colossae came to an end with the major earthquake in A.D. 60–61, the congregation there was rather short-lived. Yet out of this small chapter in the story of the spread of the gospel, a letter has been preserved that is of immense value and interest for the Christian church universal.[18]

When? AD 60.

If Paul was in prison in Rome between AD 60 and 62, then the letter should be dated during this time. If the earthquake hit in AD 60 or 61, then a good date for the writing and sending of the letter would be AD 60.

From Where? Prison.

This is one of the four prison letters of Paul. That cannot be disputed. But which imprisonment? Paul was imprisoned three times or four or five or six...? Moo writes:

> The book of Acts refers explicitly to three imprisonments of Paul: overnight in Philippi (16:19–34); for two years in Caesarea (23:23–26:32; cf. 24:27); and for two years in Rome (28:11–31;

15

cf. v. 30). But Paul's claim that he had "been in prisons" very frequently (2 Cor. 11:23) implies that he was imprisoned more often
than on these three occasions.[18]

He was imprisoned for two years in Caesarea Maritima (Caesarea by the Sea in Judea). He was then taken to Rome and kept in house arrest there. Most scholars believe that he was released and later recaptured, imprisoned, and executed in Rome while Emperor Nero reigned (AD 54–68). Some scholars also believe that Paul was imprisoned in Ephesus at one point (although this is never mentioned in Acts or Paul's writings). The suggested dates of these imprisonments are: Ephesus (c. AD 52–55), Caesarea (c. AD 57–59), house arrest in Rome (c. AD 60–62), and possible final imprisonment in Rome (c. AD 67–68).[19]

So, where was Paul when he wrote to the church in Colossae? Most scholars believe Paul was under house arrest in Rome (c. AD 60–62). Paul could have written this letter early in his imprisonment and before the earthquake in the Lycus Valley. Since Paul was in house arrest, he had the "freedom" to receive visitors and to write letters. Acts states, *"For two whole years Paul stayed there in his own rented house and welcomed all who came to see him. He proclaimed the kingdom of God and taught about the Lord Jesus Christ—with all boldness and without hindrance!"* (Acts 28:30–31). It is unlikely that while imprisoned in Caesarea Paul was afforded such luxury. So the most likely date and place of writing the letter to the Colossians is Rome while Paul was imprisoned there from AD 60 to 62.

Why? What was the occasion on which it was written?

Why would Paul write a letter to a church he did not plant and had never visited? As mentioned above, for two reasons:

1. Paul considered himself the apostle to the Gentiles. That being the case, the care of the church in Colossae fell under his purview.

2. Paul's fellow servant and minister was Epaphras. Epaphras was with Paul while he was in prison (Philemon 23 calls Epaphras a "fellow prisoner" with Paul). Epaphras had a close connection with Colossae (Colossians 4:12 informs us that he was from Colossae, and most scholars believe he planted the church there). Paul wrote to the church because Epaphras shared his concern for the church with Paul. Colossians 4:12–13 reads:

[12]Epaphras, who is one of you and a servant of Christ Jesus, sends greetings. He is always wrestling in prayer for you, that you may stand firm in all the will of God, mature and fully assured. [13]I vouch for him that he is working hard for you and for those at Laodicea and Hierapolis.

The very thing for which Epaphras was praying (that they would stand firm in all the will of God, mature and fully assured) becomes Paul's message to the church. Paul wrote the letter because of his concern for the church, but he also wrote the letter because of his close relationship with Epaphras. Moo writes, "Paul writes to a community, then, that he has 'grandfathered' through his 'son,' Epaphras."[20]

Why? What is the purpose of this letter?

Paul gives no explicit reason for the writing of the letter, but as we read it, implicit reasons for the writing of the letter are suggested. In the main, Paul is combating false teachers that are threatening the health of the church in Colossae. He writes to the church to strengthen the disciples in their battle against these false teachers. He also takes the opportunity to encourage the church because of its spiritual growth and to point out areas where they can continue to grow.

Major and Minor Themes

What is the major theme of Colossians? Christ is Supreme.

If one were to narrow the focus of the book of Colossians down to a single theme, a good suggestion for that theme would be the Supremacy of Christ. Christ is Supreme; Christ is All; Christ is Excellent. Melick writes:

> One theme predominates: the centrality of Christ. No other epistle is as Christocentric as this one. Whether the reader spends countless hours with Colossians or reads it only casually, every encounter with the text brings one face to face with the Lord whom the text introduces so well. Every occasion to read it leaves its mark indelibly on the mind.[22]

Colossians 1:15–20, "The Grand Hymn of Christ"

[15]He is the image of the invisible God, the firstborn over all creation. [16]For by him all things were created: things in heaven and on earth, visible and invisible, whether thrones or powers or rulers or authorities; all things were created by him and for him. [17]He is before all things, and in him all things hold together. [18]And he is the head of the body, the church; he is the beginning and the firstborn from among the dead, so that in everything he might have the supremacy. [19]For God was pleased to have all his fullness dwell in him, [20]and through him to reconcile to himself all things, whether things on earth or things in heaven, by making peace through his blood, shed on the cross.

Some call this passage The Great Christology. Christology means "the study of Christ." This hymn is a study of Christ, but it is also a hymn of praise. It extols the greatness and grandeur of Christ. Some scholars believe that this hymn predates the letter to the Colossians. Paul either wrote the hymn earlier in his ministry, or he borrowed it from the early church. There is no way of being certain on these points. The images in the hymn are very striking; let's look at a few of them.

1. **Christ, the Image of the Invisible God (v. 15)**
   We cannot see God. He is invisible. But we can see Christ, and when we see Christ, we see God. Christ came into the world to make God visible. How could he do that? Because he *is* God.

2. **Firstborn**
   Christ is *"the firstborn of all creation."* This does not mean that Jesus was the first created being. That idea does not fit with the context of the passage. It either means (a) since he was God, he was prior in time to everything that was created, or (b) since he was God, he has authority over all created things, or (c) both of these ideas.

   How do we know Paul does not mean Christ was the first created being? First, the very next phrase says, *"For by him all things were created."* The ability to create is a characteristic of God. Paul was not trying to say that Jesus was less than God, but that he was God. Second, however you take this phrase, you must also take the phrase *"firstborn from among the dead"* (v. 18) in the same way. "Firstborn from among the dead" cannot mean that Christ was the first resurrected being. That simply is not true. In fact, Christ, being God, brought others back from the dead before his resurrection. The phrase means that Jesus has authority over death. Same with "firstborn of all creation." Since Christ created the world, he has authority over all creation.

3. **Creation**
   "For by him all things were created." This speaks to his divinity. He created everything. Some might question, saying, "I thought God spoke everything into existence—doesn't Genesis 1 say that?" It does, and he did. God and Christ and the Spirit created everything. All three members of the Godhead were active in creation. It is sometimes described in this way, "God spoke, the Spirit moved, and Jesus redeemed." But according to Paul, Jesus did more than just redeem. Paul says, *"For by him all things were created."* With the Father and Spirit, Jesus took an active role in the creation of the world.

4. Preexistence
Christ was *"before all things and in him all things hold together"* (v. 17). Preexistence to creation is a characteristic of God. Jesus existed before creation.

5. Sovereignty
Christ was *"before all things and in him all things hold together"* (v. 17). Christ holds all things together. He is Sovereign over all creation; all creation obeys him and he holds all of it together. This includes your life, so he can help you keep your life together.

6. Resurrection
Christ is the *"firstborn from among the dead."* This means he has authority over death. He is the resurrection and the life. Lazarus came out of the tomb when Jesus called his name. At the end of time, he will call all of us by name and we will rise from the dead.

7. Deity
The ESV translates verse 19: *"For in him all the fullness of God was pleased to dwell."* This is what Paul was driving at in this passage. Jesus wasn't just a created being. He wasn't just an agent of creation. Jesus is God. All the fullness of Deity resides in him. Compare this to Colossians 2:9 which reads, *"For in Christ all the fullness of the Deity lives in bodily form."* Therefore, Christ is supreme.

8. Reconciliation
Verse 20 reads, *"...to reconcile to himself all things, whether things on earth or things in heaven, by making peace through his blood, shed on the cross."* Jesus came to reconcile all things back to God through his blood. Christ redeems humanity through his blood, but more than that, he redeems "all things" through his blood.

Colossians 2:9–10, The Grand Statement of Christ's Divinity

⁹For in Christ all the fullness of the Deity lives in bodily form, ¹⁰and you have been given fullness in Christ, who is the head over every power and authority.

No single verse in the Bible states as succinctly and precisely the fact that Jesus is God as Colossians 2:9. For anyone who wants to deny the divinity of Jesus and say that he was a created being (for example, the Jehovah Witnesses) it is difficult to get around this verse. Paul makes it clear, beyond any doubt, that all the fullness of Deity resided in Jesus. Christ is supreme.

Colossians 2:13–15, The Grand Victory

13 When you were dead in your sins and in the uncircumcision of your sinful nature, God made you alive with Christ. He forgave us all our sins, 14 having canceled the written code, with its regulations, that was against us and that stood opposed to us; he took it away, nailing it to the cross. 15 And having disarmed the powers and authorities, he made a public spectacle of them, triumphing over them by the cross.

We were dead in sin but are now alive with Christ. The supremacy of Christ is demonstrated through his triumphing over powers and authorities on the cross. This is the grand victory of Jesus. We benefit from the battles he fought and the war he won. Because of Christ, we have forgiveness of sins. The efficacy of the cross can be experienced by anyone who makes Jesus Lord.

Christ is supreme. Paul rings this bell throughout his letter. He is battling false teachers who claim their way is better than Christ. Paul lets the disciples in Colossae know that way of Christ is far superior to their way. As you read through the book of Colossians, this is abundantly clear.

Other Themes in Colossians

1. Grow to Maturity.

Paul wrote to encourage the Colossians to continue growing toward maturity. It seems the primary purpose of the book was to encourage the disciples in their growth. Paul realized that baptism was the beginning of the Christian journey and not the end. He believed in the ministry of strengthening and encouraging. That is what his letters are all about.

On Paul's missionary journeys, he went out from the sending congregation and planted churches. But what did he do on his return trip to the sending church? He could have returned a different direction than he came, thus assuring that he would plant more churches. But instead, he returned the same way that he went. He retraced his steps so that he could strengthen the churches that he had established. Paul believed in the strengthening, encouraging, and maturing ministry.

How much did Paul believe in this ministry? Enough to put his own life at risk in order to strengthen churches. As Paul returned to the cities he had left, he was often walking right back into situations where he had narrowly escaped from persecution. He risked going back into these areas in order to strengthen the brothers and sisters.

A big focus for Paul in the letter to the Colossians is to encourage the disciples in Colossae to continue to grow and mature in faith, love, and hope. Let's look at some key verses here.

In 1:10–14, Paul writes:

¹⁰And we pray this in order that you may live a life worthy of the Lord and may please him in every way: bearing fruit in every good work, growing in the knowledge of God, ¹¹being strengthened with all power according to his glorious might so that you may have great endurance and patience, and joyfully ¹²giving thanks to the Father, who has qualified you to share in the inheritance of the saints in the kingdom of light. ¹³For he has rescued us from the dominion of darkness and brought us into the kingdom of the Son he loves, ¹⁴in whom we have redemption, the forgiveness of sins.

Paul's ministry goal is stated in 1:28–29. He writes:

²⁸We proclaim him, admonishing and teaching everyone with all wisdom, so that we may present everyone perfect in Christ. ²⁹To this end I labor, struggling with all his energy, which so powerfully works in me.

Why did Paul proclaim Christ? Why did he take the time to admonish and teach the disciples? He wanted to present everyone perfect in Christ. Another word for "perfect" is "mature." Paul labored with all his energy to help disciples reach maturity. This was his ministry goal. He wasn't satisfied with just baptizing people; he wanted to see these young Christians mature in Christ.

2. Beware of False Teachers and False Doctrine.

It is not until a man finds his faith opposed and attacked that he really begins to think out the implications of that faith. It is not until the Church is confronted with some dangerous heresy that she begins to realize the riches and the wonder of orthodoxy.[22]
—William Barclay, NT scholar and author

Remember *The Odyssey*?[23] You might have read parts of it in a high school literature class. It is Homer's classic tale of the voyage of Ulysses. If you don't remember the book you might remember the wonderful retelling of the story in the movie, *O, Brother Where Art Thou?* In the book and the movie are the sirens. The sirens were half-women, half-bird creatures that inhabited an island in the Mediterranean. They sang an enchanting song that lured sailors toward their island. But once the ships left their charted course and headed toward the island, they were lured to a lethal, rocky shore upon which the ships crashed and the sailors lost their lives. The sirens would then come down from their perch and feed upon the flesh of the sailors.

Literature says that two men overcame the sirens' song. The first was Ulysses. He wanted to hear the sirens' song with his own ears. He plugged the ears of his shipmates and told them to stay on course. He had them tie his body to the main mast of the ship so that he could not get loose. As his ship sailed past the island, the sailors couldn't hear the song of the sirens and the ship was saved.

Second was Orpheus. When the Argonauts sailed past the island, Orpheus, a great musician, began to sing and play his own song. His song was so pure that the sailors did not listen to the sirens' song.

False teaching is like the sirens' song: It is deceptive by nature. It is made to tickle the ears of those who hear it. But it is deadly. It leads people off the course of God's will and into tragedy. Perhaps, like Orpheus, we need to learn to sing the music of God's word so well that other music (doctrine) doesn't entice us.

Paul takes time in this letter to warn the church in Colossae against heresy and false doctrine. He takes on the false teachers beginning in 2:4, writing, *"I tell you this so that no one may deceive you by fine-sounding arguments."* In 2:8 Paul gives a stern warning, *"See to it that no one takes you captive through hollow and deceptive philosophy, which depends on human tradition and the basic principles of this world rather than on Christ."* The idea of taking captive is literally "to take as booty of war." The false teachers wanted to capture the hearts and minds of the disciples in Colossae. Their arguments were built on human tradition and not on Christ, who is superior to any human tradition.

It is difficult to identify the exact group that might have been attacking the church with false teaching. It seems to be a syncretistic religion that blended together ideas from pagan religion and Judaism. Therefore the false doctrine that Paul wrote against in the book has been labeled The Colossian Heresy.

Concerning the heresy, R.R. Melick writes:

> The major text for determining the context is 2:8–3:4. There several matters call for attention. They include: "fullness" (*plērōma*) (2:9); "delights in false humility and the worship of angels" (2:18); "what he has seen" (2:18); "Do not handle! Do not taste! Do not touch!" (2:21); and "self-imposed worship, their false humility and their harsh treatment of the body" (2:23). Recently many have considered these as phrases from the heretical teachers themselves. If they are not actual quotes, they must be terms particularly suited to the teachings advocated by the heretics.[24]

What was this Colossian heresy? Paul never gives us a specific summary of doctrines of the false teachers. We have to infer what they were teaching from the admonitions Paul gives the disciples in Colossae concerning the false doctrine and the false teachers. Some of what Paul had to say to the church concerning the false teachers is found in 2:8–12. Paul writes:

8See to it that no one takes you captive through hollow and deceptive philosophy, which depends on human tradition and the basic principles of this world rather than on Christ.

9For in Christ all the fullness of the Deity lives in bodily form, 10and you have been given fullness in Christ, who is the head over every power and authority. 11In him you were also circumcised, in the putting off of the sinful nature, not with a circumcision done by the hands of men but with the circumcision done by Christ, 12having been buried with him in baptism and raised with him through your faith in the power of God, who raised him from the dead.

What can we learn about the Colossian heresy based on this passage?

A. Paul begins by labeling it as hollow and deceptive "philosophy" (φιλοσοφία, *philosophia*) which was built on tradition (παράδοσις, *paradosis*) and the principles of this world. "Philosophy" denotes a coherent system that has been thought through and worked out. "Tradition" speaks to the antiquity of the teaching and its general acceptance.

B. The philosophy was built on human tradition. It is easy to associate this tradition with the tradition of the scribes and Pharisees, but the heresy could also have been built on the folk tradition of the pagans.

C. The philosophy was built on *"the basic principles of this world rather than on Christ."* Here we see the elements of paganism referenced.

There are other passages to consider as well. Colossians 2:16–23 contains some of the elements of this heresy. Paul writes:

16Therefore do not let anyone judge you by what you eat or drink, or with regard to a religious festival, a New Moon celebration or a Sabbath day. 17These are a shadow of the things that were to come; the reality, however, is found in Christ. 18Do not let anyone who delights in false humility and the worship of angels disqualify you for the prize. Such a person goes into great detail about what he has seen, and his unspiritual mind puffs him up with idle notions. 19He has lost connection with the Head, from whom the whole body, supported and held together by its ligaments and sinews, grows as God causes it to grow.

20Since you died with Christ to the basic principles of this world, why, as though you still belonged to it, do you submit to its rules: 21"Do not handle! Do not taste! Do not touch!"? 22These are all destined to perish with use, because they are based on human commands and teachings. 23Such regulations indeed have an appearance of wisdom, with their self-imposed worship, their false humility and their harsh treatment of the body, but they lack any value in restraining sensual indulgence.

What do we learn about the heresy from these passages?

D. Here Paul mentions a legalism that the false teachers were attempting to impose on the disciples in Colossae. They would judge the Christians based on diet and the keeping of religious festivals. This legalism is considered a *"shadow of the things that were to come"* and not the reality found in Christ. It is difficult to conceive of anything other than Judaism being referenced here. The holy days mentioned were certainly Jewish holy days. Moo writes, "The threefold 'religious festival, New Moon celebration, or Sabbath' (*heortē, neomēnia, sabbatōn*) is a common Old Testament way of summarizing Jewish 'holy days.'"[25]

Paul gives more details as to the character of the false teachers in Colossians 2:18. He writes:

[18]Do not let anyone who delights in false humility and the worship of angels disqualify you for the prize. Such a person goes into great detail about what he has seen, and his unspiritual mind puffs him up with idle notions.

This verse gives us many details concerning the false teachers and their teaching.

E. They *"delight in false humility and the worship of angels"* (θέλων ἐν ταπεινοφροσύνῃ καὶ θρησκείᾳ τῶν ἀγγέλων). False humility is often seen as ascetic practices. Humility (ταπεινοφροσύνῃ/*tapeinophrosynē*) being the humbling of the flesh during ascetic practices, such as fasting.

F. They delight in angel worship. Was angel worship a phenomenon within Judaism? Melick answers, "Yes." He writes:

Fascination with supernatural beings characterized many groups of Jews from the time of Daniel through the Intertestamental Period. This specific infatuation was needless. In his work, Jesus dominated them. He created them (he is their head, 2:9–10; see also the hymn to Christ of 1:15–20). When many rebelled, for Paul focused here on the evil supernatural beings, Jesus conquered them, embarrassing and exposing them publicly (2:15). They deserved *no* following.[26]

G. *"Such a person goes into great detail about what he has seen, and his unspiritual mind puffs him up with idle notions"* (ἃ ἑόρακεν ἐμβατεύων). This seems to mean visions and the experience of visions.

H. Paul speaks of their legalism as *"their self-imposed worship, their false humility and their harsh treatment of the body, but they lack any value in restraining sensual indulgence.* " [See 2:23, "voluntary worship" (ἐθελοθρησκίᾳ), "humility" (ταπεινοφροσύνη), and *"severe treatment of the body"* (ἀφειδίᾳ σώματος)].

Paul continues his criticism of a false teacher in Colossians 2:19, speaking directly to one of the major problems of a heretic, writing: *"He has lost connection with the Head, from whom the whole body, supported and held together by its ligaments and sinews, grows as God causes it to grow."*

I. The idea of losing "connection with the Head," seems to imply that these false teachers were once connected with "the Head" meaning Christ. If this is the case, then Paul could have in mind disciples who were once in the church and have left to embrace false teaching and heresy.

After condemning the false teacher, Paul returns to warning the disciples in Colossae about following these heretics. In Colossians 2:20–23, Paul continues:

> *20 Since you died with Christ to the basic principles of this world, why, as though you still belonged to it, do you submit to its rules: 21 "Do not handle! Do not taste! Do not touch!"? 22 These are all destined to perish with use, because they are based on human commands and teachings. 23 Such regulations indeed have an appearance of wisdom, with their self-imposed worship, their false humility and their harsh treatment of the body, but they lack any value in restraining sensual indulgence.*

We can induce a couple more elements of the false teachers and the Colossian heresy from what Paul writes as an admonition to the disciples to stay away from the false teaching.

J. They hand down laws like: *"Don't handle, don't taste, don't even touch"* (2:21, μὴ ἅψῃ, μηδὲ λεύσῃ, μηδὲ θίλης). Those with these legalistic tendencies seem to be Judaizers.

K. Paul mentions for the second time ascetic practices. This again seems to refer to Jewish elements in the heresy.

Scholars debate as to whether this heresy was Jewish or pagan. They are divided on this issue.

O'Brien tips the scales toward the heresy being Jewish in origin, writing:

> Basically, however, it seems to have been Jewish. Evidence of this is seen in the part played in the 'philosophy' by legal ordinances, food regulations, the sabbath, new moon, and other prescriptions of the Jewish calendar.[27]

Others like Martin Dibelius posit that the heresy came from the mystery religions of the pagan Greek cults.[28] He labels the heresy as pre-Christian gnosticism.

F.F. Bruce suggests a middle-of-the-road position, stating the Colossian heresy was "more probably a Phrygian development in which a local variety of Judaism had been fused with a philosophy of non-Jewish origin—an early and simple form of gnosticism."[29]

It seems best to think of the heresy as a syncretistic fusion of paganism and Judaism. Moo writes, "We do not know nearly as much as we would like about the Colossians' own 'world.' What we do know about it suggests that it was very complex, with many religious, philosophical, and cultural movements jostling for attention.[30] As we reconstruct the Colossian heresy, this complex, multicultural setting must be taken into account.

3. Guard against Legalism.

Legalists had entered the church in Colossae. They brought their human rules along with them, "Don't handle! Don't taste! Don't touch!" Paul warns the disciples about them and challenges the disciples that they should not submit to their rules. Instead, they should understand the great situation they have as Christians. Jesus' way is far superior to that of the legalists. Paul warns the disciple not to throw away what they have been given in Jesus to fall under the yoke of legalism.

A key verse here is Colossians 2:20–23. Paul writes:

> [20]*Since you died with Christ to the basic principles of this world, why, as though you still belonged to it, do you submit to its rules:* [21]*"Do not handle! Do not taste! Do not touch!"?* [22]*These are all destined to perish with use, because they are based on human commands and teachings.* [23]*Such regulations indeed have an appearance of wisdom, with their self-imposed worship, their false humility and their harsh treatment of the body, but they lack any value in restraining sensual indulgence.*

Paul wasn't against having ethical standards and moral guidelines in life. In fact, chapters 3 and 4 are filled with guidelines, some of which are stated as commands. However, these guidelines and commands spring from Christ. The rules of the legalists don't come from such a pure source. Douglas Moo comments:

> The problem with the rules of the false teachers, however, is that they stemmed from human tradition rather than from Christ (2:8). We may, then, formulate a theology of rules from Colossians 2 along these lines: Rules must never take the place of Christ as the source of spiritual nourishment and growth; and any rules that

we propose to follow must be clearly rooted in and lead back to Christ.[31]

Paul wants the disciples to know with certainty that no rule can ever take the place of having a vibrant relationship with Jesus.

4. The Importance of the Church

Paul highlights the role of the church in Colossians. There is a movement in our culture that wants to devalue the role of the church, painting it as passé and antiquated. But Paul would disagree with that notion.

Paul speaks of the church five times in this letter, in 1:18; 1:24, 25; 4:15, 16. In 1:18, Paul writes, *"He [Christ] is the head of the body, the church; he is the beginning and the firstborn from the dead, so that in everything he might have the supremacy."* Christ is the head of the church, and thus has authority over her. He gets his work done through the church, which is his body and thus carries out the wishes of the head. Douglas Moo comments on this image of Christ as the head of the church, writing:

> The Greek word for "head" (*kephalē*) generally implies authority of some kind, and this is part of what Paul intends: Christ is the ruler of the church. But, as 2:19 strongly suggests, Christ's "headship" also involves sustenance. Just as the ancients thought of the head, physiologically, as the directing source of the body's movements, so Christ, affirms Paul, is the directing source of the body of his people. Only by staying connected to this "head," therefore, can Christians grow.[32]

Moo makes a fantastic point here. The image of Christ as head of the church implies authority and sustenance. He rules over the church, but he also provides for and nourishes her. If Christ provides sustenance for the church, then he must care for her. We take care of the ones we love. Christ loves the church; therefore he cares for her and provides for her. Anyone who belittles the church or believes the church is a passé, outmoded notion, does not have the mind of Christ.

Paul also loved and cared for the church. In 1:25 Paul calls himself a servant or minister of the church. Paul was grateful to work with the church to see the gospel advanced. Like Paul, we need to value the church today as one of the greatest things going in the dark and turbulent world in which we live.

5. Making the Colossians Aware of His Situation

Paul takes time in all his letters for the personal touch. He wants the brothers and sisters to know what is going on in his ministry. In this case, he is in prison. He wants the disciples to know that he is in jail, but that he is okay.

He is sending the letter with Tychicus, who will bring additional information to the church concerning Paul's welfare. In 4:7–8, Paul writes:

> [7] _Tychicus will tell you all the news about me. He is a dear brother, a faithful minister and fellow servant in the Lord._ [8] _I am sending him to you for the express purpose that you may know about our circumstances and that he may encourage your hearts._

Paul doesn't want the church to worry about him. He wants them to stay encouraged, so he writes them a letter and sends Tychicus with the letter for their encouragement.

6. Other Themes

There are many other themes that could be highlighted here, but we will discuss these themes as they appear in the commentary portion of the book. For example:

- Prayer—1:3, 1:9, 4:2–4, 4:12
- Eschatology—1:3–23, 2:15, 3:1
- Thanksgiving—1:3, 1:12, 2:7, 3:15, 4:2
- Reconciliation/Salvation—1:20, 1:22, 2:11–13
- Worship—3:16–17
- Christian Conduct—3:18–4:1, wives, husbands, children, parents, slaves, and masters
- The Value of Relationships—4:7–18, a list of the names of Paul's friends and associates
- Paul's Commitment to Evangelism—4:3–6

Practical Exercise: Read through the letter and circle the words "all" and "every." Go back and see how Paul used these words in his letter.

Outline of Colossians: The Supremacy of Christ

I. Theological Instruction. 1:1–3:4
 A. Greeting. 1:1–2
 B. Thanksgiving and Prayer. 1:3–14
  1. 1:3–8. Paul's Prayer of Thanks
  2. 1:9–14. Paul's Prayer of Encouragement
 C. The Supremacy of Christ. 1:15–23
  1. 1:15–20. Superior Nature The Hymn to Christ
  2. 1:21–23. Superior Reconciliation
 D. Paul's Ministry. 1:24–2:5
  1. 1:24–27. To Make the Word of God Fully Known
  2. 1:28–29. To Present Everyone Mature in Christ
  3. 2:1–5. To Encourage Your Hearts
 E. Our Walk in Christ. 2:6–15.
  1. 2:6–7. Full of Life in Christ
  2. 2:11–12. Freed From Sin; Spiritual Circumcision
  3. 2:13–15. Forgiven
 F. Free in Christ. 2:16–23
  1. 2:16–19. Let No One Disqualify You.
  2. 2:20–23. Do Not Submit to Human Regulations.

II. Ethical Teaching. 3:1–4:18
 A. The Foundation of Christian Living; The New Self. 3:1–4
 B. The Transformation of Christian Living. 3:5–17
  1. 3:5–11. Put Off.
  2. 3:12–17. Put On.
 C. Relational Matters; Household Conduct. 3:18–4:1
  1. 3:18. Wives
  2. 3:19. Husbands
  3. 3:20. Children
  4. 3:21. Fathers
  5. 3:22. Slaves
  6. 3:23–25. Slaves Specifically and Everyone in General
  7. 4:1. Masters
 D. Further Instructions. 4:2–6
  1. 4:2–4. Instructions on Prayer
  2. 4:5–6. Instructions on How to Work with Outsiders
 E. Final Greetings and Messages; Farewell. 4:7–18
  1. 4:7–9. Travel Plans: Tychicus and Onesimus
  2. 4:10–15. Greetings
  3. 4:16–17. Final Instructions
  4. 4:18. Farewell; Personal Note; Final Statement

Memory Work

A few suggestions:[33]

1:1–2
[1]Paul, an apostle of Christ Jesus by the will of God, and Timothy our brother,
[2]To the holy and faithful brothers in Christ at Colosse:
Grace and peace to you from God our Father.

1:13–14
[13]For he has rescued us from the dominion of darkness and brought us into the kingdom of the Son he loves, [14]in whom we have redemption, the forgiveness of sins.

1:15–20
[15]He is the image of the invisible God, the firstborn over all creation. [16]For by him all things were created: things in heaven and on earth, visible and invisible, whether thrones or powers or rulers or authorities; all things were created by him and for him. [17]He is before all things, and in him all things hold together. [18]And he is the head of the body, the church; he is the beginning and the firstborn from among the dead, so that in everything he might have the supremacy. [19]For God was pleased to have all his fullness dwell in him, [20]and through him to reconcile to himself all things, whether things on earth or things in heaven, by making peace through his blood, shed on the cross.

1:28–29
[28]We proclaim him, admonishing and teaching everyone with all wisdom, so that we may present everyone perfect in Christ. [29]To this end I labor, struggling with all his energy, which so powerfully works in me.

2:6–7
[6]So then, just as you received Christ Jesus as Lord, continue to live in him, [7]rooted and built up in him, strengthened in the faith as you were taught, and overflowing with thankfulness.

2:9–10

[9]For in Christ all the fullness of the Deity lives in bodily form, [10]and you have been given fullness in Christ, who is the head over every power and authority.

2:11–12

[11]In him you were also circumcised, in the putting off of the sinful nature, not with a circumcision done by the hands of men but with the circumcision done by Christ, [12]having been buried with him in baptism and raised with him through your faith in the power of God, who raised him from the dead.

2:16–17

[16]Therefore do not let anyone judge you by what you eat or drink, or with regard to a religious festival, a New Moon celebration or a Sabbath day. [17]These are a shadow of the things that were to come; the reality, however, is found in Christ.

3:1–4

[1]Since, then, you have been raised with Christ, set your hearts on things above, where Christ is seated at the right hand of God. [2]Set your minds on things above, not on earthly things. [3]For you died, and your life is now hidden with Christ in God. [4]When Christ, who is your life, appears, then you also will appear with him in glory.

3:12–14

[12]Therefore, as God's chosen people, holy and dearly loved, clothe yourselves with compassion, kindness, humility, gentleness and patience. [13]Bear with each other and forgive whatever grievances you may have against one another. Forgive as the Lord forgave you. [14]And over all these virtues put on love, which binds them all together in perfect unity.

3:15

15Let the peace of Christ rule in your hearts, since as members of one body you were called to peace. And be thankful.

3:16–17

16Let the word of Christ dwell in you richly as you teach and admonish one another with all wisdom, and as you sing psalms, hymns and spiritual songs with gratitude in your hearts to God. 17And whatever you do, whether in word or deed, do it all in the name of the Lord Jesus, giving thanks to God the Father through him.

3:18–21

18Wives, submit to your husbands, as is fitting in the Lord.

19Husbands, love your wives and do not be harsh with them.

20Children, obey your parents in everything, for this pleases the Lord.

21Fathers, do not embitter your children, or they will become discouraged.

3:23–25

23Whatever you do, work at it with all your heart, as working for the Lord, not for men, 24since you know that you will receive an inheritance from the Lord as a reward. It is the Lord Christ you are serving. 25Anyone who does wrong will be repaid for his wrong, and there is no favoritism.

4:3–4

3And pray for us, too, that God may open a door for our message, so that we may proclaim the mystery of Christ, for which I am in chains. 4Pray that I may proclaim it clearly, as I should.

4:5–6

5Be wise in the way you act toward outsiders; make the most of every opportunity. 6Let your conversation be always full of grace, seasoned with salt, so that you may know how to answer everyone.

4:18

18I, Paul, write this greeting in my own hand. Remember my chains. Grace be with you.

Class Outline for Teaching Colossians

(Eight Lessons on Colossians)

Lesson One:

Introductory Material; Major Themes

Lesson Two:

I. Theological Instruction. 1:1–3:4

A. Greeting. 1:1–2

B. Thanksgiving and Prayer. 1:3–14

1. 1:3–8. Paul's Prayer of Thanks

2. 1:9–14. Paul's Prayer of Encouragement

Lesson Three:

C. The Supremacy of Christ. 1:15–23

1. 1:15–20. Superior Nature; The Hymn to Christ

2. 1:21–23. Superior Reconciliation

Lesson Four:

D. Paul's Ministry. 1:24–2:5

1. 1:24–27. To Make the Word of God Fully Known

2. 1:28–29. To Present Everyone Mature in Christ

3. 2:1–5. To Encourage Your Hearts

Lesson Five:

E. Our Walk in Christ. 2:6–15

1. 2:6–7. Full of Life in Christ

2. 2:11–12. Freed From Sin; Spiritual Circumcision

3. 2:13–15. Forgiven

F. Free in Christ. 2:16–23

1. 2:16–19. Let No One Disqualify You.

2. 2:20–23. Do Not Submit to Human Regulations.

Lesson Six:

> II. Ethical Teaching. 3:1–4:18
>> A. The Foundation of Christian Living;
>> The New Self. 3:1–4
>> B. The Transformation of Christian Living. 3:5–17
>>> 1. 3:5–11. Put Off.
>>> 2. 3:12–17. Put On.

Lesson Seven:

>> C. Relational Matters; Household Conduct. 3:18–4:1
>>> 1. 3:18. Wives
>>> 2. 3:19. Husbands
>>> 3. 3:20. Children
>>> 4. 3:21. Fathers
>>> 5. 3:22. Slaves
>>> 6. 3:23–25. Slaves Specifically/Everyone in General
>>> 7. 4:1. Masters

Lesson Eight:

>> D. Further Instructions. 4:2–6
>>> 1. 4:2–4. Instructions on Prayer
>>> 2. 4:5–6. Instructions on How to Work with Outsiders

>> E. Final Greetings and Messages; Farewell. 4:7–18
>>> 1. 4:7–9. Travel Plans: Tychicus and Onesimus
>>> 2. 4:10–15. Greetings
>>> 3. 4:16–17. Final Instructions
>>> 4. 4:18. Farewell; Personal Note; Final Statement

Exposition of Colossians
Chapter One

I. 1:1–3:4 Theological Instruction

A. 1:1–2 Greeting

¹Παῦλος ἀπόστολος Χριστοῦ Ἰησοῦ διὰ θελήματος θεοῦ καὶ Τιμόθεος ὁ ἀδελφὸς ²τοῖς ἐν Κολοσσαῖς ἁγίοις καὶ πιστοῖς ἀδελφοῖς ἐν Χριστῷ, χάρις ὑμῖν καὶ εἰρήνη ἀπὸ θεοῦ πατρὸς ἡμῶν.³⁴

My Translation

¹Paul, an apostle of Christ Jesus according to the will of God, and Timothy our brother,

²To those in Colossae, dedicated and faithful brothers and sisters in Christ: Grace to you and peace to you from God our Father.³⁵

NIV, 1984

¹Paul, an apostle of Christ Jesus by the will of God, and Timothy our brother,

²To the holy and faithful brothers in Christ at Colosse:
Grace and peace to you from God our Father.

The Preacher's Commentary Series on Colossians opens its comments on the text of Colossians by telling a powerful story from Alex Haley's novel *Roots*. I quote this story in its entirety because it serves as an excellent preface to the text of Colossians and because I can't say it any better than the authors in this series said it.

> *Roots* was the most talked-about book in the 1970s. Millions read and millions more saw this epic story covering more than 200 years and six generations of the family of the author, Alex Haley. It centers initially in Kunta Kinte, Haley's great-great-great-great-great grandfather, as the first chapter describes the tribal customs

concerning birth, and especially the signal event of naming a child on the eighth day. The description is poignant:

> Omoro [the father] then walked out before all the assembled people of the village. Moving to his wife's side, he lifted up the infant and as all watched, whispered three times into his son's ear the name he had chosen for him. It was the first time the name had ever been spoken as the child's name, for Omoro's people felt that each human being should be the first to know who he was.

And, as if trying to place the truth of the child's identity in proper dimension, chapter one of *Roots* closes with the father taking his infant son out into the night, lifting him face-up to the heavens and proclaiming: "Behold—the only thing greater than yourself."

It was a great celebration of identity, a ritual to recall that a person might always know who he or she is. Nothing is more important—to know who we are. In Colossians, Paul addresses the question of identity. He rehearses the Good News of the gospel as the touchstone for our always remembering who we are and whose we are.[36]

As we launch into our study of the text of Colossians, let's remember that Paul is telling us who we are in this book. He does so by extolling the supremacy of Christ. Our self-esteem comes from knowing who we are and whom we serve. When we become Christians, Jesus lifts us up in his hands and holds us before the Father and the Spirit and whispers in our ears, "You are mine." That is our identity. If we know that we are Christ's, then nothing will deter us from serving him wholeheartedly all our lives. Nothing, no false teacher or false doctrine, no matter how erudite and convincing, will draw us away from Jesus. Nothing, no temptation, no matter how appealing or enticing, will cause us to stray from Jesus. Nothing. Because nothing compares to what we have found in Christ. Christ is Supreme.

1. Paul

The opening word to the letter is Paul. Paul's name also comes at the end of the letter, *"I, Paul, write this greeting in my own hand"* (4:18). There is no reason to dispute that Paul was the author of this letter.

Paul distinguishes himself as an apostle of Christ Jesus by the will of God. Apostle means "one sent on a mission." It can mean anyone sent on a mission or the technical term for the leadership role of apostle. Paul meant the latter. In the *UBS Handbook on Paul's Letter to the Colossians* Bratcher and Nida write,

"*Apostle* is literally 'messenger' and has the meaning of a representative, with the commission and authority to act in the name and on behalf of the one who has sent him; he is not simply one who delivers a message and nothing else."[37]

Christ means the "anointed one" or "Messiah." Jesus is from the Hebrew for Joshua which means "Savior." Why "Christ Jesus" versus "Jesus Christ"? This could be just a personal preference of Paul, or it could be that he is placing the emphasis on Christ, thus highlighting the Messiahship of Jesus. In this letter, Paul continually emphasizes the supremacy of Jesus as the Christ. The term "Christ" also reminded the early Christians of their Jewish roots. Moo writes, "While the title is not common in either the Old Testament or in Judaism, it was used by early Christians to identify Jesus of Nazareth as the man in whom the entire line of promise about a great Davidic king to come had reached its fulfillment."[38]

Paul is an apostle by God's will. He is not a self-appointed apostle. Paul was an apostle because God appointed him to be one. O'Brien writes, "Paul alone was the Colossians' apostle, even though he had not previously visited them in person, for he had been independently and directly commissioned by the risen Lord."[39] In his commentary, E.D. Martin mentions, "Two elements of apostleship as practiced by Paul stand out in Colossians: teaching and pastoral care."[40]

Paul is writing in conjunction with his travelling companion, Timothy. Paul recruited Timothy for his second missionary journey, and Timothy became a loyal partner with Paul in his ministry. We see here the value of mentoring/discipling relationships in the ministry of Paul. If anyone could have developed a powerful ministry as an isolated individual, it was Paul. But Paul built his ministry in connection with other brothers and sisters. This theme of teamwork will appear over and over in this letter. This connective principle stands as a great example for all of us who work in the ministry today (whether paid or volunteer). There are no "lone wolf" disciples. We all work together to build the ministry and to bring honor to God.

2. The Recipients

To whom is this letter written? To the brothers (and you can include sisters) from Colossae. (Background information about the city of Colossae was covered in the Introduction.)

Paul first calls them "saints." Some translations translate this word (ἁγίοις, *hagiois*) as "holy ones." The word means "to be set apart or to be separate." All Christians are to be separate from the world. Part of the problem in Colossae was that the Christians there were accepting syncretistic religions into their fellowship so they lost their distinctiveness from the world. Paul points this out at the very beginning of his letter, reminding the Christians of their call to holiness.

C.F.D. Moule points out that ἁγίοις, *hagiois*, holy ones, signifies the devotion of the disciples in Colossae. He writes, "ἁγίοις is perhaps best rendered 'dedicated', 'God's own', because it represents the OT conception of 'the dedicated ones.'"[41] So we aren't just separated from the world, but we are separated to be holy unto the Lord.

Next, the disciples are faithful. The word "faithful" (πιστοῖς, *pistois*) can mean "full of faith" or it can mean "trustworthy." Here it probably is emphasizing the disciples' commitment to follow Jesus in the midst of a syncretistic society. Paul does not usually include this adjective in the opening of his letters. To find it here puts emphasis on the idea that the disciples in Colossae are in a battle with the false teachers, but they are staying faithful in the battle.

Paul also calls the disciples "brothers." You can also add sisters. In Paul's day it was typical to write to the male audience understanding that the female audience would be implied. If Paul were writing today, he would most likely change his writing style to fit within our social convention and become "all things to all people." Therefore, it is appropriate to add sister here, and I do so in my translation. Paul speaks to the familial and relational aspects of the church in using terms like brothers and sisters. The church is family. Martin writes, "By calling them *brothers and sisters*, Paul draws attention to their link with others of the Christian family. Christians are not meant to be alone or unattached."[42]

The opening address is typically Pauline: *"Grace and peace to you from God our Father."* "Grace" (χάρις, *charis*) was often used in letters as we use the word "hello." It was often just a greeting. But in the context of the church, it carried the added weight of "unmerited favor" or "undeserved/unearned favor from God." It was a typical Roman greeting.

"Peace" (εἰρήνη, *eirēnē*) was a more Jewish greeting. It came from the Hebrew *shalom,* which meant "wholeness" or "wellness." In the Greek mind "peace" had a different nuance. O'Brien writes, "εἰρήνη ('peace') in secular Greek…indicated the antithesis to war, or the situation resulting from the cessation of war. It denoted the state of law and order from which the blessings of prosperity would arise."[43] Bratcher and Nida write:

> *Peace* may often be best expressed metaphorically, for example, "may God cause you to have a quiet heart" or "…to sit down in your hearts." This emphasis of *peace* in this type of context is not, however mere tranquility or so-called "peace of mind." It is far more all-embracing and therefore should suggest what is often spoken of in English as "the good life."[44]

Grace and peace come from God our Father. Mentioning the idea of God as father speaks to the nature of God as a giver and a nurturer. As father, God is the origin and agent of grace and peace to the church and all the saints.

Practical Exercise: Take a moment to write a letter filled with grace and peace to one of your brothers and sisters encouraging their holiness and faithfulness.

Practical Exercise: Take note of how rich the Bible is. See the great themes that you can discover in just two verses of the Bible. Study these themes throughout the week.

- Sunday—Apostleship; leadership in the church
- Monday—The will of God; the sovereignty of God
- Tuesday—Holiness
- Wednesday—Faithfulness
- Thursday—Brothers and sisters; relationships in the church
- Friday—Grace
- Saturday—Peace
  Take this theme and see how it is used throughout this book.

B. Thanksgiving and Prayer. 1:3–14.

1. 1:3–8 Paul's Prayer of Thanks; Faith, Love, and Hope

³Εὐχαριστοῦμεν τῷ θεῷ πατρὶ τοῦ κυρίου ἡμῶν Ἰησοῦ Χριστοῦ πάντοτε περὶ ὑμῶν προσευχόμενοι, ⁴ἀκούσαντες τὴν πίστιν ὑμῶν ἐν Χριστῷ Ἰησοῦ καὶ τὴν ἀγάπην ἣν ἔχετε εἰς πάντας τοὺς ἁγίους ⁵διὰ τὴν ἐλπίδα τὴν ἀποκειμένην ὑμῖν ἐν τοῖς οὐρανοῖς, ἣν προηκούσατε ἐν τῷ λόγῳ τῆς ἀληθείας τοῦ εὐαγγελίου 6τοῦ παρόντος εἰς ὑμᾶς, καθὼς καὶ ἐν παντὶ τῷ κόσμῳ ἐστὶν καρποφορούμενον καὶ αὐξανόμενον καθὼς καὶ ἐν ὑμῖν, ἀφ' ἧς ἡμέρας ἠκούσατε καὶ ἐπέγνωτε τὴν χάριν τοῦ θεοῦ ἐν ἀληθείᾳ· ⁷καθὼς ἐμάθετε ἀπὸ Ἐπαφρᾶ τοῦ ἀγαπητοῦ συνδούλου ἡμῶν, ὅς ἐστιν πιστὸς ὑπὲρ ὑμῶν διάκονος τοῦ Χριστοῦ, ⁸ὁ καὶ δηλώσας ἡμῖν τὴν ὑμῶν ἀγάπην ἐν πνεύματι.

My Translation

³We always thank God the Father of our Lord Jesus Christ when we pray for you, ⁴having heard of your faith in Christ Jesus and of the love which you have for all the saints ⁵because of the hope that is reserved for you in the heavens and that you have heard about before in the word of truth: the gospel ⁶that has come to all of you; just as all over the world this gospel is bearing fruit and

increasing, just as it has been doing from the day you heard it and understood God's grace in truth—[7]just as you learned it from Epaphras, our dear fellow servant, who is a faithful minister of Christ on our behalf, [8]and who also revealed to us your love in the Spirit.

NIV, 1984

[3]We always thank God, the Father of our Lord Jesus Christ, when we pray for you, [4]because we have heard of your faith in Christ Jesus and of the love you have for all the saints— [5]the faith and love that spring from the hope that is stored up for you in heaven and that you have already heard about in the word of truth, the gospel [6]that has come to you. All over the world this gospel is bearing fruit and growing, just as it has been doing among you since the day you heard it and understood God's grace in all its truth. [7]You learned it from Epaphras, our dear fellow servant, who is a faithful minister of Christ on our behalf, [8]and who also told us of your love in the Spirit.

Notes

V3. Paul begins with a prayer of thanksgiving. Verses 3–8 form one sentence in the Greek text, with a minor pause at the end of verse 6.[45] It's as if Paul starts thinking of reasons he is grateful and has a difficult time stopping. Look at whom Paul is thanking. Verse 3 reads, *"We always thank God."* Paul directs his attention toward God. That is always a good place to begin. Melick writes, "The expression 'we thank God' occurs frequently in the Pauline Epistles. The term implies both a statement of thanksgiving for what is received from God and an element of praise for God's character which originated it."[46]

For Paul to begin with thanksgiving is very typical of his correspondence. But let's not think this is perfunctory. This prayer of thanksgiving meant something to Paul; it was the heart of Paul. He was grateful for what God had done for the disciples at Colossae. He also knew that the church in Colossae was in a crucible: The disciples were waging war against false teachers. Paul was very grateful that God was still working in the church there, and he openly expressed his grateful heart to the church. This stands as an example for us to explore how grateful we are before God.

Paul was thankful for all the churches. The one at Colossae was not a major church, not what some would call a "pillar" church. In this region of the world the church in Ephesus would have been considered a "pillar" church. But Paul was thankful for churches of all sizes.

Paul says "we" give thanks. Some call this the "epistletory plural" and believe it should be translated in the singular, "I give thanks." However, we should also consider that Paul truly meant to include others in the "we" because Paul was a team player. O'Brien writes, "It is also possible that the plural 'we give thanks whenever we pray' may draw attention to the regular gathering together for prayer by Paul and his colleagues to give thanks to God for the Colossian Christians."[47]

Paul doesn't direct his thanksgiving to the disciples but literally to *"God, the Father of our Lord Jesus Christ."* God as Father demonstrates what type of God he is. It speaks to his nature—he is a nurturing, caring God who is our Father. He is a redeeming God because he is the father who gave us our Lord Jesus Christ. The wording that Paul uses here is out of the ordinary. Douglas Moo suggests, "Perhaps, in a letter that elevates Christ, Paul wants at the outset to anchor the person of Christ firmly to God the Father."[48]

The title "Lord Jesus Christ" contains the elements of Jesus being our master (Lord/Κύριος/*kurios*), savior (Jesus/Ἰησοῦς/*Iēsous*), and messiah/king (Christ/Χριστός/*Christos*). That God is father of our Lord Jesus Christ demonstrates that God in no longer just the father of the Hebrew nation, but he is father of *our* Lord Jesus Christ, and thus by proxy, anyone who has made Jesus their Lord and Christ, including the gentiles.[49] William Hendriksen writes, "Note also that beautiful word of appropriating faith, namely, *our*: 'the Father of *our* Lord Jesus Christ.' Hence, in the sublimest and most comforting sense, he is *our* Father. What a reason for thanksgiving!"[50]

"Always…when we pray" is to say that the church in Colossae was always on Paul's mind. As a Jewish Christian, Paul would pray at least three times a day (some Jews prayed five times a day). During those times of prayer, he would mention the church in Colossae to the Father. Paul always had the church on his mind. He was preoccupied by what was happening in the churches. What preoccupies your mind? Is it spiritual ideas and spiritual concerns?

Paul was a man of prayer. This is obvious in all his letters. Here we see that Paul prayed continually for disciples in all the churches. Melick summarizes what can be learned from Paul's prayer in this opening, by writing:

> Several factors appear regarding Paul's prayers. First, they were continual. The church was regularly in Paul's mind and thoughts. Second, the prayer was directed to God. Finally, the prayers were intercessory, "when we pray for you." This phrase indicates the prayers involved people more than events.[51]

V4. Paul mentions two ways the disciples in Colossae have demonstrated their commitment to Jesus: through faith and love. James D.G. Dunn writes, "To be noted also is the degree to which the vertical ("faith in Christ") was integrated with the horizontal ("love for the saints"). Paul would never have wanted these two to fall apart."[52] This vertical faith (relationship with God) must lead to a horizontal love (relationship with others). The vertical and horizontal relationships both spring from hope. Faith, love, and hope must be evident in the lives of all disciples.

Before Paul brings up the areas where the disciples in Colossae need to focus and grow, he begins by mentioning positive characteristics in their ministry and reasons why he is grateful for them. Hendriksen writes:

There were dangers threatening the church. Certain weaknesses, moreover, are clearly implied (3:5–11; cf. 2:4, 8, etc.). But before Paul even begins to refer to these things he first of all assures those to whom this letter is sent that he is convinced that the work of God's grace is evident in their lives. What a lesson for every parent, counselor, teacher, and pastor, especially in cases where warning or even rebuke would appear to be in order! There is such a thing as Christian tact.[53]

Hendriksen makes an important point here. As mentioned before, Paul's note of thanksgiving isn't just a perfunctory comment used to get his pen moving so that he can talk about the things he wants to talk about. Paul genuinely sees growth in the disciples in Colossae and wants to commend them for their growth. We would do well to imitate Paul's approach: First commendation, then reproof. First encouragement, then correction.

> **Practical Exercise:** During the next week, be aware of how you correct others. Make a concerted effort to praise strengths before you point out weaknesses. Encourage before you correct. Commend before you reprove. Practice this habit over the next few weeks until it becomes who you are.

Paul specifically says he has heard of their faith. We infer from this that Paul did not plant the church in Colossae. Even though he did not plant the church there, he still had great concern for the disciples in Colossae. He cared enough to listen carefully to reports that came from Colossae and to write a letter to help the church there. Paul had concern for all the churches.

As was just mentioned, Paul highlights three essential traits of Christian character that should be obvious in the life of every Christian: faith, love, and hope. These three characteristics are mentioned at the end of 1 Corinthians 13, *"And now these three remain: faith, hope and love. But the greatest of these is love." The Bible Knowledge Commentary* writes, "Faith is the soul looking *upward* to God; love looks *outward* to others; hope looks *forward* to the future. Faith rests on the past work of Christ; love works in the present; and hope anticipates the future."[54]

Paul begins with faith, then he moves on to love and hope. But we will notice in the next verse that faith and love are grounded in hope. Bratcher and Nida add this practical point on faith and love, writing:

Since *faith* in this context is a matter of active trust and confidence, it may be appropriate to translate *your faith in Christ Jesus* as "how you trust Christ Jesus" or "how you have put your confidence in Christ Jesus." Similarly, of *your love for all God's people* may be rendered as "how you love all God's people."[55]

It seems to me that Bratcher and Nida provide an excellent distinction between faith as confidence in Christ and love as directed toward people. But we should also remember that these two ideas are bound together in our hope for heaven, in fact they spring from that hope.

Faith must be active and the activity of faith is love. Paul mentions a specific type of ἀγάπην/*agape* love here—one that is directed toward all the saints, the brothers and sisters in the churches. Melick describes this love as having two characteristics. He writes, "First, it was sacrificial. The term *agapē* reminded them of the sacrificial love of Christ for them. Second, within the Christian community it was indiscriminate. The love was directed to all the saints."[56]

For Paul the local church was part of a larger whole, a worldwide group of churches for which Jesus died. Paul was committed to the whole and to each local church that made up the whole. This is evident from this letter to the disciples in Colossae, a church that Paul neither planted nor visited on his previous missionary journeys. He now encourages the love of the disciples in Colossae to be an *agape* love for "all" the saints or all God's people. Dunn writes:

> But it is clear that for Paul the self-sacrifice of Christ is the definitive expression of this "love"... Presumably, therefore, this is what was in mind here—an active concern for one another among the Colossian Christians which did not stop short at self-sacrifice of personal interests—and not just for one another, if the "all the saints" is to be taken seriously. Here may be indicated a network of mutual support and encouragement as Christians moved among the different towns in Asia Minor.[57]

Dunn speaks of a "network of mutual support and encouragement." It would be proper to think of the churches across Asia Minor as a network of churches. Thus, the local church should not exist selfishly thinking only of its own concerns, but the local church was a part of a larger group of churches and the local church should demonstrate Jesus' self-sacrificing love for all the churches.

Paul often mentions in his letters the connection between faith and love. This reminds us of Galatians 5:6 where Paul writes, *"For in Christ Jesus neither circumcision nor uncircumcision has any value. The only thing that counts is faith expressing itself through love."* Max Anders writes:

> Faith is only the beginning. Faith in Jesus Christ should produce inclusive love for others in the faith. The false teachers at Colossae were telling the Colossians that the fruit or evidence of spirituality was keeping rules, being initiated into secret knowledge, or having

ecstatic experiences. Paul counters this by saying that the real fruit of faith is love.[58]

V5. The Greek here begins with "because of the hope," which is reflected in my translation above. This differs from the NIV, which states that faith and love spring from hope. Hope could refer back to thanksgiving, or it could be applied to faith and love. The interpreter has to make a choice here. Although I do translate the text quite literally at this point, I feel the NIV expresses the thought of Paul here by connecting faith and love with hope; therefore, I will follow that line of thinking in my following comments.

Faith and Hope Springing from Love

> Ever more people today have the means to live, but no meaning to live for.[59]
>
> —Victor Frankl, psychologist

To live a happy, healthy life, people need hope. Victor Frankl was a psychologist who studied hope and meaning while he was in a Nazi concentration camp. He is the author of *Man's Search for Meaning*. Frankl noticed in the concentration camp that when people had a reason for hope, they stayed motivated. For example, if a man knew his wife or children were still alive, then he would fight to survive. But when that same man discovered that his wife and children were dead, he would stop fighting to survive and would soon die.

We need hope. It is a natural motivator. Think about this: Sometimes dog owners play a game with their dogs where they act as if they are going to give the dog a toy, but then they jerk the toy away at the last second. Then they might hide the toy under their arm or in their lap. The dog goes crazy looking for the toy, perhaps circling around its owner time and again looking for it. They'll sniff for the toy, bark, and keep on looking with manic enthusiasm. Dogs seem to never tire of this game.

However, when you try this same game with a little child, the child will play for a while, but then he or she will get frustrated and stop playing the game. Humans don't like to be fooled. We don't like to be "toyed with." We like to know that at the end of our effort, there is some payoff. At the end of a task, if there is no sense of accomplishment or no reward, then we quickly grow tired of the job and will often abandon the task. We need some hope that after our work is done, there will be something to show for our labor.

We are hopeful people. When hope is taken away, we lose motivation. Proverbs 13:12 that reads: *"Hope deferred makes the heart sick, but a longing fulfilled is a tree of life."*

Paul says that faith and love spring from hope. That is saying that the source of faith and love is hope. That makes hope incredibly important.

What do you look forward to? A better job, finishing college, getting married, having a baby, buying a house, purchasing a new car, going on vacation, retirement?

These aren't bad things. They are good things, but if they are the only things that we look forward to, then that's not good. We all need hope beyond this life. The greatest hope we can have is the hope for heaven, and Paul speaks of a hope stored in heaven.

What is hope? More specifically, what is the Christian hope that Paul mentions here? William Hendriksen writes, "Christian hope is not mere wishing. It is a fervent yearning, confident expectation, and patient waiting for the fulfillment of God's promises, a full *Christ-centered* (cf. Col. 1:27) assurance that these promises will indeed be realized."[60]

Christian hope is a "fervent yearning, confident expectation, and patient waiting." It is the assurance that through Christ we will realize our hopes. Christian hope fuels our motivation to live a life that pleases God and helps others.

Since hope is so important, we have to be careful where we put our hope. Where do people put their hope? In relationships, money, things, leisure activities, jobs, careers, diplomas, power, drugs, alcohol, and pleasure.

We shouldn't put our hope in the world.

We should put our hope in heaven.

Colossians 1:5–6 teaches us three things about hope:

(A) In order to mature in Christ, you need hope.

I think most of us would agree that Christians need faith and they need love. Paul here commends the disciples in Colossae because they had faith in Jesus and love for all the saints. That's great. Those attributes are needed if you want to succeed as a disciple. I don't know of anyone who would say you could be a faithless Christian or a loveless disciple. However, we don't talk as much about hope.

But Paul says here that our faith in Christ Jesus and our love for all the saints spring from our hope that is stored in heaven. In other words, the hope of heaven causes our faith and love to grow.

Do you want to increase in your faith and love? Then you need to grow in your hope for heaven. In order to mature in Christ, you need hope. Hopeful people are positive people. They are people with a plan. They tend to make things happen instead of standing idly by watching things happen.

Someone once said, "There are only three types of people in the world: one, those who make things happen; two, those who watch things happen, and three, those who say, 'What happened?'" We want to be in category one. These are people who hold firmly to the hope that they can make a difference in the world. They believe you can change the world one life at a time. They believe that God can change anyone. They believe that there is more to this world than this world. They believe one person with God is a majority. They believe in growth. They believe they can mature in Christ. They believe in hope. Be that person.

(B) Hope is a present reality.

Hope is stored in heaven. This word "stored" is the word used for storing a valuable coin for safekeeping. Our hope is presently stored for us in heaven.

1 Peter 1:3–5 reads:

[3]Praise be to the God and Father of our Lord Jesus Christ! In his great mercy he has given us new birth into a living hope through the resurrection of Jesus Christ from the dead, [4]and into an inheritance that can never perish, spoil or fade—kept in heaven for you, [5]who through faith are shielded by God's power until the coming of the salvation that is ready to be revealed in the last time.

Peter tells us that our inheritance is kept for us in heaven. That means it is safe and secure. It will be there when we need it. Therefore, we should walk securely in the here and now because of what we have in store for us in the hereafter.

For example, what if somebody told you, "Listen, I've been watching you from a distance and I want you to know that I decided to do something today to help you out a bit."

"What's that?" you ask.

"I deposited $100,000.00 in your checking account this morning. It's already cleared the bank, and you can use it however you wish. You're welcome." Then he or she walks away. (Now that didn't just happen so don't get too excited).

That bit of news would probably put a bounce in your step. Instead of eating at Taco Bell, you might go a little nicer Mexican restaurant. You might even stop by the mall and pick up a few things you've been putting off buying (like a new computer). You might go to a movie, order popcorn and a soda, and stay for a second movie. You might be a bit more generous with people. If you truly knew that the reality was that you have $100,000.00 in your bank account today that wasn't there yesterday, it would probably change the way you live your life today.

If we truly believe in the reality of heaven, then it will impact how we live our lives in the here and now. Here are two illustrations of how the reality of heaven becomes a present reality and helps us in the present.

First, look at this illustration from the lives of the early disciples. Hebrews 10:32–34 reads:

[32]Remember those earlier days after you had received the light, when you stood your ground in a great contest in the face of suffering. [33]Sometimes

you were publicly exposed to insult and persecution; at other times you stood side by side with those who were so treated. ³⁴*You sympathized with those in prison and joyfully accepted the confiscation of your property, because you knew that you yourselves had better and lasting possessions.*

Look at verse 34. The early disciples "*joyfully accepted the confiscation of their property,*" because they knew they "*had better and lasting possessions.*" Where were those better and lasting possessions? In heaven. The present reality of heaven caused them not to get nailed down to possessions on this earth. Some of us are so possessed by our possessions that we hardly have room to think about heaven. We've created our heaven here. Not the early Christians. They joyfully accepted the confiscation of their property. We have to say "No" to the voices that tie us to this earth. Possessions, things, credit card debt, bigger houses, nicer cars, manicured lawns, the white picket fence—these are all things that can tie us down to the earth. The present reality of heaven helps us realize that things don't make us truly happy because you can't buy happiness with "things." The early disciples were happy/joyful when their things were taken away. They had better and lasting possessions in heaven. The present reality of heaven changed their lives.

Consider Hebrews 11:24–26. It reads:

²⁴*By faith Moses, when he had grown up, refused to be known as the son of Pharaoh's daughter.* ²⁵*He chose to be mistreated along with the people of God rather than to enjoy the pleasures of sin for a short time.* ²⁶*He regarded disgrace for the sake of Christ as of greater value than the treasures of Egypt, because he was looking ahead to his reward.*

The reward of heaven became a present reality for Moses. It changed the way he lived his life in the here and now. So much so that Moses was willing to be mistreated with the people of God rather than enjoy the pleasures of sin for a short time. Moses had long-range vision. He looked in the distance and saw heaven, thus giving up temporary pleasure in the here and now. Are you a glutton for pleasure in the here and now? If you aren't careful, cravings for pleasure will destroy your long-range vision and you will fail to see heaven. We have to say "No" to sin in the here and now in order to stay focused on heaven. When we are focused on heaven, it helps us to say "No" to sin and pleasure.

Our hope for heaven becomes a present reality and it helps us live Godly lives in the present.

(C) Hope is based on the gospel.

We learn about the hope we have in heaven from the gospel, the word of truth, something we have already received. To stay connected with hope that is stored in heaven, it is important that we stay connected with the gospel to keep heaven fresh in our minds.

The gospel is dynamic. As Paul says in Romans 1:16, *"it is the power of God for salvation."* The gospel is the good news of our salvation. We learned this good news from reading the word of truth, the Bible. By staying in the Word, it reminds us that there is more to this life than this life and there is more to this world than this world. The Word keeps us in touch with the fact that this life is just a prelude to eternity. It is a constant reminder that there is a home beyond that is much better than the home we have here. The gospel teaches us about heaven and deepens our conviction of the realness of heaven, thus impacting our present reality.

Notice it doesn't take Paul long in the letter to mention truth. That's because he is combating error in this letter. What is the source of truth? It is the word of truth, the gospel. He mentions this idea of the truth of the gospel twice in this opening. You repeat things for emphasis. Paul emphasizes that truth comes from the word of God, which is the gospel.

We have to take time to hear the gospel. We have all kinds of things that bid for our attention. Newspapers, magazines, radio stations, iPhones, iPods, iPads, iTunes, Xboxes, PlayStations, TV shows, movies, Netflix, the NFL, NBA, WNBA, NHL, and MLB. We have multiple DVR's around the house to record shows we will never have time to watch. All of these things can be fine, but they can be distractions if we allow them to take us away from the gospel, the word of truth. If we pay too much attention to them, then they can become a hindrance to our spiritual growth.

When you look up distraction in the dictionary, the first definition is "a: diversion of the attention."[61] That's bad, but not too bad. The second definition is scary, "b: mental derangement."[62] A diversion of attention can become a mental derangement. That's why it is so important that we focus on the right things in life. A big part of our focus should be the gospel, the word of truth. Staying in the word helps us stay anchored to the hope of heaven, and that will help us make heaven a reality in the here and now.

Faith and love spring from hope. If we live our lives in the here and now as if we know for certain there is a hereafter, then it will change the way we live for the better. Grab hold of the hope stored in heaven and stay focused on that hope every day.

Some scholars mention that Paul does not express the same eschatology in this letter that he used in 1 and 2 Thessalonians. Eschatology is the study of last things like the end of time, the resurrection of the saints, heaven, hell, eternity, and so on. Some would go so far as to say that since the eschatology of 1 and 2 Thessalonians differs from that of Colossians, Paul is not the author of Colossians. Paul doesn't mention eschatology often in this letter to Colossae, but when he does, it is the same eschatology as expressed in his earlier letters: Our hope is in the future as we hold to the promises of God. Our hope is in heaven. Our hope is grounded in the truth of the gospel. But this future hope is grounded in the present. It is something that is already claimed in this life. Our passport has already been stamped; we are just waiting for the day of departure.

Our daily lives ought to be different because of the hope we have right now. The reality of heaven ought to affect the way we live life today. Faith and love spring from hope.

V6. Paul emphasizes the effectiveness of the gospel in the local setting of Colossae (they have faith, love, and hope because of the gospel), but Paul also mentions that the gospel has gone all over the world. The gospel is effective. When it is preached, people become disciples.

What does Paul mean when he says the gospel is bearing fruit all over the word? It probably means the gospel had spread to the major cities in the known world by that point (AD 60).

The gospel was bearing fruit and increasing. It was effective. When the gospel is preached, it bears fruit and increases. Sometimes we focus too much on the bearing fruit and increasing when we should be focused on the preaching. If we let the word do its thing, then it is going to bear fruit and increase.

Moo suggests that Paul is reaching back to the OT theme of humanity multiplying around the world and the nation Israel growing and increasing because of God's blessing.[63] This blessing has now been transferred to the church, which is increasing around the world. Moo writes:

> Paul may, then, be deliberately echoing a biblical-theological motif according to which God's original mandate to humans finds preliminary fulfillment in the nation of Israel but ultimate fulfillment in the worldwide transformation of people into the image of God by means of their incorporation into Christ, *the* "image of God."[64]

"You…understood God's grace in all its truth" can mean the disciples understood the substantive truth of the gospel expressed in grace. Or, it can mean they understood grace in all its truth. Truth and grace are both important. Truth without grace breeds self-righteous Pharisees. Grace without truth breeds liberal-hearted Universalists. So we need to understand both truth as it is expressed through grace and grace in all its truth.

"Knowing" and "understanding" in the Bible imply more than just intellectual knowledge. Bratcher and Nida write:

> *To know* is in Greek a compound verb, which may carry the connotation of knowing thoroughly, completely. The use of *know* in this context suggests something more than mere intellectual perception or "knowing about." The implication is "having some experience of." This is in line with such biblical expressions

as "knowing God," which certainly involves more than mere intellectual knowledge about God.[65]

Years ago, my good friend and fellow teacher, Gordon Ferguson, wrote a book about the letter to the Romans. The book description included the idea that, with its emphasis on God's grace, "once you get Romans, God gets you. Got Romans?" (That last was taken from the old "Got milk?" TV commercials where you see various celebrities with a white milk mustache above their mouth.) To really get God you have to get grace. What is grace? Anders writes, "Mercy is when God doesn't give us what we do deserve. Grace is God giving us what we don't deserve. He gives us heaven when we deserve hell; he grants us forgiveness when we deserve to be forgotten; he offers us life when we deserve death. It's all grace."[66] That is grace. Getting what we don't deserve. Do you "get" grace"?

Paul contrasts the gospel message to the false teaching of the heretics here. The gospel message is spreading and increasing around the world, whereas the heretics have a local message that is confined to Colossae. The gospel message has truth and grace, which the disciples have experienced through a changed life. The heretics have a message of lies and legalism without any power to change people's lives.

V7–8. Epaphras, who was from Colossae, taught the disciples in Colossae the grace of God. Epaphras reported to Paul what was happening in Colossae. That is why Paul wrote this letter. Epaphras seems to have been the one who originally preached the message of truth to Colossae. Dunn writes:

> But it may have been Paul's missionary strategy to concentrate his own energies in major cities, while sending out mission teams to towns in the region (cf. Acts 19:10). It is not too fanciful to imagine Epaphras, anxious to share the good news with his own townsfolk, volunteering to evangelize Colossae and devoting himself to laboring for the gospel there and in the nearby cities of Laodicea and Hierapolis (4:13).[67]

Epaphras had an interest in the church because he was invested in the church in Colossae. Anders writes:

> The most significant day in the history of Colosse was not the day Xerxes rested in the city on his march against Greece, nor was it the day Cyrus marched his Greek army through the city. No, the most significant day in the history of Colosse was the day Epaphras came to town and planted the seed of the gospel. No banners unfurled in the wind, nor did trumpets blare in the breeze;

but lives were changed and destinies were eternally altered when the gospel was planted.[68]

The disciples learned the gospel from Epaphras. O'Brien writes, "The term 'learned' (ἐμάθετε, *emataete*) probably indicates that Epaphras had given them systematic instruction in the gospel rather than some flimsy outline and that these Colossians had committed themselves as disciples to that teaching (cf. 2:6, 7)."[69]

Paul speaks very positively of Epaphras. He calls him a beloved (Ἀγαπητός/ *agapatos*) fellow slave (σύνδουλος/*sundoulos*). 'Beloved" emphasizes the close bond between Paul and Epaphras, a bond built upon the realization that both men have voluntarily become slaves to Jesus their Lord. Paul also calls Epaphras a "faithful servant" (διάκονος/*diakonos*). "Faithful" can denote either a committed believer or a trustworthy and reliable servant. "Servant" literally means "waiter at a table," but it is often used as "minister" in Paul's writings. It is the word used for deacon in 1 Timothy 3. Epaphras was a reliable minister so Paul commissioned him to go back to his hometown of Colossae and plant the church there. Now Epaphras served on Paul's behalf, making sure the apostle stayed informed of the health of the church in Colossae.

Paul has already mentioned one of his coworkers, Timothy, in his letter. Now he mentions Epaphras as a fellow slave and faithful minister. Paul believed in a team ministry. He shared his work with other reliable servants. *The Preacher's Commentary* notes, "In his letters Paul mentions fourteen fellow workers, four fellow prisoners of war, two fellow soldiers, two fellow slaves, and one yokefellow. Enough for us to know that Paul knew his was not a solo ministry."[70]

Epaphras revealed to Paul the love the disciples of Colossae had in the Spirit. Some commentaries say that the book of Colossians is devoid of the Holy Spirit. That is not true. Here is a direct reference to the Holy Spirit. The epistle does not mention the Spirit as much as some of the other letters of Paul, but to say the Spirit is not found in Colossians is wrong. True, the Spirit is only referred to directly in this one verse, but he is in every sentence that Paul wrote.

Paul was truly thankful for what was going on in the church in Colossae. Sometimes we find it difficult to be grateful for what is going on in our own lives, much less to broaden our thanksgiving radar to include the lives of others disciples and other churches around the world. Paul's thanksgiving radar was calibrated to detect Christians all over the world. This is an upward call for us.

Practical Exercise: List all the ways you are thankful. Begin in a personal way, thanking God for all the ways he has blessed you personally. Then spread that attitude of gratitude toward the church. Pray to God mentioning all the reasons you are grateful to him for the church.

2. 1:9–14. Paul's Prayer of Encouragement

⁹Διὰ τοῦτο καὶ ἡμεῖς, ἀφ᾽ ἧς ἡμέρας ἠκούσαμεν, οὐ παυόμεθα ὑπὲρ ὑμῶν προσευχόμενοι καὶ προσευχόμενοι, ἵνα πληρωθῆτε τὴν ἐπίγνωσιν τοῦ θελήματος αὐτοῦ ἐν πάσῃ σοφίᾳ καὶ συνέσει πνευματικῇ, ¹⁰περιπατῆσαι ἀξίως τοῦ κυρίου εἰς πᾶσαν ἀρεσκείαν, ἐν παντὶ ἔργῳ ἀγαθῷ καρποφοροῦντες καὶ αὐξανόμενοι τῇ ἐπιγνώσει τοῦ θεοῦ, ¹¹ἐν πάσῃ δυνάμει δυναμούμενοι κατὰ τὸ κράτος τῆς δόξης αὐτοῦ εἰς πᾶσαν ὑπομονὴν καὶ μακροθυμίαν. μετὰ χαρᾶς ¹²εὐχαριστοῦντες τῷ πατρὶ τῷ ἱκανώσαντι ὑμᾶς εἰς τὴν μερίδα τοῦ κλήρου τῶν ἁγίων ἐν τῷ φωτί· ¹³ὃς ἐρρύσατο ἡμᾶς ἐκ τῆς ἐξουσίας τοῦ σκότους καὶ μετέστησεν εἰς τὴν βασιλείαν τοῦ υἱοῦ τῆς ἀγάπης αὐτοῦ, ¹⁴ἐν ᾧ ἔχομεν τὴν ἀπολύτρωσιν, τὴν ἄφεσιν τῶν ἁμαρτιῶν·

My Translation

⁹Because of this, since the day we heard about you, we ourselves have not stopped earnestly praying on your behalf asking God to fill you with the knowledge of his will in all spiritual wisdom and understanding. ¹⁰And we pray so that you may walk worthy of the Lord, always doing what makes him happy: bearing fruit in every good work and increasing in the knowledge of God; ¹¹being strengthened with all power according to his glorious might so that you may have great endurance and patience, and joyfully ¹²giving thanks to the Father, who has qualified you to share in the inheritance of the saints in the kingdom of light. ¹³For he has rescued us from the tyranny of darkness and translated us into the kingdom of the Son he loves, ¹⁴in whom we have redemption, the forgiveness of sins.

NIV, 1984

⁹For this reason, since the day we heard about you, we have not stopped praying for you and asking God to fill you with the knowledge of his will through all spiritual wisdom and understanding. ¹⁰And we pray this in order that you may live a life worthy of the Lord and may please him in every way: bearing fruit in every good work, growing in the knowledge of God, ¹¹being strengthened with all power according to his glorious might so that you may have great endurance and patience, and joyfully ¹²giving thanks to the Father, who has qualified you to share in the inheritance of the saints in the kingdom of light. ¹³For he has rescued us from the dominion of darkness and brought us into the kingdom of the Son he loves, ¹⁴in whom we have redemption, the forgiveness of sins.

Notes

V9. As we have seen, Paul offers thanksgiving to God the Father for the disciples at Colossae. Now, he adds that he offers regular intercession for them as well. Paul believed in prayer. Hendriksen writes, "The apostle was a firm believer in 'the fellowship of prayer': a. he (and those associated with him) praying for those addressed, and b. the latter in turn being requested to pray for him."[71]

Paul uses two different words for prayer in verse 9, "praying" (προσευχόμενοι, *proseuchomenoi*) and "asking" (αἰτούμενοι, *aitoumenoi*). The first is a more general word for prayer. It is the word Paul uses most in his writings to refer to the general life of prayer. The second is a more specific word, which is linked to intercession. Intercession is petitioning God on the behalf of other people. In this case, Paul petitions God specifically to fill the disciples *"with the knowledge of his will in all spiritual wisdom and understanding."* O'Brien writes, "Paul's actual petition is for the discernment of God's will and the power to perform it."[72]

How do we know the will of God for our lives? How can we discern God's will? This is a tough question. We are always praying to discern God's will, but it isn't easy to know what God's will is for our lives. Paul gives us some helpful advice and guidance in this passage to help us discern the will of God for us.

Special Study: How to Discern the Will of God

(A) To discern the will of God, we have to be controlled by the will of God. Paul asks God to fill the disciples with the knowledge of his will. "To be filled with" means to be controlled by. Disciples are to be controlled by the knowledge of God's will. "Knowledge" goes beyond intellectual knowledge. Wisdom and understanding are used as synonyms here. Knowledge of God's will comes from wisdom and understanding. Wisdom and understanding come from doing. To know God's will, we need to be doing God's will. The more we are controlled by the knowledge of God's will, the more we will be able to discern his will for our lives.

I'm always baffled by the guy who asks me to pray for God's will about a job choice, when the same guy hasn't committed his life to living for God every day. I usually answer, 'Obey God's will for areas where you know his will, then seek his will in other areas." We know God wants us to give up sin. That's his will. Start there. We know God wants us to commit our lives to follow Jesus. That's his will. Begin there. If you want to know God's will, you have to begin by being controlled by his will. Dunnam and Ogilvie write, "The greatest problem in life is not to know what to do, but to do it—to have the will and the power to act according to what we know."[73]

Paul wants the disciples to know the will of God in the sense that his will controls their lives. Bratcher and Nida write about God's will, stating:

> *His will* is, in this context, God's design, purpose, plan, intention for his people. *The knowledge of his will* is really "to experience what God wants for you." This may be expressed as "to experience what God wants you to do," but more likely as "to experience what God wants you to experience."[74]

What does God want you to experience? For certain, the lordship of Jesus in your life. Repentance of sin. The forgiveness of sins through baptism. These are a given. If you want to know the will of God for your life, begin by giving God control of your life. Not just once when you decide to make Jesus Lord, but every day through being a disciple of Jesus.

In other words, you must make righteous decisions every day. If you are choosing sin, then you aren't choosing the will of God. That is one way to discern if you are doing God's will. Ask yourself, "Is this a righteous choice or a sinful choice?"

(B) To discern the will of God, we need to know the word of God. God has revealed a huge portion of his will to us through his word. His will is found in his Scriptures. But we have to read the word in the right manner. Knowledge of the Word has to be practical knowledge and knowledge that is practiced. Richard Melick writes, "Knowledge of God's mind comes from spiritual resources. Getting to know God is qualitatively different from other quests. The human responsibility is to place oneself in an environment conducive to spiritual growth where God can reveal his mind."[75] One of the greatest "spiritual resources" that God has given us so that he "can reveal his mind" is his word. Whoever wants to know the will of God must spend time contemplating the mind of God in his word.

But not all choices are written down for us in the Bible. Not all choices are choices between righteousness and sin. Sometimes we want to know answers to questions like: What school should I attend? Which job should I take? Where should I live? How many children should we have? Where should I spend my vacation? These are all good questions. They all fit within the realm of the will of God. How do we know what we should do in these situations?

(C) A third way to discern the will is God is through faithful prayer. Paul is praying for the disciples to be filled with the knowledge of God's will. Therefore, Paul sees a correlation between praying and knowing the will of God. James says that wisdom comes from faithful prayer, stating in James 1:5–8:

⁵If any of you lacks wisdom, he should ask God, who gives generously to all without finding fault, and it will be given to him. ⁶But when he asks, he must believe and not doubt, because he who doubts is like a wave of the sea, blown and tossed by the wind. ⁷That man should not think he will receive anything from the Lord; ⁸he is a double-minded man, unstable in all he does.

James says that wisdom is a gift of God, and God gives this gift generously to all who ask with faith. Wisdom comes from faithful prayer.

(D) To discern the will of God, you need to learn life's lessons. In other words, experience teaches us God's will. Wisdom and understanding are gained from experience. We can discern the will of God over time in our life experiences. For example, you might be a person who knows that if you don't get a certain amount of sleep, then you are going to be grumpy, moody, and emotional the next day. Experience tells you that it is God's will that you get the sleep you need. If for some reason you have to stay up late (maybe your child is sick or you are up late studying the Bible with someone), then experience tells you to keep a close watch over your moods and emotions the next day because you are going to be on edge. Life teaches us these types of lessons. We learn the will of God through experience.

Also, there are people around us who have already learned spiritual lessons from life, and they can share their guidance and wisdom with us. We have to be open to learning from them. Some call this discipling. It doesn't matter what you call it. You can call it discipling, mentoring, or practicing "one another" relationships. The label isn't important; getting advice from older, more experienced disciples is important. This is an avenue God has given us for gaining wisdom from experience.

This doesn't mean it is always easy to discern the will of God. Sometimes it is easy: If something is sinful, then that's not God's will. But what if you have a choice to make between two good things? How do you discern the will of God in this instance? Paul says—pray, gain knowledge, and gain wisdom and understanding. When we gain wisdom and understanding through prayer and experience, that wisdom and understanding can lead us to God's will for our lives. Bratcher and Nida write, "Since *wisdom and understanding* are essentially the means by which the believers in Colossae would experience God's will, this relationship may be expressed as a causative, 'being wise and having understanding will cause you to know God's will.'"[76]

Perhaps Paul brings up "knowledge" here because he knows that the disciples are facing the challenge of the Gnostics presenting a false concept of knowledge in Colossae. Paul will speak about knowledge several times in the letter. His opening salvo clarifies that the knowledge God seeks is an obedient knowledge that is based upon his will. O'Brien writes:

> Paul's use of "knowledge" (ἐπίγνωσις) here might be by way of contrast with the much-canvassed *gnosis* of the false teachers. Heretical gnosis was speculative and theoretical while the knowledge for which the apostle prayed concerned the "will of God" (θέλημα θεοῦ; cf. Rom 12:2; Eph 5:17; 1 Thess 4:3; 5:18)—it was comprehensive and demanded an obedience visible in a person's actions.[77]

V10–11. We are to walk worthily or to live a live worthy of the Lord. We are to please him in every way. This is our goal. It's good to have a goal. If you don't, then you don't know what to strive for in life. Life is aimless without goals. Paul makes it clear to the disciples in Colossae that their goal is to live a life worthy of God and to please him. That's a great goal for each day and a great slogan for the day.

> **Practical Exercise:** Get a note card and write on it: "My goal today is to live a life worthy of the Lord and to please him in every way." Place this note where you can see it every morning. Write this goal on the opening page of your Bible. Keep this goal in your mind throughout the day. Now live out the goal. Imagine making God happy. Imagine Jesus smiling down on you from heaven. That's your goal.

How do you walk worthy of the Lord and please the Lord? Paul uses four participles to describe how: (1) "bearing fruit" (καρποφοροῦντες, *karpophoroutes*, v. 10), (2) "increasing in the knowledge of God" (αὐξανόμενοι, *auxanomenoi*, v. 10), (3) "being strengthened" (δυναμούμενοι, *dunamoumenoi*, v. 11), and (4) "giving thanks" (εὐχαριστοῦντες, *eucaristountes*, v. 12).

(1) Bearing fruit

We please God by bearing fruit in every good work. Often fruit is equated with making other disciples. That is one way of bearing fruit, but it isn't the only way. We bear fruit every time we do a good work for God. Helping the poor is bearing fruit. Encouraging a struggling disciple is bearing fruit. Living out the fruit of the Spirit in our lives is bearing fruit. We don't bear fruit to earn salvation. We bear fruit because we want to live a worthy life and please the Lord. We bear fruit because we are grateful for our salvation.

(2) Increasing in knowledge of God

We please God by increasing our knowledge of him. We study God's character and nature. We meditate on who he is. The more we think about who God is, the more we become like him. Thus we live lives that are worthy of him, and we please him. When was the last time you did a Bible study on the nature and character of God? When we study God (not in a philosophical way searching for esoteric knowledge, but in a relational way), the more we will understand how we can please him with our lives.

> **Practical Exercise:** Take a week (or a month or a year) and study out the nature and character of God. Learn who God is. The more you know about God, the more you will learn what it means to please him.

V11. (3) Being strengthened

We please God by being strengthened with all power according to his glorious might. When we become stronger disciples, this pleases God. Of course we don't become strong on our own; God's might strengthens us. Our power comes from his glorious might.

We also grow strong as we grow in endurance and patience. When we face trials and overcome those trials, this produces endurance and patience. This is the formula that James gives for growth in James 1:2–4, where he writes:

> *2Consider it pure joy, my brothers, whenever you face trials of many kinds,
> 3because you know that the testing of your faith develops perseverance.
> 4Perseverance must finish its work so that you may be mature and complete, not lacking anything.*

We are to grow in endurance and patience. Endurance (ὑπομονή, *hupomona*) means "steadfastness." It is the word for an army that holds out against the enemy in battle. Hendriksen writes, "Endurance is the grace to bear up under, the bravery of perseverance in the performance of one's God-given task in spite of every hardship and trial, the refusal to succumb to despair or cowardice."[78] This word is often used in relation to trials and situations we face in life.

Paul uses another word for patience: μακροθυμία, *makrothumia,* meaning "longsuffering." Hendriksen states, "*Longsuffering* characterizes the person who, in relation to those who oppose or molest him, exercises patience, refusing to yield to passion or to outbursts of anger."[79] In the Scriptures it is used to describe God's patience with humanity. This word is often used in relation to people who cause us pain and suffering. We must stay faithful in face of both circumstances that can test us and people who challenge us. Both endurance and patience are needed. Both are gifts from God.

V12. (4) **Giving thanks.** We please God by giving thanks to the Father. God is pleased when we have a grateful heart. He loves it when we have the attitude of gratitude.

One thing we have to be grateful for is that God has qualified us to share in the inheritance of the saints in the kingdom of light. We don't have to stay trapped in the tyranny of darkness. We can be a part of the kingdom of light. This word *kingdom* has taken a beating in recent years in our movement of churches. That's because it was misused in the past. But it is a good word and we should reclaim it. We get to live in God's kingdom right now. The *kingdom* means "the rule and reign of God." Whenever we serve Jesus as the Lord of our lives, we are a part of the kingdom of God. God's kingdom is full of light. It's a good place to be. Some theologians call this realized eschatology. Since eschatology is the study of the last things, realized eschatology means that we get to have a taste of the last things in the present. We should give God thanks for allowing us to glimpse eternity while living in the temporal.

Of eschatology that is realized in the present, O'Brien writes:

> The aorist tenses point to an eschatology that is truly realized (i.e. God had *already* qualified [ἱκανώσαντι] the Colossians to share in the inheritance, he had *already* delivered [ἐρρύσατο] them from this alien power and had *already* transferred [μετέστησεν] them to his Son's kingdom), while by contrast, the present tense of verse 14, "we have" (ἔχομεν), stresses the continued results of the redemption wrought in the past.[80]

As disciples, we experience some of the future glory of God in the present. This gives us reason for hope and thanksgiving. Paul continues this thought in the next two verses.

V13–14. In face of trials and persecution, we should joyfully give thanks to the Father. Why should we be thankful? Paul mentions three reasons here. He says we should be thankful because (a) God has rescued us from the tyranny of darkness, (b) he has translated us into the kingdom of the Son he loves, and (c) he has given us redemption, the forgiveness of sins.

We have been rescued from the tyranny of darkness. Max Anders writes, "Paul uses a stark word (*ruomai*) to describe God's deliverance of the believer from darkness. The force of this word indicates that the believer was in acute danger and has been delivered from an alien power in a highly dangerous situation."[81] This is an arresting image. We were in severe danger being held hostage by an alien power, then God rescued us through Jesus. Do you feel rescued?

When I was a teenager I was a lifeguard for a couple of summers at church camp and a Boy Scout camp. At scout camp the lifeguard duties were tough for two reasons. First, the kids were swimming in a lake, which meant that if a kid went underwater, he was lost from sight. As a lifeguard, you had to be extremely vigilant watching the swimmers. Second, the kids were crazy. They kept trying to drown each other. Fortunately, I only had to rescue swimmers twice. Once I didn't even go into the water. I watched as a kid fell into water that was over his head. I knew he couldn't swim, so I ran to the kid, grabbed him by the hair, and jerked him onto the dock. I grabbed a head of hair and pulled as hard as I could. Now you might think that someone who just had his hair jerked might be upset, but you would be wrong. The kid didn't say, "Hey, you pulled my hair!" This kid was grateful because I snatched him out of deep water.

While all of us were going under and drowning in sin, God reached down, grabbed us, and pulled us out of the darkness. Why be thankful? Be grateful that God brought you to safety. We were taken from darkness into light. Hendriksen writes poetically of the transformation that God gave us when he snatched us out of the darkness and brought us into light. He writes:

> He brought us out of the dark and dismal realm of false ideas and chimerical ideals into the sun-bathed land of clear knowledge and realistic expectation; out of the bewildering sphere of perverted cravings and selfish hankerings into the blissful realm of holy yearnings and glorious self-denials; out of the miserable dungeon of intolerable bonds and heart-rending cries into the magnificent palace of glorious liberty and joyful songs.[82]

Be thankful for where he has brought you—into the kingdom of the Son he loves. We are presently in the kingdom of God. But also there is a future kingdom still to come. This is the "already, not yet" of the Kingdom. In the present we are "already" a part of God's kingdom as it has been manifest on the earth. But beyond this world there exists a manifestation of the kingdom where God reigns with the heavenly hosts in eternal glory. This is the "not yet" of the Kingdom. The church is part of the kingdom of God. It is part of the "already" manifestation of God's kingdom, but the Kingdom is bigger, larger, and more comprehensive than the church. The eternal kingdom of God is made up of the "already" and the "not yet" of the Kingdom.

At some point in the future, the Kingdom in the "here and now" will be collected into the Kingdom in the "ever after." It is exciting to think that we can be a part of God's kingdom in the here and now. The Kingdom is already among us. But also the eternal kingdom of God is something that we look forward to and long to discover. It is the undiscovered country that we long to see. It is the sweet by-and-by that we eagerly anticipate. It is the "not yet" that we pray will come quickly. So we have something in the here and now (the "already") to be extremely excited about. We also have something in the "ever after" (the "not yet") to look forward to. That is the brilliance of God's kingdom.

Be thankful for redemption, the forgiveness of sins. Redemption is a metaphor that comes from the first-century marketplace. Slavery was a huge part of the Roman culture.[83] When a slave was redeemed, someone paid the price for his or her freedom. That's the image that Paul uses here. Jesus paid the price for our freedom when he died on the cross for our sins. Through his death, we have the forgiveness of sins. Paul uses this image of redemption to remind us that we should be grateful for what Jesus did to give us salvation.

Anders lists five metaphors or images of salvation that Paul uses in his letters:

1. **From the court room** (justification) Romans 3:21–31.
   The sinner stands before God accused and guilty. God declares the sinner righteous.

2. **From the marketplace** (redemption) 1 Corinthians 6:20...
   The sinner stands before God as a slave. God grants freedom by payment of a ransom.

3. **From the bank** (forgiveness) Ephesians 1:7.
   The sinner stands before God in debt, and the debt, having been paid by another, is canceled.

4. **From the home** (adoption) Ephesians 1:5...
   The sinner stands before God as a stranger; God makes the sinner a member of his family.

5. **From the battlefield** (reconciliation) 2 Corinthians 5:18.
   The sinner stands before God as an enemy and becomes a friend when God makes peace.[84]

All of these images stand as a reminder that God did something for us that we could not do for ourselves. He snatched us out of darkness. He redeemed us from our sins and reconciled us to himself. We should always be grateful to God for what he has done for us. Paul never lost sight of this fact. He knew that he was a sinner saved by God's grace. We shouldn't lose sight of it either.

Practical Exercise: In this section of his letter, Paul mentions that he makes intercession in prayer for the disciples in Colossae. Make a list of people for whom you can make regular intercession, and list their needs. Begin today to make regular intercession for them.

Jesus, I Come[85]
By William T. Sleeper
Published 1887

Out of my bondage, sorrow and night,
Jesus, I come, Jesus, I come;
Into Thy freedom, gladness and light,
Jesus, I come to Thee;
Out of my sickness into Thy health,
Out of my want and into Thy wealth,
Out of my sin and into Thyself,
Jesus, I come to Thee.
Out of the fear and dread of the tomb,
Jesus, I come, Jesus, I come;
Into the joy and light of Thy home,
Jesus, I come to Thee;
Out of the depths of ruin untold,
Into the peace of Thy sheltering fold,
Ever Thy glorious face to behold,
Jesus, I come to Thee.

C. 1:15–23. The Supremacy of Christ

1. 1:15–20. Superior Nature; The Hymn to Christ

[15]ὅς ἐστιν εἰκὼν τοῦ θεοῦ τοῦ ἀοράτου, πρωτότοκος πάσης κτίσεως, [16]ὅτι ἐν αὐτῷ ἐκτίσθη τὰ πάντα ἐν τοῖς οὐρανοῖς καὶ ἐπὶ τῆς γῆς, τὰ ὁρατὰ καὶ τὰ ἀόρατα, εἴτε θρόνοι εἴτε κυριότητες εἴτε ἀρχαὶ εἴτε ἐξουσίαι· τὰ πάντα δι' αὐτοῦ καὶ εἰς αὐτὸν ἔκτισται· [17]καὶ αὐτός ἐστιν πρὸ πάντων καὶ τὰ πάντα ἐν αὐτῷ συνέστηκεν, [18]καὶ αὐτός ἐστιν ἡ κεφαλὴ τοῦ σώματος τῆς ἐκκλησίας· ὅς ἐστιν ἀρχή, πρωτότοκος ἐκ τῶν νεκρῶν, ἵνα γένηται ἐν πᾶσιν αὐτὸς πρωτεύων, [19]ὅτι ἐν αὐτῷ εὐδόκησεν πᾶν τὸ πλήρωμα κατοικῆσαι [20]καὶ δι' αὐτοῦ ἀποκαταλλάξαι τὰ πάντα εἰς αὐτόν, εἰρηνοποιήσας διὰ τοῦ αἵματος τοῦ σταυροῦ αὐτοῦ, [δι' αὐτοῦ] εἴτε τὰ ἐπὶ τῆς γῆς εἴτε τὰ ἐν τοῖς οὐρανοῖς.

My Translation
[15]He is the image of the invisible God, the firstborn over all creation. [16]For by him all things in heaven and on earth were created: visible and invisible, whether thrones or dominions or rulers or powers; all things were created through him and for him. [17]He is before all things, and all things hold together in him.

[18]And he is the head of the body, the church; he is the beginning and the firstborn from the dead, so that in everything he might have the supremacy

(be first). [19]For God was determined to have all his fullness live in him, [20]and through him to reconcile all things to himself, whether things on earth or in heaven, making peace through his blood on the cross.

NIV, 1984

[15]He is the image of the invisible God, the firstborn over all creation. [16]For by him all things were created: things in heaven and on earth, visible and invisible, whether thrones or powers or rulers or authorities; all things were created by him and for him. [17]He is before all things, and in him all things hold together. [18]And he is the head of the body, the church; he is the beginning and the first-born from among the dead, so that in everything he might have the supremacy. [19]For God was pleased to have all his fullness dwell in him, [20]and through him to reconcile to himself all things, whether things on earth or things in heaven, by making peace through his blood, shed on the cross.

> **Practical Exercise:** Before you read this section, take a few minutes and see how many superlatives Paul uses in these few verses to speak of Christ. Make a list and then compare your list with what you read below.

> Honestly ask yourself, "Does Jesus have absolute supremacy in my life?"[86]
>
> —Max Anders

Notes

Paul moves to a hymn that extols the supremacy of Jesus. Some believe this hymn was composed by someone other than Paul and used by the early church in its worship and that Paul later added this hymn to his letter.[87] But Paul could easily have composed it, either for this letter or as a general hymn to expound the supremacy of Christ.

The use of the word "hymn" is much different from the way we tend to use it today. In this context, hymn is used as a credo of the early church. Certainly Paul places this paragraph here as he opens his letter to emphasize the importance of what he is saying. It follows his introduction and becomes the first and most important theme introduced in the letter, that is, the supremacy of Christ.

Ernest Martin gives his literal translation of the passage, which highlights some of the key concepts found in this Hymn to Christ.[88] He writes:

(15)
    WHO IS the image of the invisible God,
        THE FIRSTBORN of ALL creation,

(16)
> for in him were created ALL things
> in the heavens and on the earth,
> things visible and things invisible,
> whether thrones or dominions or rulers or authorities;
>> ALL things through him and for him were created;

(17)
and HE IS before ALL things,
and ALL things in him hold together,

(18)
and HE IS the head of the body, the church;
WHO IS the beginning,
> THE FIRSTBORN of the dead,
>> so that in ALL things he might be first,

(19)
> for in him ALL the fullness was pleased to dwell,

(20)
> and through him to reconcile ALL things to himself,
>> having made peace through the blood of his cross,
through him (that is), whether things on the earth or things in the heavens.

In adding this hymn to his letter Paul battles against the views of the false teachers concerning Jesus. Anders writes:

> When Paul wrote to the Colossians, he was countering a clever company of false teachers who sought to replace the Colossians' enthusiastic devotion to Christ with only a mild approval of him. They didn't encourage anyone to forget Jesus altogether; they just said he wasn't the only show in town.[89]

V15. How many superlatives about Jesus can we find in this hymn? Let's keep count.

First, Paul begins by saying that Jesus is the image of the invisible God. God is invisible; however, because of Jesus, we get to see an image of God. The word for "image" (εἰκὼν/ *eikōn*) is the word used for the likeness or stamp on the coins of Rome. These stamps were portraits of various emperors or politicians. Jesus is the portrait of God. God's image was stamped on Jesus. Hebrews 1:3 expresses the same idea with these words: *"The Son is the radiance of God's glory and the exact representation of his being, sustaining all things by his powerful word."* One commentary notes:

An *eikōn* was a representation, or reproduction with precise likeness. A portrait of a person's likeness or an image of a sovereign or hero on a coin was an *eikōn*. Paul says Jesus Christ was that—a representation of God the Creator-Father. But more. The word *eikōn* also means manifestation. More than being in the likeness of God, as are all persons created, Jesus was God Himself in human incarnation.[90]

John would later say the same thing when he wrote, *"The Word became flesh and made his dwelling among us"* (John 1:14). This is the idea of the incarnation. Jesus took on flesh so we could see what God is like.

I remember the story of the little girl who asked her Mom what God was like. Her mom replied by saying that God is love, God is compassion, God is good, and God is caring.

The little girl replied, "Yes, but what does God look like?"

The mom answered, "No one knows, because God is invisible."

The little girl said, "I want a God who has some skin on him."

There are times when all of us want a God with a little skin on him because we want to picture what he is like. That is where the incarnation helps. Jesus is God with skin on him. He is the image of the invisible God.

Second, Jesus is the firstborn over all creation. "Firstborn" in the Old Testament can mean first in temporal order, but it also means first in rank. It also denotes the chosen one of God or the one to whom God shows special favor or love. So what does it mean in this context?

Some interpret this phrase to mean that Jesus was the first created being, that he was not God; he was only a created being. But we have to be careful here. One rule of interpretation is to the let the Bible interpret itself. Look at the verse in context and see if the context doesn't tell you what the problematic phrase means. Here, look at what Paul says after he introduces Jesus as the firstborn over all creation. He adds, *"For by him all things were created."* According to Genesis 1, that was the role of God. God spoke the world into existence. Paul does not mean that Jesus was the first created being and less than God. Paul is saying that Jesus created the world and therefore is superior to everything that was created. The firstborn in the Jewish mind is the position of authority. Firstborn over all creation means that Jesus has authority over all creation.

Compare this verse to Psalm 89:27: *"I will also appoint him my firstborn, the most exalted of the kings of the earth."* The firstborn of God is the "most" exalted king. Firstborn is a place of authority, a position of superiority. Jesus is the King of kings. Jesus is the Lord over creation. Jesus is superior to the created order.

Another rule of interpretation is that we must compare Scripture with

Scripture. Use parallel passages. In this case, in verse 18, Paul says that Jesus is the firstborn from among the dead. That doesn't mean that Jesus was the first person to rise from the dead. Elijah brought the widow of Zarephath's son back from the dead.[91] Jesus brought Lazarus back from the dead (John 11:38–44). Paul could not have meant Jesus was the first resurrected being. He meant Jesus had authority over death. However we take "firstborn from among the dead," we need to be consistent and take "firstborn over all creation" in the same way. In both instances, Paul is talking about authority—authority over creation and over death.

V16. *Third,* all things were created by Jesus. He is the creator. Only God creates. Paul here equates Jesus with God. J.R.R. Tolkien, whom many consider to be the most influential author of the twentieth century, made a distinction in his literature between creation and "subcreation." God creates; man sub-creates. This is an important distinction. If only God creates, and all things were created by Jesus, then Jesus is God.

Jesus created "all things." Therefore, he is superior to all things. Moo writes, "The universality expressed in 'all things' (*ta panta*) is a leitmotif of the 'hymn,' the construction here suggesting a collective sense: 'the entire universe.'"[92] In other words, Jesus created the entire universe and the entire universe is subject to him.

Since Jesus created the world, he has authority over all creation including thrones, powers, rulers, and authorities. Some commentators point out that these four categories are classes of spiritual beings (beings in the heavenly realms, both good and evil). One aspect of the heresy at Colossae is the worship of angels and other spiritual beings. Moo writes:

> The existence of spiritual beings of various sorts and their critical impact on the affairs of human beings were fundamental components of the ancient worldview. This belief was apparently an important catalyst for the Colossian false teaching, and Paul's emphasis here on Christ's supremacy to these powers reminds the Colossians that they are utterly unable to rival Christ in any way.[93]

Paul here demonstrates that Jesus has authority over creation and over all the spiritual beings in the heavenly realms.

V17. *Fourth,* Jesus is before all things. Before the world, Jesus existed. He was before the universe. This "preexistence" of Jesus is another way of saying that Jesus is God. One attribute of God is that God has always been. If Jesus has always existed, then he is God.

This is also another way to say that the universe is subject to Jesus. Since Jesus was before all things, he has authority over all things and all things are subject to him.

Fifth, in Jesus all things hold together. Jesus holds the universe together. He is Sovereign over all creation. O'Brien writes, "He is the sustainer of the universe and the unifying principle of its life. Apart from his *continuous* sustaining activity…all would disintegrate."[94] Moo writes, "What holds the universe together is not an idea or a virtue, but a person: the resurrected Christ. Without him, electrons would not continue to circle nuclei, gravity would cease to work, the planets would not stay in their orbits."[95]

Christ is supreme. Jesus holds everything together. Here we have another characteristic that we think of as only applying to God, but Paul applies this characteristic to Jesus. Jesus is divine.

If Jesus can hold the universe together, can't he hold our lives together? Of course he can. All of us have some sort of chaos in our lives, but Jesus can help us with that. We need to surrender our chaos to his order.

> **Practical Exercise:** Take a moment to think of everything in your life that you consider chaotic. For example: your schedule, your finances, your children, your marriage, your education, your job, your laundry, your desk, your appearance, or your life. Get specific. Mention things that you might consider small things—your refrigerator, your garage, or your makeup mirror. Now take a moment to surrender all those things to Jesus who "holds all things together."

V. 18. *Sixth,* Jesus is the head of the body, the church. Jesus is over all of creation. He is also over the church. He is Sovereign over the church; he is the head of the body. The image denotes that Jesus has authority over the church. The term for church (ἐκκλησία, *ekklasia*) means an assembly. It was used in Greek literature in terms of calling an army to assembly. Paul uses the word sixty-two times in his epistles.

Some people don't like church today. They say the church is an outdated model. Perhaps this is because they haven't seen the church as it is expressed in the New Testament. Jesus still believes in the church. He is its head, and as head, he sustains the church; he gives it sustenance.

Seventh, Jesus is the beginning and the firstborn from among the dead. Just as Jesus was the beginning and firstborn over creation, he is now the beginning and the firstborn over the "new" creation, which is the resurrection. Moo writes:

> The resurrection of Christ initiates this end-time resurrection; his resurrection guarantees and, indeed, stimulates the resurrection of all who follow (1 Cor. 15:20; cf. Acts 26:23; Matt. 27:52–53). In this sense, he is not only the first one to experience resurrection;

he is the "founder" of the new order of resurrection.[96]

"Firstborn" doesn't speak to time, but to rank. Jesus has authority over death. Jesus conquered death. He is superior to death. Therefore, in everything Jesus has supremacy.

V. 19. *Eighth,* all the fullness of God dwells in Jesus. There is some difficulty in knowing how to translate the phrase "all the fullness." Since it is in the neuter case, it is difficult to know what it modifies. It could be translated as (1) a subject, "all the fullness was pleased to dwell," (2) an object, "God was pleased to have all his fullness dwell," or (3) an appositive, "God in all his fullness." The first option is the most literal. The third is also very literal, but you do have to supply the word "God" here because it is not in the Greek text. To me, however, the second option seems to translate the thought that Paul is making here.

Paul states that all the fullness of God resides in Christ. Christ is divine. Christ is supreme. O'Brien writes, "He (Jesus) is the 'place'…in whom God in all his fullness was pleased to take up his residence… All the attributes and activities of God—his spirit, word, wisdom and glory—are perfectly displayed in Christ."[97]

V. 20. *Ninth,* all things are reconciled through Jesus. Paul's last point is his most important. Paul is not teaching Universalism here. He is not saying that evil will be saved. In 2:25, he makes a point that Christ triumphs over powers and authorities through the cross; he doesn't redeem them. Paul is saying that everything will be put in its place. Moo writes, "Colossians 1:20 teaches, then, not 'cosmic salvation' or even 'cosmic redemption,' but 'cosmic restoration' or 'renewal.' Through the work of Christ on the cross, God has brought his entire rebellious creation back under the rule of his sovereign power."[98]

Since Jesus is Sovereign over all, he allows evil to play its part in this world; but ultimately good will triumph over evil, and all things will be reconciled through Jesus.

Look over this list. I count at least nine superlatives of Jesus. Paul includes this hymn because he wants the disciples to understand how great, majestic, noble, magnificent, gallant, heroic, regal, powerful, grand, marvelous, splendid, wonderful, superb, immense, mighty, grand, big, and supreme Jesus is. It is always good to take time to reflect upon the might and majesty of Christ.

Practical Exercise: Think of ways that you can creatively say that Jesus is supreme. Write your own hymn of the supremacy to Jesus.

2. 1:21–23. Superior Reconciliation

²¹Καὶ ὑμᾶς ποτε ὄντας ἀπηλλοτριωμένους καὶ ἐχθροὺς τῇ διανοίᾳ ἐν τοῖς ἔργοις τοῖς πονηροῖς, ²²νυνὶ δὲ ἀποκατήλλαξεν ἐν τῷ σώματι τῆς σαρκὸς αὐτοῦ διὰ τοῦ θανάτου παραστῆσαι ὑμᾶς ἁγίους καὶ ἀμώμους καὶ ἀνεγκλήτους κατενώπιον αὐτοῦ, ²³εἴ γε ἐπιμένετε τῇ πίστει τεθεμελιωμένοι καὶ ἑδραῖοι καὶ μὴ μετακινούμενοι ἀπὸ τῆς ἐλπίδος τοῦ εὐαγγελίου οὗ ἠκούσατε, τοῦ κηρυχθέντος ἐν πάσῃ κτίσει τῇ ὑπὸ τὸν οὐρανόν, οὗ ἐγενόμην ἐγὼ Παῦλος διάκονος.

My Translation

²¹And you formerly were estranged from God and were enemies in your minds through your evil deeds. ²²But now he has reconciled you in his physical body through death to present you holy, blameless, and without blemish in his sight, ²³indeed, if you remain in faith, established and firm, not moved from the hope in the gospel, which you have heard, the gospel preached to all humanity under heaven of which I, Paul, have become a servant/minister.

NIV, 1984

²¹Once you were alienated from God and were enemies in your minds because of your evil behavior. ²²But now he has reconciled you by Christ's physical body through death to present you holy in his sight, without blemish and free from accusation— ²³if you continue in your faith, established and firm, not moved from the hope held out in the gospel. This is the gospel that you heard and that has been proclaimed to every creature under heaven, and of which I, Paul, have become a servant.

Notes
(A) Remember Who You Were.

V. 21. *"Once you were alienated from God and were enemies in your minds because of your evil behavior."*

Paul says, "Once you were."

Paul begins with "and you." He wants the disciples in Colossae to know that he is speaking directly to them here. They were estranged from God. They were enemies in their minds through their evil behavior.

Sometimes when we listen to sermons or lessons, we are thinking about others who should be hearing the sermon instead of thinking of ourselves. Paul wants each disciple to realize what was his or her condition before Christ entered the picture. He speaks of this as something they used to be ("you formerly were").

Paul starts with "And you formerly," and moves to "but now...you." See the contrast. Paul wants the disciples to see how far they have come. Once they were enemies, now they are friends. Once God had to reconcile them to himself, but now they are a part of God's ministry of reconciliation in the world. It is very important that we see the transformation that God brings to our lives. This idea of "once...but now" is very important to Paul.

First, each of them was alienated or estranged from God. To be estranged is to be out of harmony with God. We understand what it means to be estranged from a friend or a relative. Before we were reconciled to God through Jesus, this is how we were with God.

Second, each of them was an enemy of God in their minds through evil deeds. This second term is even stronger. Not only were we out of harmony, but we were the enemies of God because our thoughts were hostile to his thought and our deeds were evil. Since our minds were hostile to God, we committed evil deeds.

We need to remember from where we have come. George Santayana wrote in his *Reason in Common Sense*, "Those who cannot remember the past are condemned to repeat it."[99] This can be true of your personal history as well.

We need to remember what it felt like to be alienated from God. "Alienated" means "to be cut off or separated." Elizabeth Barrett Browning, the poet, was cut off from her parents because she married someone of whom they did not approve. She sent them letters every day for ten years to ask them to accept her back. One day a box came from her parents. It was filled with all her letters, unopened. That's what it means to be alienated. And that's how we were with God.

Alienation from God leads to a hostile mind and evil actions. You remember when your mind was hostile. You were filled with negativity, bitterness, hatred, lust, racist thoughts, uncontrolled urges, greed, pride, and rage. Your mind was full of sinful thoughts all the time. That's a horrible place to be. Yet, that's where you are when you are alienated from God.

Have you ever been to Times Square in New York when it was really busy, like between Christmas and New Year's when there are thousands of people on the street? It's a sea of humanity. You can't walk in a straight line. You have to constantly dodge people around you. The whole place is full of people, a steady stream of people, person after person after person. That's how your mind was filled with sin when you were alienated from God. You were hostile. Sinful thoughts filled your mind: First lust, then anger, then hatred, then pride, then greed. Sin after sin after sin filled your mind. That's what it is like to be alienated from God.

We were all in really bad shape. I really enjoy the writings of G.K. Chesterton. He was a deep thinker who had a wonderful sense of humor. Once a question was asked in the *The Times of London*. The question said, "What's Wrong with the World?" Chesterton sent in this reply, "I am. Yours truly, G.K. Chesterton." At one point, we all were the problem with the world. We were also the problem with our own world. We wanted to blame others. That's the easy thing to do—shift the blame, to say, "It's not my fault; if you had had my parents, you'd be just as messed up as I am." But the problem was each of us. That's because we were alienated from God, hostile in our minds, and full of evil deeds.

Sin did this; it separated us from God (Isaiah 59:1–2). God wouldn't hear us. He couldn't even look at us. We chose sin, and that separated us from God.

> [1]Surely the arm of the LORD is not too short to save,
>   nor his ear too dull to hear.
> [2]But your iniquities have separated
>   you from your God;
> your sins have hidden his face from you,
>   so that he will not hear.

Here's another reminder from Paul of who we were. Ephesians 2:12–13 reads:

> [12]Remember that at that time you were separate from Christ, excluded from citizenship in Israel and foreigners to the covenants of the promise, without hope and without God in the world. [13]But now in Christ Jesus you who once were far away have been brought near by the blood of Christ.

We shouldn't forget who we were. It reminds us that we never want to go back there again. It reminds of how far we have come.

(B) Remember Who Christ Is.

V. 22. *"But now he has reconciled you by Christ's physical body through death to present you holy in his sight, without blemish and free from accusation."*
Follow Paul's line of reasoning here:
Once you were alienated.
"But now he." He who? God.
You were alienated, but now God. Now God what?
You were alienated, but now God has reconciled you. How?
You were alienated, but now God has reconciled you by Christ's physical body through death. Why?
You were alienated, but now God has reconciled you by Christ's physical body through death to present you holy in his sight, without blemish and free from accusation.
Wow![100]
But Christ reconciled us to God in his physical body through his death. We couldn't save ourselves, so Jesus became the sacrifice for our sins. For those false teachers who would say that Jesus never took on flesh (this is known as

Docetism), Paul makes it clear that Jesus lived in a physical body. Literally, the phrase reads, "in the body of his flesh."

The purpose of the death of Jesus was to present us holy, blameless, and without reproach before God. Some place these terms within the sacrificial system of Israel. But O'Brien points out that the verb "to present" was often used in a legal setting in the sense of bringing someone to court. He adds:

> The last term "irreproachable" (ἀνέγκλητος), which probably determines the meaning of the other two...does not belong to the context of cultic statements. It was a judicial word (which came to be used in everyday speech ...) denoting a person or thing against which there could be no ἔγκλημα and which was "free from reproach," "without stain."[101]

Through the death of Jesus, we have been cleared of all wrongdoing. We are found not guilty.

But we can still be guilty souls. We have to learn to let go of our past mistakes. Christ doesn't want us to keep beating ourselves up over them. We have to learn to forgive ourselves in the same way that Christ has forgiven us.

2 Corinthians 5:21 states, *"God made him who knew no sin to be sin for us, so that in him we might become the righteousness of God."*

We were alienated, but Jesus became sin for us and brought us back to God. This is an amazing thought—that Jesus died for me.

Charles Wesley wrote "And Can It Be?"[102]

And can it be that I should gain
an interest in the Savior's blood!
Died he for me? who caused his pain!
For me? who him to death pursued?
Amazing love! How can it be
that thou, my God, should'st die for me?

Long my imprisoned spirit lay
fast bound in sin and nature's night.
Thine eye diffused a quick'ning ray:
I woke the dungeon flamed with light!
My chains fell off, my heart was free,
I rose, went forth and followed Thee.
Amazing love! How can it be
that Thou, my God, should'st die for me!

We should never forget the price that Jesus paid for our freedom. When we choose Jesus, we are reconciled to God. No more alienation. No more hostile mind. No more evil deeds. We receive blessing upon blessing because we choose Jesus. God forgives us of our sins. As for the separation that existed between God and us, Jesus closes that gulf. Jesus takes away our hostile mind. Blessing after blessing after blessing.

I read a story about a man who loved his son more than anything. This man collected very expensive paintings, but none of them compared with the love he had for his son. His son went off to war and was killed in action. A good friend of the man's son sent the father a portrait of his son that he drew while the son was a soldier. The man valued that portrait more than any other painting in his collection.

When the man died, all his paintings were to be sold at auction. The first painting up for bid was the portrait of the man's son drawn by his army friend. The auctioneer started the bidding. The portrait went for $10.00. The auctioneer said, "Sold for $10.00." Before the next painting was presented, the man in charge of the auction approached the podium. The man said, "According to the wishes of the owner of these paintings, all the paintings go to the person who bought the portrait of his son. The owner stipulated in his will: 'Whoever takes my son, takes all.' The auction is now over."[103]

"Whoever takes my son takes all." We need to remember who Christ is and what he has done for us. Whoever takes Jesus receives all the blessings that come with Jesus. Remember what Christ has done for you.

> **Practical Exercise:** What past mistakes do you have a difficult
> time throwing away? Make a list and then present the list to God.
> Listen as God declares you to be "Not Guilty" of all these past
> wrongs. Now burn the list or throw it in the garbage.

(C) Remember Who You Are.

V. 23. *If you continue in your faith, established and firm, not moved from the hope held out in the gospel. This is the gospel that you heard and that has been proclaimed to every creature under heaven, and of which I, Paul, have become a servant."*

Paul begins this passage with a gigantic, colossal two-letter word, "If." We have been reconciled, but that doesn't mean we have our ticket punched and we are ready to fly to heaven.

Paul says, "if you continue in your faith." Some see this statement as the purpose clause for which Paul penned the letter, to make sure the Colossians continued in their faith and grew to maturity. Moo writes, "As we have seen, in v. 23 Paul introduces—albeit somewhat obliquely—the central concern of the letter: to encourage the Colossian Christians to resist the blandishments of the false teachers and to continue to grow in their knowledge of Christ."[104]

The word "if" does remind us that salvation is always conditional. The Bible does not teach "once saved always saved." God wants us to be secure in our salvation, but he also wants us to be aware that we can stray from the mark. So Paul writes, "If you remain in faith." Paul expects this warning to be taken seriously. Moo writes:

> Paul would clearly want his words here to be taken with great seriousness. He wants to confront the Colossians with the reality that their eventual salvation depends on their remaining faithful to Christ and to the true gospel. Only by continuing in their faith can they hope to find a favorable verdict from God on the day of judgment. We have in this verse, then, a real warning. This warning, along with many similar ones, presents the "human responsibility" side in the biblical portrayal of final salvation. God does, indeed, by his grace and through his Spirit, work to preserve his people so that they will be vindicated in the judgment; but, at the same time, God's people are responsible to persevere in their faith if they expect to see that vindication.[105]

Faith here is synonymous with the gospel, which was preached around the world. This faith must be "established and firm, not moved." The metaphor is that of a solid building with a firm foundation. O'Brien writes:

> Paul's terms "stable and steadfast" (τεθεμελιωμένοι καὶ ἑδραῖοι) are metaphors of strength and security used in connection with a house (cf. Matt 7:24–27). Both the foundation (the noun θεμέλιον is akin to this verb) ought to be well established and the structure firm (ἑδραῖος).[106]

This reminds me of the hymn, "How Firm a Foundation." It was written by John Keith and published in 1787. This beautiful hymn goes:

> How firm a foundation, ye saints of the Lord,
> Is laid for your faith in his excellent word!
> What more can he say than to you he hath said—
> To you who for refuge to Jesus have fled?
>
> "Fear not, I am with thee, oh, be not dismayed,
> For I am thy God, and will still give thee aid;
> I'll strengthen thee, help thee, and cause thee to stand,
> Upheld by My gracious, omnipotent hand.

"When through the deep waters I call thee to go,
The rivers of sorrow shall not overflow;
For I will be with thee thy trouble to bless,
And sanctify to thee thy deepest distress.

"When through fiery trials thy pathway shall lie,
My grace, all-sufficient, shall be thy supply;
The flame shall not harm thee; I only design
Thy dross to consume and thy gold to refine.

"The soul that on Jesus doth lean for repose,
I will not, I will not, desert to his foes;
That soul, though all hell should endeavor to shake,
I'll never, no never, no never forsake."

In what sense has this gospel been preached "to every creature under heaven"? Are we to take this literally? Does Paul mean that the gospel reached every person under heaven by AD 60 or 61? In my opinion, this is not likely. I believe Paul is using a hyperbole to express that the gospel has spread to the four corners of the world and thus the gospel has spread to all humanity. Certainly the major cities had been reached with the gospel. Certainly it had gone north, south, east, and west. Symbolically, the gospel had been preached to every creature under heaven.

Paul closes by mentioning that he is a servant or minister (διάκονος, *diakonos*) of this gospel. Paul was grateful to be connected with spreading the gospel throughout the world.

Remember. Remember who you were. Remember who Christ is. Remember who you are.

While I was writing this book, Leigh and I attended the funeral of a dear friend who was a faithful disciple of Jesus for over six decades. Her name was Jeaneen Lile. She was married to Harold Lile for over fifty years. Jeaneen was one reason Harold was an elder. She was an amazing wife and mother and a Proverbs 31 woman.

Jeaneen was one of the most consistent, powerful, committed, and faithful disciples I have ever known. Her memorial service lasted two and a half hours. It could have gone on all night, so many people wanted to share.

At one point, someone asked anyone who felt like Harold and Jeaneen had made them a part of their family to stand. Over 100 people stood up. When I asked for Leigh's hand in marriage, I had to ask her dad for permission, but I also had to ask the Liles for permission, because Leigh had become a part of their family. Jeaneen never preached a sermon nor was she a lead speaker at a women's day. She was a wife, a mother, and a disciple. She was an older woman who trained younger women how to be wives and mothers. She loved people deeply. She knew who she was. She left a legacy that lives beyond her. She has influenced a hundred who will influence thousands who will influence tens of thousands. Her legacy will never die; it will live on in eternity.

We all need to remember who we are.

If you are familiar with the Disney movie *The Lion King*, then you know that young Simba's father Mufasa dies and his wicked uncle Scar takes over the pride. Simba goes into exile. He should be the next king of the pride, but he forgets who he is. So Mufasa comes to Simba in a vision. The script reads:

> Mufasa's ghost: [from above] Simba.
> Adult Simba: Father?
> Mufasa's ghost: [appears among the stars] Simba, you have forgotten me.
> Adult Simba: No. How could I?
> Mufasa's ghost: You have forgotten who you are and so have forgotten me. Look inside yourself, Simba. You are more than what you have become. You must take your place in the Circle of Life.
> Adult Simba: How can I go back? I'm not who I used to be.
> Mufasa's ghost: *Remember who you are. You are my son, and the one true king. Remember...*[107]

We all need to remember who we were, who Christ is, but, mostly, who we are. Remember.

> **Practical Exercise:** The gospel is to reach every human under heaven. Think of places where the gospel still needs to reach. Pray for these areas throughout the week. Perhaps you can find a world missions calendar. Keep this calendar in front of you so that you can pray for world missions every day.

(D) Paul's Ministry. 1:24–2:5.

In this section, Paul describes and defines his personal ministry. In his ministry, Paul desires to accomplish three things: 1) to make the word of God fully known, 2) to present everyone mature in Christ, and 3) to encourage the hearts of the disciples in Colossae.

Paul then takes a few moments to encourage the disciples in Colossae and to state the purpose of writing the letter (vv. 2:1–5). He is writing so the disciples might stay strong and fight against the false teachers who are trying to decimate the church in Colossae. He writes encouraging the disciples to contend for the faith.

Douglas Moo sees a chiastic structure in this section. In a chiasm, the author works from the outside in. Therefore, the middle section in the chiasm become the main point the author wishes to stress. In this case, the main idea is "to contend." Moo outlines the chiasm as follows:[108]

A		"Rejoice" (*chairō*), "flesh" (*sarx*)	1:24
	B	"make known," "riches," "mystery"	1:27
		C	"contend"	1:29
		C'	"contending"	2:1
	B'	"knowledge," "riches," "mystery"	2:2
A'		"delight" (*chairō*), "body" (*sarx*)	2:5

1. 1:24–27. To Make the Word of God Fully Known

²⁴Νῦν χαίρω ἐν τοῖς παθήμασιν ὑπὲρ ὑμῶν καὶ ἀνταναπληρῶ τὰ ὑστερήματα τῶν θλίψεων τοῦ Χριστοῦ ἐν τῇ σαρκί μου ὑπὲρ τοῦ σώματος αὐτοῦ, ὅ ἐστιν ἡ ἐκκλησία, ²⁵ἧς ἐγενόμην ἐγὼ διάκονος κατὰ τὴν οἰκονομίαν τοῦ θεοῦ τὴν δοθεῖσάν μοι εἰς ὑμᾶς πληρῶσαι τὸν λόγον τοῦ θεοῦ, ²⁶τὸ μυστήριον τὸ ἀποκεκρυμμένον ἀπὸ τῶν αἰώνων καὶ ἀπὸ τῶν γενεῶν — νῦν δὲ ἐφανερώθη τοῖς ἁγίοις αὐτοῦ, ²⁷οἷς ἠθέλησεν ὁ θεὸς γνωρίσαι τί τὸ πλοῦτος τῆς δόξης τοῦ μυστηρίου τούτου ἐν τοῖς ἔθνεσιν, ὅ ἐστιν Χριστὸς ἐν ὑμῖν, ἡ ἐλπὶς τῆς δόξης·

My Translation
²⁴Now I rejoice in the suffering on your behalf and I fill what is lacking in regard to Christ's afflictions in my flesh on behalf of his body, which is the church. ²⁵I have become its servant/minister according to the stewardship God gave me to complete the Word of God in you, ²⁶the mystery that has been hidden from the ages and the generations, but now has been made manifest to the saints ²⁷to whom God has wished to make known the glorious riches of this mystery to the Gentiles, which is Christ in you—the hope of glory.

NIV, 1984
²⁴Now I rejoice in what was suffered for you, and I fill up in my flesh what is still lacking in regard to Christ's afflictions, for the sake of his body, which is the church. ²⁵I have become its servant by the commission God gave me to present to you the word of God in its fullness— ²⁶the mystery that has been kept hidden for ages and generations, but is now disclosed to the saints. ²⁷To them God has chosen to make known among the Gentiles the glorious riches of this mystery, which is Christ in you, the hope of glory.

Notes

Paul speaks of his ministry here. He considers his ministry given to him by God. What was that ministry? What do you think of when you think of ministry today? Often we think of a series of elaborate church buildings complete with gymnasiums and large-screen televisions, plush carpets and beautiful, oaken pews. I just came back from my hometown of Columbia, Tennessee. There is a war going on in Columbia, the war to see who can build the most elaborate church building. It is quite a competition. In order to compete with the church next to you, you have to top their building project. If they build a gym, then you have to build a gym plus a pool. If they have a giant screen at the front of the auditorium, then you have to get one a foot larger. The war never ends. Was that the ministry of Paul?

Paul's ministry was not defined by buildings; his ministry was defined by suffering. Look at verse 24: *"Now I rejoice in the suffering on your behalf and I fill what is lacking in regard to Christ's afflictions in my flesh on behalf of his body, which is the church."*

I believe one of the most destructive false teachings that exist today is prosperity theology. Prosperity theology is the belief that if you follow the teachings of Jesus, then he will prosper you in this life to the point that your life will be satisfied in every way in the here and now. Prosperity theology teaches:

- You will find total satisfaction in your career.
- You will never be less than completely satisfied in your marriage.
- God will take care of all your bills and you will enjoy material prosperity in life.
- God will take care of your physical infirmities and maladies.
- You children will grow up to love the Lord and will never give you a moment of heartache.
- In other words, the happily ever after that you read about in the fairy tales will become a part of your life in the here and now.

There are many problems biblically with this false teaching. First, it isn't taught in the Bible. Second, it wasn't the experience of Jesus in his life. Third, it wasn't the experience of Paul in his life. Fourth, it's not the experience of many disciples today.

Paul didn't believe in prosperity theology. He believed in the theology of suffering with Jesus. He delineates that theology in this section of Colossians.

V. 24. In Max Anders' commentary on Colossians, he writes, "In his effort to keep believers from falling prey to the seductive sounds of false teaching, Paul tells us the truth about authentic ministry. It involves suffering. Its aim is maturity. It's hard work."[109]

Paul was in prison as he wrote this letter. His ministry was a ministry of suffering. O'Brien writes, "The word πάθυημα (*pathuama*), meaning "suffering," "affliction," or "misfortune," was used from the time of the Greek tragedians onward to denote that which befell a man and had to be accepted by him."[110] Paul saw his suffering as connected with the affliction of Jesus.

This smacks against the proponents of prosperity theology today—though they be many and though they be loud, they aren't correct. Life in Jesus is not always a bed of roses. Often it is the thorns. Paul was a prime example of the suffering Christian. He suffered because he was doing the right thing: spreading the good news of the Kingdom. Therefore he used the phrase, *"suffering on your behalf."* He also said, *"I fill what is lacking in regard to Christ's afflictions in my flesh on behalf of his body, which is the church."* It's not that Paul enjoyed suffering. He wasn't a masochist. He knew his suffering was for a purpose—to fill what was lacking in the church. He suffered because he was working to build up the church.

It is difficult to know what Paul meant by "I fill what is lacking in regard to Christ's afflictions in my flesh." Concerning the term "fill what is lacking," Richard Melick writes:

> Paul used an unusual term for "fill up," occurring only here in all of Scripture. The basic root means "to fill," as to fill in substance or content. The preposition "again" (*ana*) is prefixed to the root, and another Greek preposition, "in place of" (*anti*), is added to it. Together, the word literally conveys the idea of "completing in place of" or "complete for someone else." The word seems to demand the ideas of exchange or vicariousness and repetition.[111]

How could the suffering of Paul fill in or complete the afflictions of Jesus? This is difficult to know. Perhaps Paul meant that since Jesus was no longer here on earth to suffer, that Paul suffered in Christ's place. This is one possible explanation. Hendriksen writes:

> But since *he* (Jesus) is no longer physically present on earth, their arrows, which are meant especially for *him*, strike his followers. It is in that sense that all true believers are in his stead supplying what, as the enemies see it, is lacking in the afflictions which Jesus endured. Christ's afflictions overflow toward us.[112]

Certainly, Paul is not speaking of the suffering that Jesus did for salvation, or redemptive suffering. Christ completed salvation through his suffering. Ernest D. Martin writes:

> A distinction may be made between suffering that saves and suffering that edifies. The work of redemption has been fully

accomplished in Christ, but Christ's ongoing suffering to bring believers to perfection is shared by Christ's servants. As Paul applies the principle to himself, he suffers, not for his own benefit, but for the edifying benefit of others.[113]

Martin introduces another aspect to the discussion of suffering which Paul might have meant in this instance, suffering "for the edifying benefit of others."

So Paul suffered for Jesus because Jesus wasn't there to suffer, and he suffered to edify the church. In this way he completed the afflictions of Jesus through his suffering. Suffering is a part of the age of the Messiah. Since we are in the last days, we will suffer. Since Christ has gone back to heaven, we suffer until he returns. This is the nature of the age in which we live. O'Brien writes of this suffering in the Messianic age, stating:

> All Christians participate in these sufferings; through them they enter the kingdom of God (Acts 14:22; cf. 1 Thess. 3:3, 7). Suffering with Christ is a necessary prerequisite to being glorified with him (Rom. 8:17, εἴπερ συμπάσχομεν ἵνα καί συνδοξασθῶμεν). But none of these afflictions is able to separate the believer from the love of God in Christ Jesus (Rom 8:38, 39).[114]

Paul describes his sufferings in 2 Corinthians 6:3–10:

> [3]We put no stumbling block in anyone's path, so that our ministry will not be discredited. [4]Rather, as servants of God we commend ourselves in every way: in great endurance; in troubles, hardships and distresses; [5]in beatings, imprisonments and riots; in hard work, sleepless nights and hunger; [6]in purity, understanding, patience and kindness; in the Holy Spirit and in sincere love; [7]in truthful speech and in the power of God; with weapons of righteousness in the right hand and in the left; [8]through glory and dishonor, bad report and good report; genuine, yet regarded as impostors; [9]known, yet regarded as unknown; dying, and yet we live on; beaten, and yet not killed; [10]sorrowful, yet always rejoicing; poor, yet making many rich; having nothing, and yet possessing everything.

Paul boasts of his sufferings in 2 Corinthians 11:16–29:

> [16]I repeat: Let no one take me for a fool. But if you do, then receive me just as you would a fool, so that I may do a little boasting. [17]In this self-confident boasting I am not talking as the Lord would, but as a fool. [18]Since many are boasting in the way the world does, I too will boast. [19]You gladly put up with fools since you are so wise! [20]In fact, you even put up with anyone who enslaves you or exploits you or takes advantage of you or pushes

himself forward or slaps you in the face. ²¹To my shame I admit that we were too weak for that!

What anyone else dares to boast about—I am speaking as a fool—I also dare to boast about. ²²Are they Hebrews? So am I. Are they Israelites? So am I. Are they Abraham's descendants? So am I. ²³Are they servants of Christ? (I am out of my mind to talk like this.) I am more. I have worked much harder, been in prison more frequently, been flogged more severely, and been exposed to death again and again. ²⁴Five times I received from the Jews the forty lashes minus one. ²⁵Three times I was beaten with rods, once I was stoned, three times I was shipwrecked, I spent a night and a day in the open sea, ²⁶I have been constantly on the move. I have been in danger from rivers, in danger from bandits, in danger from my own countrymen, in danger from Gentiles; in danger in the city, in danger in the country, in danger at sea; and in danger from false brothers. ²⁷I have labored and toiled and have often gone without sleep; I have known hunger and thirst and have often gone without food; I have been cold and naked. ²⁸Besides everything else, I face daily the pressure of my concern for all the churches. ²⁹Who is weak, and I do not feel weak? Who is led into sin, and I do not inwardly burn?

When I was a young disciple and a young man, I had the idealistic thought that life would always be hunky-dory for me. I grew up in a happy home without any real struggles or major issues in my life. I assumed that all of my life would go this way. All would be smooth sailing. After all, didn't Jesus say, *"The thief comes only to steal and kill and destroy; I have come that they may have life, and have it to the full."¹¹⁵* I believed that Jesus promised me life to the full, so the rest of my life would be lived without any major turbulence or any major bumps. I believed the fullness of life meant:

- a satisfying job;
- no conflicts in marriage;
- a life without health issues;
- and few or no financial worries.

This was a naive view of life. If I had read the Bible more closely, then I would have realized that God never promised all these things in the here and now.

Now I'm in my mid-fifties. I've had moments where my job stressed me to the point where I experienced anxiety attacks and insomnia. My wife Leigh and I have had to work through various conflicts in our marriage. We've faced many trying times as parents. Leigh and I have both had our health issues. Plus, Leigh was the major caregiver for her mother who suffered for almost a decade with dementia and Alzheimer's. And, of course there have been many financial worries over the years. I earned every gray hair on my head.

Life in the here and now was never supposed to be the "happily ever after." There have been many happy moments. We have picture albums filled with photographs of those happy moments. But there have also been times when we have suffered, struggled, and felt pain. But through the trials and tribulations, we have also grown. A tree becomes stronger because of the wind. This is also true of the Christian who withstands the storms of life.

V. 25. Paul saw his ministry as a gift or an administration from God. The word "ministry" (διάκονος, *diakonos*) doesn't mean fulltime, paid ministry. At times, Paul was a fulltime, paid minister. At other times, he was a fulltime, volunteer minister. At all times, he was a fulltime minister. The word minister means "servant," and Paul was always a servant. Whether he was getting compensated or not, Paul was a minister/servant in the church.

He saw this as his calling. Another word for it is stewardship. A steward stands in place of the king when the king is absent. In *The Return of the King* (Volume III of *The Lord of the Rings* trilogy by J.R.R. Tolkien), Denethor II was the steward of Gondor. He wasn't the king of Gondor; he was only its steward. But he was entrusted with the care of Gondor until the return of the king (Aragon Elessar). Likewise, the stewardship of the church had been entrusted to Paul's care (and is entrusted to our care) until King Jesus returned. We have to understand the weight and import of the role of steward. Paul understood. Therefore, he was willing to say in the previous verse, *"I fill what is lacking in regard to Christ's afflictions in my flesh on behalf of his body, which is the church."*

But what was the goal or purpose of his stewardship? It was this: *"to complete the Word of God in you."* O'Brien writes, "The verb πληρόω covers a wide range of meanings: 'to fill, make full, fulfill, complete or finish'… Here it carries the sense of 'doing fully,' or 'carrying to completion' the divine commission."[116] Paul saw it as his divine commission to complete his preaching of the word of God to the churches. He saw this as his stewardship before God.

V. 26. Paul considered the revelation of Jesus as the Christ to the Gentiles as a mystery that was revealed to the saints. Paul liked this word "mystery" (μυστήριον, *mustarion*) and used it twenty-one times in his letters. It seems to be most closely tied with Old Testament passages speaking of God as being the revealer of mysteries. These mysteries don't usually equate to end-of-time themes in the ministry of Paul. More often, they are connected to Jesus as he reveals the true will of God on the earth. This is certainly the reference that Paul makes here. This mystery, hidden from the ages, is revealed to God's saints (his holy ones, see 1:4).

The Jews used this word "mystery" to speak to the special revelation that they as a people had received from God concerning his will to Abraham, Isaac, and Jacob and the promise of a future Messiah who would be a priest like Melchizedek and a king like David.

The word "mystery" was a favorite of the mystery cults of the pagan religions. It was also a favorite word of the Gnostics. Both groups taught that they had been given the answers to mysteries that were passed down from one generation to the next in guarded secrecy. Therefore, if you wanted to learn the answers to these mysteries, you had to join their group. They shared these revelations a little at a time, so if you wanted to learn the answers to the larger mysteries of life, you had to devote years and years to their order.

This same tactic is used with great effect by new-age religious teachers today. Religious leaders pretend that they have been given the secret to spiritual life. Only those initiated into their system can learn their secrets. This is part of the appeal of new-age religions.

Paul let the disciples in Colossae know that teachers who claim to have the revelation of mysteries and the answers to secrets should not be trusted. The disciples should not be intimidated by these charlatans. Why? Because the mystery of God had been revealed to them in Christ Jesus. They have already discovered the truth of spiritual living in Jesus.

In school, teachers give tests, but they don't give you answer keys to those tests. They expect the students to know or to discover the answers. They use the answer keys to grade the tests. In Christ, God has given us the answer key. All the mysteries of living a spiritual life are answered in the revelation of Jesus.

Ernest D. Martin considers all the references to the mystery used by Paul in Colossians. He brings them together in the following:

1. The secret is associated with the *word of God* (1:25), meaning the gospel message (as in 1 Thess. 2:13).

2. The secret was *hidden throughout the ages and generations,* known only to God, but is now made known.

3. The secret *has now been revealed to his saints* (God's people) as an integral part of the revealed message of the new era of salvation history.

4. The secret has been disclosed because *God chose* to reveal it, unveiling his sovereign purposes.

5. The secret is described in terms of *the riches of [its] glory,* expressing how wonderful the revealed message is.

6. The secret is to be made known openly *among the Gentiles,* who are most directly affected by the revealed secret. This is the new dimension.

7. The secret is simply stated as *Christ in you,* and *you* refers to the Gentiles as full participants in God's purposes, with assurance of a glorious destiny in the age to come (1:5; 3:4).[117]

The mystery is not to be selfishly clung onto by the Colossians, but they are to proclaim it to others. It is not for sale or for profit; it is to be freely given to others. This was one of the differences between the mystery found in Christ and the mystery of pagan religious cults. In the pagan mystery cults they kept the key to the mystery to themselves; they guarded their secret. In Christianity, the disciples of Jesus freely shared the revelation of the mystery of God with everyone. The same is true today. As disciples of Jesus we are to freely share what we have discovered about spiritual life in Jesus. It is not a secret that we keep to ourselves. It is a mystery that we share with others.

Also, the mystery is not meant for some elite group in the church, initiates who have entered a special circle of revelation. The mystery is for the saints, all the disciples in the church. O'Brien writes, "They are not some select group of initiates, but are those who have heard and received the word of God, for it is in the effective preaching and teaching of the gospel that the revelation of the mystery takes place."[118]

V. 27. Paul speaks more of the mystery in verse 27.

Special Study: What Do We Know of This Mystery?

(A) The mystery contains "glorious riches." This mystery is not a cheap parlor trick like you would find in one of the mystery religions or one of the new-age cults today. The mystery in Christ is gloriously rich. If you have experienced it, then you know what Paul is talking about. Forgiveness of sins is rich. The diverse, encouraging family that we have found in the church is a blessing. The friendships that God gives us in Christ can't be found anywhere else. The confidence and joy that we have in Jesus is surpassingly brilliant.

(B) The mystery has to do with God revealing his will to the Gentiles. The Jews were waiting for a Messiah. They were waiting for the promise made to Abraham, Isaac, and Jacob to be fulfilled in a Christ-figure. But the Gentiles weren't expecting such a wonderful gift. This made the mystery all the more special to them.

(C) The basic content of the mystery is that God now allows Christ (the Supreme One) to live in the saints, with a special note that this revelation is also for the Gentiles. Christ isn't just revealed to the Gentiles; he takes up residence in them.

(D) Also, the content of the mystery is Christ, the hope of glory. Christ lives with the saints in the present. Therefore, the hope of glory is not some far-off hope that we cannot attain until the end of time. We can begin living in God's hope now. This is realized eschatology. A bit of heaven comes into this world for us to enjoy in the here and now. Melick writes:

> The expression means that Christ was their hope of receiving and participating in glory. Because of what he did—his death and resurrection—the Gentiles could expect to share in glory. Here again Paul stated that the only hope of glory is Christ. Gentiles, like Jews, must rely on him for their salvation.[119]

The hereafter once again creeps into the here and now as we realize our hope of glory in Christ.

The mystery is Christ himself. The mystery has been revealed in Christ. Through Christ we are given the key of knowledge of the mystery of God. Christ is the revelation of the mystery, and he is our hope of glory. All of this once again demonstrates the high Christology of Paul, which is consistent throughout this letter. Moo writes, "The strongly christological orientation of Colossians is seen again in Paul's definition of the mystery: *Christ in you, the hope of glory* (see also 2:2; 4:3). Only in these verses in Colossians does Paul equate the mystery with Christ."[120]

What is the mystery of God in Christ? Paul sums it up nicely in Galatians 2:20:, *"I have been crucified with Christ; it is no longer I who live, but Christ who lives in me; and the life I now live in the flesh I live by faith in the Son of God, who loved me and gave himself for me."*[121] The mystery of God is Christ; Christ who now lives in the life of every disciple.

Practical Exercise: Spend some time journaling. List ways that you have suffered in life, and then list the lessons you learned through the suffering. It might be difficult to recall the times of suffering, but it will be a great benefit to recognize the lesson God taught you through them.

2. 1:28–29. To Present Everyone Mature in Christ

²⁸ὃν ἡμεῖς καταγγέλλομεν νουθετοῦντες πάντα ἄνθρωπον καὶ διδάσκοντες πάντα ἄνθρωπον ἐν πάσῃ σοφίᾳ, ἵνα παραστήσωμεν πάντα ἄνθρωπον τέλειον ἐν Χριστῷ· ²⁹εἰς ὃ καὶ κοπιῶ ἀγωνιζόμενος κατὰ τὴν ἐνέργειαν αὐτοῦ τὴν ἐνεργουμένην ἐν ἐμοὶ ἐν δυνάμει.

My Translation

²⁸We proclaim him, instructing and teaching every person with all wisdom, in order that we may present every person mature in Christ. ²⁹For this I labor, struggling with his energy, with which he so powerfully energizes me.

NIV, 1984

²⁸We proclaim him, admonishing and teaching everyone with all wisdom, so that we may present everyone perfect in Christ. ²⁹To this end I labor, struggling with all his energy, which so powerfully works in me.

Notes

Several places in this letter are what I consider high-water marks for Paul and his theological presentation. We looked at one of these high-water marks earlier when we studied the Christological hymn (1:15–20). Now we look at a second one. Paul gives the purpose of the proclamation of Christ at this point in his letter. It is always good to know why you are doing something. The knowledge of the "Why?" is the key to proper motivation. The "Why?" behind the proclamation of Christ is so that everyone may become mature in Christ. The goal of Paul's ministry was the maturing of disciples.

This is a key verse in the area of spiritual formation. Spiritual formation is the practice of the spiritual disciplines like prayer, fasting, meditation, fellowship, and Bible study for the purpose of forming Christ in our lives. Henri H.M. Nouwen, theologian and spiritual writer and an expert in this field, has written, "We need some very concrete spiritual disciplines to help us fully appropriate and internalize our joys and sorrows and find in them our unique way to spiritual freedom."[122] Spiritual disciplines lead to spiritual freedom, which is maturity in Christ.

What is your goal as a disciple of Jesus? I believe our ultimate goal should be this: to be like Jesus. When the apostle Paul wrote to the churches of Galatia, he told them, *"I am again in the pains of childbirth until Christ is formed in you* (Galatians 4:19, emphasis added)." Paul's goal was nothing less than to see Christ formed in the hearts and lives of each disciple. This is the goal of spiritual formation.

Many great books have been written about the spiritual disciplines.[123] Each book lists the spiritual disciplines a little differently and in a different order. The following is my list of the spiritual disciplines.

The Spiritual Disciplines

(A) Learning Dependence on God
(1) Prayer
(2) Fasting
(3) Meditation
    Silence; Solitude; Reflection
(4) Bible Study
    Journaling; Memorization
(5) Worship
    Celebration
(6) Surrender
    Trust; Submission; Obedience; Guidance;
    Suffering; Self-Denial
(7) Repentance
    Confession

(B) Learning Interdependence with Others
(8) The One-Another Way
    Fellowship; Mentoring/Discipling; Confession
(9) Evangelism
    Missions
(10) Simplicity
    Frugality
(11) Service
    The Servant Heart; Sacrifice; Giving
(12) Sanctifying the Ordinary
    24/7 Discipleship; Living an Everyday,
    Ordinary Life for God

The power of the spiritual disciplines comes not from the disciplines themselves, but from God. Dallas Willard writes:

> At the center of biblical teaching, then, is the idea of an all-loving and all-powerful God who is *in action*, for us and with us. He is not passive. He is not distant. He is not indifferent. 'He will not allow your foot to slip; He who keeps you will not slumber' (Psalm 121:3 NASB[124]).[125]

This should not be "self-effort;" it should be "God-effort." Keith Meyer writes, "Now the disciplines are not ways to prove my spirituality but ways to immerse myself in God's grace and his love for me."[126]

Again, the goal of the spiritual disciplines and spiritual formation is maturity in Christ. It is the same goal that Paul states as his goal for the proclamation of Christ. Disciples should mature. They should reach the point where they can stand on their own two feet spiritually and make solid spiritual decisions about their lives. This is the goal of Paul's ministry.

V. 28. What was Paul's mission? What was the purpose of his ministry? In today's world "mission statements" are important. It is important to know what your goals are and why those goals exist. In my opinion, in this passage Paul gives the readers a concise statement of his mission. What was Paul's ultimate goal? Simply put: *"to present every person mature in Christ."*

Paul's mission wasn't just to baptize people, although baptism was important. Today, it has been downplayed by the evangelical world until it has become little more than an afterthought in the conversion process. Paul had a much higher view of baptism than that. In Colossians 2:11–12, he wrote:

> *[11]In him (in Christ) you were also circumcised, in the putting off of the sinful nature, not with a circumcision done by the hands of men but with the circumcision done by Christ, [12]having been buried with him in baptism and raised with him through your faith in the power of God, who raised him from the dead.*

Paul equated baptism with circumcision. Through baptism we are connected to the death and resurrection of Jesus. Baptism is central in the conversion process; it isn't an afterthought. But baptism wasn't the ultimate goal of Paul's preaching and ministry. Paul's ultimate goal was to see every Christian reach his or her full potential in Christ.

What is the goal? To present everyone mature/perfect in Christ. This word τέλειος, *teleios* (perfect/mature) is difficult to translate. Moo writes,

> "Perfect" is too strong, "mature" too weak. Rarely does the word in the New Testament have the sense of our English "perfect," with its connotations of absoluteness.... "Mature," on the other hand, is too relative, inviting us to think that we are *teleios* as long as we are doing a bit better than some other Christians we could name.... *Teleios* connotes the quality of being so wholehearted in one's devotion to the Lord that one can be said to be blameless in conduct.[127]

I believe that in our religious society the word "perfect" is too closely associated with perfectionism to make it an adequate translation for *teleios*; therefore, I always use "mature" when I translate this word

How would this be accomplished? How could Paul present everyone mature in Christ? Paul uses three verbs to explain how he would accomplish this task. All of these verbs are in the present tense signifying the continuing, lasting effect of their action. The three verbs are: proclaim, admonish, and teach.

Special Study: How Do We Help Someone Mature?

(A) Proclaim (καταγγέλλω, *katangello*)

Paul proclaimed Jesus. He proclaimed the mystery of Christ. Proclamation was an important part of the mission. This became a technical term for preaching or the proclamation of Christ on the mission field.

But to build a ministry, we can't just preach Jesus and expect people to grow on their own. This is where the next two verbs come into play. In order to help people to mature, we have to admonish and teach them. Preaching is the easy part. When we admonish and teach people, we have to roll up our sleeves and really work.

(B) Admonish (νουθετοῦντες, *nouthetountes*)

This verb is used of instruction and warning. The thought behind this verb is the idea of putting someone in proper order. O'Brien writes that this verb "had to do with setting the mind of someone in proper order, correcting him or putting him right."[128] After we preach Christ to someone, we have to help the person go through a "mind-change" to help him or her think like a new person. This implies training. As a parent trains a child to think properly, disciples help other disciples correct their thinking about the world. Hendriksen writes, "For him (Paul) to *admonish* meant *to warn, to stimulate,* and *to encourage.* He would actually *plead* with people to be reconciled to God (2 Cor. 5:20). He would at times even shed tears (cf. Acts 20:19, 31; 2 Cor. 2:4; Phil. 3:18)."[129] When you admonish someone, you are compelled to be in his or her life. You need to look in someone's eyes in order to warn a person about sin. You need to reach out and give someone a hug in order to encourage him or her.

(C) Teach (διδάσκοντες, *didaskontes*)

Teaching is the practical and theoretical instruction that leads to growth. Melick writes, "'Teaching' complements 'admonishing.' 'Teaching' is the orderly presentation of Christian truth for converts so that they may know how to grow."[130] Teaching is about growth.

Teaching and admonishment ought to go "hand in glove." When we warn, we also instruct. Hendriksen writes:

> It should be stressed in this connection that there was no wide gulf between Paul's *admonishing* and his *teaching*. For him *abstract* doctrine did not exist. Neither did Christian ethics suspend in mid-air. On the contrary, Paul's teaching was done with a view to admonishing; his admonishing was rooted in teaching.[131]

All three verbs are about growth. The goal of proclaiming, admonishing, and teaching is to help disciples grow to maturity. But the last two of these three verbs imply that we must be involved in people's lives. We are to proclaim the gospel, but we don't stop there. We take the next step, which is to admonish and teach disciples in areas that are specific to their growth as Christians. What is the ultimate goal of this work? We want everyone to grow, to become mature in Christ.

It is important to ask ourselves how we are doing in the church today with these three verbs: proclaiming, admonishing, and teaching. We might be doing fine with proclamation, but how are we doing in admonishing and teaching people toward maturity? Are we helping people to grow and mature in Christ?

Our ministry can't end with preaching. It can begin with preaching, but it must move on to admonishing and teaching others to grow. To have a balanced ministry, we must evaluate our ministries and ask, "Are we preaching, admonishing, and teaching people in this ministry?"

V. 29. Paul recognized that helping people reach maturity in Christ was hard work. He writes, *"For this I labor."* This word, "struggle" or "labor," was used of an athlete who struggles to win the prize. Hencriksen writes, "With a reference to himself Paul continues, for which I am laboring, that is, *toiling* to the point of weariness and exhaustion."[132] Ernest Martin writes:

> The word *toil* denotes hard work, exertion, as with an athlete straining to the limits in training. *Struggle,* a word also used regarding an athletic contest, further describes the toil as a deeply intense effort to achieve a goal. The Greek word is the one from which the English word *agonize* is derived. *Agonizing* aptly conveys the meaning of the word in this verse (and in 2:1), expressing the rigorous demand on physical and emotional energy in Paul's expenditure of himself.[133]

Have you even fought hard in an athletic competition until you reached the point where you were out of energy? In running, they call it hitting the wall. During those times, it's good to have something that will help you push through that tough time. It might be a mantra like, "Yes, I can!" Or, you might break through the wall by receiving an encouraging word from a coach or a fan that lifts your spirit. You might reach in your pocket for some energy gel that will help you to push through the tough moment. For Paul, his energy gel was Christ. Jesus helped him through the tough times.

But Paul didn't labor with his own energy, but with the energy that came from Jesus. Notice Paul's words here, *"For this I labor, struggling with his energy, with which he so powerfully energizes me."* Paul repeats the word energy here. He uses it in the noun form and the verb form. Christ's energy energized him.

Dunn writes, "'Ενέργεια (*energea,* energy) means basically 'activity,' and so also the 'energy' that accomplishes activity; similarly the verb ἐνεργέω (*energeo,* energize), 'be at work' and so 'produce, be effective.'"[134] Christ gave Paul the energy to keep working with people until they became mature.

Have you ever wondered how Paul was able to accomplish so much in his life? He led mission teams, travelled, preached, taught, wrote, trained others, escaped persecution, and stayed spiritually strong through it all. How could he do all this? Hendriksen asks and answers this question, writing, "The question has often been asked, 'How was it possible for *one* man (and a man with a thorn in the flesh!), even with the help of fellow-workers, to accomplish so much?' The answer is contained in the words of Paul himself: (striving) by his energy working powerfully within me."[135] Paul didn't try to do it on his own. He realized he was part of Team Jesus. He tapped into the energy which only Jesus can give.

As we work with people, we must make sure that we aren't working with our own energy, but we are working with the energy of Christ. How do we do this? It begins with staying connected with Jesus and making sure that we are deeply spiritual men and women. This is where the spiritual disciplines like prayer, meditation, Bible study, worship, fellowship, fasting, discipling, evangelism, and simplicity enter the picture. These tools for spiritual growth help us stay connected with Jesus. The better we stay connected with Jesus, the more we will be able to help others reach maturity in Christ.

Practical Exercise: Take a close look at your personal ministry. Paul's ministry included preaching, admonishing, and teaching. Does your ministry consist of these three elements? If so, where are you weakest and where are you strongest? In what ways can your ministry grow in each of these three areas?

Do the same exercise with the ministry within your local church. Does your ministry consist of these three elements: preaching, admonishing, and teaching? If so, where is your local ministry the weakest and where is it the strongest? In what ways can your local ministry grow in each of these three areas?

Exposition of Colossians
Chapter Two

3. 2:1–5. To Encourage Your Hearts

The Purpose of the Letter

¹Θέλω γὰρ ὑμᾶς εἰδέναι ἡλίκον ἀγῶνα ἔχω ὑπὲρ ὑμῶν καὶ τῶν ἐν Λαοδικείᾳ καὶ ὅσοι οὐχ ἑόρακαν τὸ πρόσωπόν μου ἐν σαρκί, ²ἵνα παρακληθῶσιν αἱ καρδίαι αὐτῶν συμβιβασθέντες ἐν ἀγάπῃ καὶ εἰς πᾶν πλοῦτος τῆς πληροφορίας τῆς συνέσεως, εἰς ἐπίγνωσιν τοῦ μυστηρίου τοῦ θεοῦ, Χριστοῦ, ³ἐν ᾧ εἰσιν πάντες οἱ θησαυροὶ τῆς σοφίας καὶ γνώσεως ἀπόκρυφοι. ⁴Τοῦτο λέγω, ἵνα μηδεὶς ὑμᾶς παραλογίζηται ἐν πιθανολογίᾳ. ⁵εἰ γὰρ καὶ τῇ σαρκὶ ἄπειμι, ἀλλὰ τῷ πνεύματι σὺν ὑμῖν εἰμι, χαίρων καὶ βλέπων ὑμῶν τὴν τάξιν καὶ τὸ στερέωμα τῆς εἰς Χριστὸν πίστεως ὑμῶν.

My Translation

¹I wish for you to know how much I am struggling for your behalf and for those in Laodicea, and for all who have not seen my face in the flesh. ²My purpose is that they may be encouraged in their hearts since you have been knit together in love, in order that they may have the full riches of complete understanding, in the knowledge of the mystery of God, which is, Christ. ³In Christ all the treasures of wisdom and knowledge are hidden. ⁴I tell you this in order that no one may deceive you by fine-sounding arguments. ⁵For though I am absent from you in body, I am with you in spirit and I rejoice to see how orderly you are and how firm in Christ is your faith.

NIV, 1984

¹I want you to know how much I am struggling for you and for those at Laodicea, and for all who have not met me personally. ²My purpose is that they may be encouraged in heart and united in love, so that they may have the full riches of complete understanding, in order that they may know the mystery of God, namely, Christ, ³in whom are hidden all the treasures of wisdom and

knowledge. ⁴I tell you this so that no one may deceive you by fine-sounding arguments. ⁵For though I am absent from you in body, I am present with you in spirit and delight to see how orderly you are and how firm your faith in Christ is.

Notes

Paul lets the disciples in Colossae know the reason for his writing, listing three reasons:

1. *"I wish for you to know how much I am struggling for your behalf"* (v. 1).

2. *"My purpose is that they may be encouraged in their hearts since you have been knit together in love"* (v. 2).

3. *"I tell you this in order that no one may deceive you by fine-sounding arguments"* (v. 4).

The disciples are facing battles against false teachers and false doctrines. Paul admonishes them to hold onto what they have found in Jesus, because in Jesus they have discovered a true treasure. In this chapter, Paul doesn't just refer to the heresy in Colossae as he does in chapter 1, but he goes on to speak in general terms of the types of teachings that the disciples are battling in Colossae. They should not give in to:

1. **Deceitful philosophy,** 2:1–10

2. **Judaic ritualism,** 2:11–17

3. **Angel worship,** 2:18–19

4. **Ascetic practices,** 2:20–23

Since we have found the real treasure in Jesus, we are free from these other deceptive and false doctrines. Let's never trade what is real for a shadow. Christ is supreme. To trade Christ for anything is a bad trade. Don't make that trade. Hold onto Christ. Hendriksen writes:

> The Colossians need not, must not, look for any source of happiness or of holiness outside of Christ. Do false teachers boast about their wisdom and their knowledge? Or about that of the angels? Neither man nor angel nor any other creature has anything at all to offer which cannot be found in *incomparably superior essence and an infinite degree in Christ.*[136]

Douglas J. Moo notes that there is a possible chiasm in these first five verses, writing

...with vv. 1 and 5 focusing on the readers, vv. 2a and 4 on the reaction Paul hopes to stimulate from h s readers, and vv. 2b and 3 on the central truth to which his readers need to respond: Christ, the mystery of God, the repository of *"all the treasures of wisdom and knowledge."*[137]

Thus, the structure would look like this:

> V. 1. The readers
> V. 2a. Paul's hope to stimulate the readers
> V. 2b. Christ, the mystery of God
> V. 3. Christ, the treasure of wisdom and knowledge
> V. 4. Paul's hope to stimulate the readers
> V. 5. The readers

The central truth in this section (and in the entire book of Colossians) is found here—Christ is the treasure. In his commentary on Colossians, Anders relates this story found in Elie Weisel's *Souls on Fire*:

In faraway Krakau, in days when sleep was often disturbed by dreams, there lived one Isaac, son of Yechel. Isaac was a poor man whose family seldom ate their fill. One night in a vivid dream, he saw the distant city of Prague. He saw a river flowing through the city, and under a particular bridge he saw a buried treasure. When he woke the next morning, the dream had not faded. Its clear and vivid images remained etched on his mind. That night the dream returned. And the next night. Every nigh: for two weeks, Isaac had the same dream in which he saw the city of Prague, the river, the bridge, and the buried treasure hidden beneath the bridge.

Finally, he decided to walk all the way to Prague to see for himself if the dream might be real. After several days he arrived in the city. Even though he had never been there, he recognized it and knew it well from his dreams. He found the bridge, went under it to search for the treasure, and then suddenly was grabbed firmly at the back of his neck by a soldier who dragged him away to prison for interrogation.

The soldier sat him in a chair and said, "All right, Jew, what were you doing prowling around under that bridge?" Not knowing what else to say, Isaac decided to tell the truth, "I had a dream that there was buried treasure under that bridge, and I was looking for it."

Immediately, the soldier burst into mocking laughter, "You stupid Jew, don't you know that you can't believe what you see in your dreams? Why, for the last two weeks I myself have had a dream every night that far away in the city of Krakau, in the house of some Jew by the name of Isaac, son of Yechel, there is a treasure buried beneath the sink in his house. Wouldn't it be the most idiotic of actions if I were to go all the way to Krakau to look for some Jew that doesn't exist? Or there may be a thousand Isaacs, son of Yechel. I could waste a lifetime looking for a treasure that isn't there." With uproarious laughter, the soldier stood him up, opened the door, gave him a good kick, and let him go.

Naturally, Isaac, son of Yechel, walked back to Krakau, back to his own house, where he looked beneath the sink in his own kitchen, found the treasure buried there, and lived to a ripe old age as a rich man. The treasure was at home all along.[138]

This story is an analogy to our search for wisdom and knowledge. Paul doesn't want the disciples in Colossae to go on a treasure hunt for wisdom and knowledge somewhere outside the church when they have already discovered the real treasure in Christ. He warns them against the appeal of false doctrine.

Notes

V. 1. Paul writes to let them know that he is struggling along with them. Even though it is likely that Paul had never met them face to face, their struggles were still his struggles. He mentions Laodicea, some ten miles away; and he most likely also has in mind Hierapolis, located fifteen miles away.

Some scholars debate the point as to whether Paul had been in Colossae before. William Hendriksen writes, "On his way to Ephesus, Paul followed the natural route which via Colossae led to Ephesus. He passed through Colossae, and may even have spent a night there. Whether or not he did we simply do not know."[139] Hendriksen is correct, "We simply do not know." However, it seems more likely that Paul never met the disciples in Colossae or visited their town. This is why he mentions Epaphras in his letter. Epaphras was Paul's connection to Colossae.

Paul was writing them from prison. This would have been a good opportunity to let them know how much he had suffered over the last few months and years. But Paul is not focused on self here. His focus is on others. At different times Paul does rehearse his litany of suffering and struggles for Jesus. But this was never done for self-pity. It was to defend his apostleship in 2 Corinthians. Paul is not interested in comparing war wounds. He is writing to inspire others to persevere because at the end of their suffering, glory will come.

V. 2. Paul is writing to (1) encourage their hearts since they have been knit together in love, and (2) enrich their understanding so that it is a complete understanding in the knowledge of the mystery of God, which is Christ. Melick writes, "Christian growth is a group task!"[140] If we, as a community, are knit together in love and if we, as a people of God, have a mature understanding of the knowledge of the mystery of God in Christ, then we won't we drawn to deceitful and hollow philosophies.

Ernest D. Martin mentions three pastoral goals of Paul: encouragement, unity in love, and confident understanding.[141]

Paul's Pastoral Goals: Encouragement, Unity in Love, and Confidence from Understanding

(A) Encouragement (παρακληθῶσιν, *paraklathosin*) expresses the idea of holding off despair and discouragement from the disciples. It also has the positive connotation of placing courage in people's hearts. The heart in ancient culture was often thought of as the seat of the emotions, but it was also considered the source of the personality of the person (or the person as a whole). Thus Moo writes, "'Encouraged in heart' or 'to have hearts encouraged' is therefore a way of referring to an encouragement that touches the deepest part of our being and that effects every aspect of our persons."[142]

(B) Unity comes from being knit together in love. Think of tendons of the body, which hold all the muscles onto the bones. This is what love does in the body of Christ. Dunn writes:

> Unlike the previous prayer for the Colossians, which could be understood simply in individual terms (1:9–14), the hope here is also for their well-being as a community. The encouragement is thought of not in terms of a sequence of individuals being individually encouraged but of an encouragement which facilitates and is facilitated by their experience of being "held together in love."[143]

(C) Finally, an understanding of Jesus based on both knowledge and wisdom will keep us confident in Christ so that we will not stray toward deceptive philosophies or false teachings. This idea has been mentioned before and will be mentioned again. Why? Repetition is a great pneumonic device. Moo writes:

> But "awkwardness" is in the eye of the beholder (or the reader), and the repetition of ideas may be emphatic rather than simply repetitious. Paul is again piling up words in order to hammer home the truth that Christ, and Christ alone, is the source of every conceivable bit of spiritual knowledge worth having.[144]

V. 3. Paul continues his theme of the supremacy of Christ by writing, *"In Christ all the treasures of wisdom and knowledge are hidden."* This is the central point of the chiasm, and the point that Paul is hoping to drive home to the disciples. They need not search for wisdom and knowledge anywhere else, because they have already found it in Christ. Moo writes:

> This verse is the christological high point of the letter. It does not match the "hymn" of 1:15–20 for exalted language in reference to Christ, but it expresses beautifully and compactly the cutting-edge christological point that is Paul's driving concern: Christ is the one in whom is to be found *all* that one needs in order to understand spiritual reality and to lead a life pleasing to God.[145]

Christ is the source of all knowledge and wisdom. I distinguish between knowledge and wisdom this way. Knowledge is the accumulation of facts, which can be applied to life in order to make wise choices. Wisdom is the ability to apply knowledge to everyday situations so that you can make prudent choices. Knowledge is more theoretical than wisdom. Wisdom is more practical than knowledge. One should not be separated from the other. Moo writes, "'Wisdom,' of course, refers to practical knowledge, the ability to understand reality from God's perspective and to act on that understanding. 'Knowledge,' on the other hand, has a more intellectual focus."[146]

You've probably seen people who have tons of knowledge (book sense) but are dumb as a rock when it comes to making wise choices in life. However, I've met people who are illiterate and have no book knowledge, but they excel in their relationships with people and know how to live life to the full. In the first church where I served there was an elder who could barely read or write, but who was full of the wisdom of Christ. This was the Arkland Church of Christ in Sawdust, Tennessee.[147] This elder was a farmer and had very little formal education. But he knew his Bible as well as anyone I've ever met. His source of wisdom and knowledge was Christ. He was a great leader in his home, his community, and the church.

V. 4. Paul gives the reason for his writing. He says that he writes so that no one may deceive them with fine-sounding arguments. Of "fine-sounding arguments," Moo writes, "This phrase translates a single Greek word (*pithanologia*), which has a neutral meaning, 'plausible arguments' (ESV); 'persuasive argument' (NASB).[148]

Someone has come into Colossae attempting to pull the disciples away from the truth. Paul writes because the church in Colossae is under attack by false teachers. Paul took that seriously. He writes this letter to remind the church in Colossae that Christ is supreme.

V. 5. Even though Paul isn't there in person, he is there in spirit. Paul is grateful that they are still orderly (τάξι, *taxi*) and firm (στερέωμα, *stepeoma*) in their faith (firmness in faith). Both could be military images. If so, then "orderly" would signify soldiers standing in military formation and "firm" would designate a military fortress or buttress. Dunn writes, "The former denotes an 'arrangement,' something set in orderly fashion.... The latter term, στερέωμα, means basically 'what is made firm or thick,' hence 'basis, foundation, or solid body.'"[149]

The false teachers have made inroads into the church in Colossae, but the disciples haven't totally given in to the false teaching. Paul encourages them for their strength. He encourages them to stay orderly and firm. O'Brien writes, "The praise given to the congregation suggests that, although it was troubled by false teachers,...the church was still basically sound in the faith, preserving the apostolic message and persisting in it."[150]

In order to stand against false teachers, we must take an orderly and firm approach toward false teaching. How can we stand against false teachers?

First, we must understand the truth of God's word. If we know what the Bible says, then we won't topple at every fine-sounding argument. Max Anders writes:

> How can we learn to recognize deception when it is intentionally cloaked in the appearance of truth? Here is how that problem is handled in the banking industry. Bank tellers attend a training class to learn how to identify counterfeit money. During the entire course of training they never study a counterfeit bill. Instead, they spend all their time studying the genuine article. They learn to recognize the texture of the paper, the colors of the ink, the clarity of the images, and the design of the bill. When they finish their training, the tellers have such an intimate knowledge of authentic currency that counterfeits are obvious by comparison.[151]

Second, we must be aware of the schemes and methods of false teachers. False arguments rarely look totally false. If they did, then they would be rejected in a moment. False teaching is usually built around a kernel of truth. If we understand this, then we will be prepared to differentiate between what is false and what is true.

Third, we must be vigilant. We live in a syncretistic, pluralistic, postmodern age in which tolerance is preached from every street corner. Today we are expected to accept everyone's lifestyle and everyone's beliefs. It has become a part of our society that every idea needs to be heard no matter how ludicrous and false it might be. About the only idea that isn't tolerated is when someone says they measure truth based on the teachings of Jesus. Say that and watch tolerant people become very intolerant. NT scholar, D.A. Carson, has written a book entitled *The Intolerance of Tolerance.* I think that is a great title for a book. It's a comment on how tolerant our society is to everything except Bible-believing Christians. Disciples of Jesus must remain strong in their conviction that truth is revealed in Scripture.

We have to remain vigilant against false teaching. Complacency can cause us to let down our guard until false doctrine fills our mind. Max Anders quotes Paul Fox as saying, "The greatest danger regarding cults…is complacency—considering ourselves and our children to be immune from their attraction. If Christ is not the center of a Christian's life, that Christian is ripe for another spirit…."[152] So to fight against false teaching, we must remain vigilant.

The main point that Paul is making here is this: If you have Christ, you have the greatest treasure of all. Don't trade Christ for a cheap imitation. If you trade what you have discovered in Christ for false teaching, then you've made a terrible trade.

> **Practical Exercise:** In verse 2, Paul talks about the importance of encouragement. What can you do today to encourage a disciple? Now, go do it.

E. Our Walk in Christ. 2:6–15.

What does this picture of Jesus teach us? Three things: We are (1) to be full of life in Christ, (2) to be freed from sin, and (3) to be forgiven.

Before we move on to discuss the material in this section of Colossians, let me first mention a point on Bible study. There are at least two ways to read the Bible.

1. Read large sections of Scripture and see the general flow of Scripture.

2. Read the Bible verse by verse and pay attention to what is being said in each verse.

When reading through Colossians it is important to read the Bible following both of these principles. We need to understand the general flow of what Paul is saying as he moves from one topic to the next in his letter. We need to pay attention to the major themes and minor themes and see how Paul weaves them together in a beautiful tapestry that extols the supremacy of Christ. It is also good to pay attention to the smaller details of the letter, because these little details are like beautiful gems that deserve our attention. So we read looking at the broad brushstrokes of Paul's pen and the close detail work of his pencil. These first two chapters of Colossians are more theoretical and theological.

Chapters 3–4 are more practical. Practice of ministry should always be based on good theology.

Paul just stated that the treasure of the Christian life is that we have Christ in us—the hope of glory. But what does it mean to have Christ in us? If we walk/live in Christ, how will that be demonstrated in our lives? Paul is talking about growing spiritually in this section. To walk/live in Christ is to mature in Christ. In this section, verses 6–15, Paul describes what it means to walk/live in Christ and thus, how we can grow spiritually. He says it means three things: (1) We are full of life of Christ. (2) We are forgiven in Christ. (3) We are free in Christ.

1. 2:6–10. Full of Life in Christ

⁶Ὡς οὖν παρελάβετε τὸν Χριστὸν Ἰησοῦν τὸν κύριον, ἐν αὐτῷ περιπατεῖτε, ⁷ἐρριζωμένοι καὶ ἐποικοδομούμενοι ἐν αὐτῷ καὶ βεβαιούμενοι τῇ πίστει καθὼς ἐδιδάχθητε, περισσεύοντες ἐν εὐχαριστίᾳ. ⁸βλέπετε μή τις ὑμᾶς ἔσται ὁ συλαγωγῶν διὰ τῆς φιλοσοφίας καὶ κενῆς ἀπάτης κατὰ τὴν παράδοσιν τῶν ἀνθρώπων, κατὰ τὰ στοιχεῖα τοῦ κόσμου καὶ οὐ κατὰ Χριστόν· ⁹ὅτι ἐν αὐτῷ κατοικεῖ πᾶν τὸ πλήρωμα τῆς θεότητος σωματικῶς, ¹⁰καὶ ἐστὲ ἐν αὐτῷ πεπληρωμένοι, ὅς ἐστιν ἡ κεφαλὴ πάσης ἀρχῆς καὶ ἐξουσίας.

My Translation

⁶Therefore, just as you received Christ Jesus as Lord, continue to live in him, ⁷rooted and built up in him. Be strengthened in the faith you were taught, and overflow with thanksgiving.

⁸See to it that no one captures you like a prisoner of war through empty and deceptive philosophy, which depends on human tradition and the fundamental propositions of this world rather than on Christ.

⁹Because in Christ all the fullness of the Deity lives in bodily form, ¹⁰and you have been given fullness in Christ, who is the head over every power and authority.

NIV, 1984

⁶So then, just as you received Christ Jesus as Lord, continue to live in him, ⁷rooted and built up in him, strengthened in the faith as you were taught, and overflowing with thankfulness.

⁸See to it that no one takes you captive through hollow and deceptive philosophy, which depends on human tradition and the basic principles of this world rather than on Christ.

⁹For in Christ all the fullness of the Deity lives in bodily form, ¹⁰and you have been given fullness in Christ, who is the head over every power and authority.

Notes

Vv. 6–7. Dunn proposes that the theme of the book is stated in verses 6 and 7.[153] Moo calls it—the heart of matter.[154] O'Brien states:

> In the paragraph commencing with verse 6 we come to the heart of the letter.... Here Paul gives a careful exposition of his teaching (sometimes drawing on traditional materials) for purposes of positive instruction and by way of a corrective to the false teaching. Verses 6 and 7 occupy a pivotal position: (a) they set forth the positive instruction that serves as a basis for the attack on the Colossian heresy, and this is because (b) they summarize much of what has preceded: so the Christological statement, "Christ Jesus the Lord," draws attention to the one who is at the center of the mystery (1:27) and the subject of the magnificent hymn (1:15–20).... In the space of a few brief words the apostle encapsulates many of the important ideas already spelled out in the letter, drives them home to the hearts of his readers by means of an "indicative-imperative" formulation and prepares to confront them with sharp alternatives (v. 8) that will demand of them clear unequivocal decisions.[155]

Therefore, we should pay close attention to verses 6–7. You might want to memorize these verses. Paul develops the theme found in these two verses in the following section of the letter, 2:8–4:6.

When we break down verses 6–7, what are the major thoughts that Paul is expressing here?

(A) *"Therefore, just as you received Christ Jesus as Lord, continue to live in him."* The first thought that Paul expresses here is this: Since we have received Jesus as Lord, we must continue to walk/live in him. Before we walk in Christ, we must first make Jesus the Lord of our lives. What does it mean to make Jesus the Lord of your life? It means that he is master or ruler. That is where everything in your spiritual life begins. Lordship is an important concept. If Jesus is Lord, what does that make us? We are his servants. Another word for that is slave. Jesus directs our lives and we live for his glory. This is lordship.

Of course, making Jesus Lord does not negate the need for faith, repentance, or baptism. Paul will focus on the role of baptism in verses 11–12. To receive Jesus as Lord *includes* faith, repentance, and baptism.

What does Paul mean when he speaks of receiving Jesus as Lord? Douglas Moo writes:

> Paul's choice of the verb "receive" in the first clause is significant. This verb (*paralambanō*) is usually used by Paul to refer to the

> 'receiving' or 'accepting' of tradition about Christ and his signifi-
> cance.... In keeping with the christological focus of this letter, how-
> ever, Paul refers here not to the receiving of teaching, or tradition,
> or the word of God (cf. 1 Thess. 2:13), but of Christ himself....
> To 'receive Christ'—in this verse at least—is not only a matter of
> believing 'in' his person; it also involves a commitment to the ap-
> ostolic teaching about Christ and his significance.[156]

So receiving Christ is to receive the person and teaching of Christ. That implies that we must come to Christ in the way that he asks to come to him; namely, through faith, repentance, and baptism. Having said that, I would quickly add that the main emphasis of this opening phrase is the idea of receiving Jesus the person as the Lord of our lives.

(B) Once we receive Jesus as Lord, we go on to live/walk in him. Max Anders writes, "'Live' literally means walk. Step by step, day by day, we are to conduct our affairs in conscious submission to the lordship of Jesus Christ. Life is a journey, and we are not expected to sprint through it. We are just to make steady progress."[157]

Follow the progression here—we receive Jesus as Lord and we walk in him. This is what discipleship is all about—making Jesus the Lord of our lives and walking daily in Jesus. How is that going for you? Do you find yourself walking in the steps of Jesus every day?

I remember a time when Leigh and I visited New Delhi, India. We went to the place where Mohandas Gandhi had lived and where he would walk from the house to the garden in the back to meditate. This is where Gandhi was as-sassinated.[158] In the yard there are clay footprints that represent the footprints of Gandhi. You can literally walk where Gandhi walked.

In the Holy Lands, you can visit dozens of sites that relate to the Bible. My favorites are the ones where Jesus would have walked, for example, the syn-agogue at Capernaum or the steps at the Southern Temple Mount. When you walk on these locations, you have a sense that you are walking where Jesus did.

But we need to walk in the steps of Jesus every day. How do we do that? That leads to Paul's next idea: How do we walk in Jesus?

(C) How do we walk/live in him? William Hendriksen writes, "By a series of four participles ('rooted,' 'being built up,' 'being established,' 'and overflow-ing'), the first a *perfect passive* and the other three *present*, Paul now shows what this living *in Christ* (that is, *in vital union with him*) means."[159]

To live/walk in Jesus is described by these four participles.

(1) Rooted (ῥιζόω, *hridzoo*)

This participle is a perfect passive participle indicating a condition that exists because of a past action. The passive voice notes that God performed the action (known as a divine passive). Paul uses a metaphor from horticulture: rooted, like a plant is rooted in the ground. The disciples are rooted in Christ because of what God has done for them in the past. The past action is their conversion when they received Christ (2:6). By receiving Christ as Lord, they have a foundation for life. A tree digs its roots deep into the soil to get nutrition. The disciple digs his or her roots deep into Jesus because he provides spiritual nutrition. Roots keep a tree from toppling over in the winds and storms. The roots of a disciple will keep him or her solid through turbulent times. We have to make sure we are rooted in Jesus.

(2) Built up (ἐποικοδομέω, *'epoikodomeo*)

Here we have a present passive participle, indicating that God continues to build up disciples. Paul uses a metaphor from architecture: constructing a building. Building up implies that you are building upon something. The root and solid foundation of the Christian's life is Jesus Christ as Lord. Paul moves from an image from horticulture to an image from architecture. We must be built up in Jesus. We must continue to grow.

(3) Strengthened (βεβαιόω, *bebaioo*), also translated as "established"

Paul used a metaphor from the field of law. Dunn notes that this word was "commonly used to denote the formal or legal guarantee required in the transfer of property or good."[160] In this case the end result of the transfer is a strengthening of the faith. Again, it is the divine passive intimating that God is doing the strengthening. Moo writes, "With this participle, Paul summarizes what he expects to happen as a result of the first two: by sticking to their roots and being built up, the readers will be established in faith."[161] The sphere in which God strengthened them was in the faith that they were taught.

(4) Overflowing (Περισσεύω, *perisseuo*)

Because they are rooted, built up, and strengthened, they will overflow with thanksgiving. Paul often emphasized the role of thanksgiving in the disciple's life. Melick writes:

> Paul frequently employed thankfulness as one of the litmus tests of Christian health. He assumed that Christians would live in an attitude of thankfulness for the many blessings bestowed upon them. By contrast, one of the first indicators of departure from God is a lack of thanksgiving (e.g., Rom 1:21ff.).[162]

I've discovered in my over thirty years of ministry that what Dr. Melick writes is true. The people that do the best spiritually are the people who keep an attitude of gratitude. When people become ungrateful, they are in a bad place spiritually. We should overflow with thanksgiving. And if Christ is in us, then thanksgiving will flow from our hearts.

(D) 2:8–19. Concerning Doctrine and False Teaching

Paul has been discussing the life we live in Christ. But he also speaks to the threat against that life from false teachers. Thus, Paul deals directly with two doctrines in verses 8–19, the doctrine of salvation and the doctrine of sanctification. These two doctrines deal with how a person is saved and how a person stays saved. The false teachers attacked these doctrines by focusing primarily on three areas: the keeping of the law, angel worship, and ascetic practices. Paul will address all three of these topics in this section.

Concerning this false teaching, Melick writes:

> The theological threat concerned two major tenets of the Christian faith. These were soteriology, the person and work of Christ specifically related to the cross, and sanctification, the application of the cross to the development of personal purity. In this portion of the epistle, Paul addressed the theological foundations of both of these subjects. Thus the text presents the *theology* of salvation (2:8–15) and the *theology* of sanctification (2:16–19).[163]

2:8–15. The Doctrine of Salvation

V. 8. Paul moves on to speak a word of warning to his readers: "See to it" or "Watch out." He delineates the nature and source of the false teaching. The nature is that the false teaching is deceptive, tricky, false, hollow, crafty, and empty. It would lure the listener into a trap. Once the trap was released, the listener would become a captive to the doctrine. This word "captive" is used of prisoners of war or of the plunder of war. It is a word that is seldom used, and it contains a strong image to warn the readers of the nature of false teaching.

The source of the false teaching was twofold. Max Anders writes, "Paul provided the Colossians with the two origins of this philosophy, neither of which is Christ. First, Paul says this empty deception is based on human tradition.... The second source of this empty deception was the basic principles of this world."[164] Also, Paul notes that the philosophy was not of Christ. So, Paul opposed the philosophy for three reasons:

1. It was based on human tradition.

2. It was based on elemental principles of this world.

3. It was not of Christ.

Paul is not against the study of philosophy *per se*, but he gives warning to those who would base their lives on empty, hollow philosophy. Paul himself was a thinking man who understood the qualities of nice argumentation. We see Paul quote various philosophers in his writings. He doesn't mind philosophy, but he does mind false teachers using deceptive philosophy to win converts. Moo writes:

> Paul has no intention of criticizing "philosophy" as such, but only the kind of philosophy being propagated by the Colossian false teachers. Our use of the word "philosophy" is narrower than was the case in Paul's day, when it could be applied to virtually any system of thought."[165]

The first source of the deceptive philosophy was human tradition. This can mean any type of human speculation. Not all tradition is wrong. But when you base theology on human tradition, this is wrong.

The second source, *"the fundamental propositions of this world,"* is more difficult to define. In fact, Moo writes, "the meaning of the phrase that Paul uses here, *ta stoicheia tou kosmou* ("the elements of the world"), is one of the more intractable problems in New Testament interpretation."[166] There are three suggestions as to what the term means: (1) Some see it as the elements of the universe: fire, water, earth, and air. (2) Others see it as the foundational principles of an area of study. The term *stoicheia* is used of the alphabet. The term can be used as the elementary rudiments of any field of study. (3) Still others see the term as applying to spiritual beings. This relates to the worship of angels, which Paul discusses in the following verses. Of these three views, I like the second one the best. I believe Paul is warning the disciples not to get drawn into philosophy devoted to foundational principles of Judaism or gnosticism. These types of teachings were drawing people away from Christ and fit the context of what Paul says in the rest of this letter.

Some have traced this deceitful philosophy back to Judaism and the Judaizers whom Paul battled time and again throughout his life. Certainly the teachings of the Judaizers is in Paul's mind throughout this letter. Hendriksen writes:

> This was not *apostolic* tradition, nor was it tradition that belonged to the main stream of *Judaism*, though it did have something in common with Judaism and embraced some of the latter's tenets. It was rather a mixture of Christianity, Judaistic Ceremonialism, Angelolatry, and Asceticism, as verses 11–23 indicate.[167]

V. 9. Next we have this beautiful and clear statement concerning the divinity of Jesus: *"Because in Christ all the fullness of the Deity lives in bodily form."*

This verse states the divinity of Jesus as succinctly as any verse in the New Testament. I would say it is the single most direct statement of the divinity of

Jesus in the Bible. Ernest Martin writes, "Coupling the word *whole* with *fullness* amplifies the claim, making it even stronger than the similar one in 1:19. *Deity* further explains what fullness Paul has in mind. *Deity* means divine essence, a stronger term than divine nature."[168] Melick writes, "Paul meant that the fullness of deity dwells in Christ. The expression is unusual, but the God-man relationship cannot be expressed well in human language. The fullness of deity was Paul's way of stating that Jesus is every bit God."[169]

This one verse makes many claims:

- Jesus is God in the body.
- Jesus is God and man.
- Jesus is fully human and fully divine.
- All the fullness of God dwells in Jesus in bodily form.
- Jesus possesses the fullness of God.

As God dwelt in the Holy of Holies in the Old Testament, now the fullness of the Deity dwells in Jesus. Hendriksen writes:

> When the apostle thus describes Christ he has in mind the latter's *deity*, not just his *divinity*. He is referring to the Son's complete equality of essence with the Father and the Holy Spirit, his *consubstantiality*, not his *similarity*. He is saying that this plenitude of deity has its abiding residence in Christ, and this *bodily*.[170]

But what does Paul mean when he writes, *"the fullness of the Deity 'lives' in bodily form"*? "Lives" is the present tense. What is the meaning here? Melick writes:

> The point of tension is that the verb "lives" occurs in the present tense so that Paul stated that Jesus *now* has the fullness of deity in bodily form. Many, therefore, have taken the expression "bodily" in a spiritual or metaphorical sense. They say it means something like "totally."[171]

The problem with that is that Paul generally used the word "body" (*sōma*) for the real body. Thus, with Lightfoot, it seems best to understand that the fullness of God lives in Jesus in bodily form. In the "form" of Christ we have the reality of God. Another possible solution here is that Paul is using the historical present. Therefore, Paul is saying that the fullness of deity "lived" in bodily form in Christ.

Max Anders lists other passages where the divinity of Christ is affirmed throughout the Bible. He writes:

Christ Possesses the Attributes of Deity
1. Eternity (John 8:58; 17:5; Isa. 9:6; Mic. 5:2)
2. Omnipresence (Matt. 18:20; 28:20; John 3:13; 1:50)
3. Omniscience (Matt. 16:21; Luke 6:8; John 2:24, 25; 6:64; 21:17)
4. Omnipotence (Matt. 28:18; Mark 5:11–15; Phil. 3:21)
5. Immutability (Heb. 1:10–12; 13:8)
6. All attributes of deity belong to Christ (Col. 2:9)

Christ Performs the Work of Deity
1. Creation (John 1:3, 10; Col. 1:16; Heb. 1:2)
2. Preservation (Col. 1:17; Heb. 1:3)
3. Forgiveness of sins (Mark 2:1–12; Luke 5:24; Col. 3:13)
4. Power to raise the dead (John 5:21; 11:43)
5. Judgment of the world (John 5:22, 27; 2 Cor. 5:10)

Christ Accepted the Worship Due Deity
1. John 5:23
2. Luke 24:52

Christ Is Given the Titles of Deity
1. Son of God (Matt. 26:63–64; Mark 1:1; John 10:36)
2. Son of man (Dan. 7:13; Mark 2:10)
3. YHWH (Luke 1:76 [compare Mal. 3:1]; Rom. 10:13 [compare Joel 2:32])
4. God (John 1:1, 18; 20:28; Heb. 1:8)

Jesus Claimed to Be God
1. By claiming to be YHWH (Luke 1:76)
2. By accepting worship (Matt. 28; John 9)
3. By identifying himself with God in context of monotheism (John 10:30; 17:5).
4. By explicit claims (John 8:58)
5. By claiming to do what only God can do (John 5:19–27; Matt. 12:5–8)
6. By accepting the titles of deity (John 20:28; Matt. 16:16)

Messianic Proof of Christ's Deity
1. The Old Testament says "Messiah is God."
    Isaiah 7:14: Immanuel
    Isaiah 9:6: Mighty God
    Isaiah 40:10: Lord God
    Daniel 7:13–28: Ancient of Days

Micah 5:2: From Everlasting
Zechariah 12:10: YHWH
Zechariah 14:16: LORD of Hosts (or LORD Almighty)
Psalm 45:6: God (Heb. 1:8)
Psalm 110:1: LORD—(Matt. 22)
Psalm 118:22: Stone (used 4 times in New Testament)
2. Jesus is Messiah (Hebrew basis for Greek christos or Christ)
   Matthew 16:16–17, 20
   Mark 8:29
   Luke 9:20
   Jesus alone fulfills all the prophecies.
3. Therefore Jesus is God.[172]

V. 10. The fullness of God dwells in Christ, and we have been given fullness in Christ. Therefore, we should not be drawn to false teaching. Also, Christ is head over every power and authority. Therefore, there is no better place to turn in life than to Christ. Moo believes that the power and authority mentioned here are spiritual beings.[173] That could be the case, but it doesn't have to be. It could mean that Jesus is the head (the authority) over anything that has power or authority. "Head" emphasized authority. This could also be a metaphor to say that as the head leads the body, so Jesus leads anything that has power or authority. It could also mean that anything with power and authority emanates from Jesus. The point is this: Since Christ is the head over power and authority, Jesus is the supreme authority in life.

Practical Exercise: Compose a single statement that declares that Jesus is God. See if you can write a sentence that states the divinity of Jesus as simply and eloquently as Paul does in verse 9.

2. 2:11–12 Freed From Sin; Spiritual Circumcision

[11]ἐν ᾧ καὶ περιετμήθητε περιτομῇ ἀχειροποιήτῳ ἐν τῇ ἀπεκδύσει τοῦ σώματος τῆς σαρκός, ἐν τῇ περιτομῇ τοῦ Χριστοῦ, [12]συνταφέντες αὐτῷ ἐν τῷ βαπτισμῷ, ἐν ᾧ καὶ συνηγέρθητε διὰ τῆς πίστεως τῆς ἐνεργείας τοῦ θεοῦ τοῦ ἐγείραντος αὐτὸν ἐκ νεκρῶν·

My Translation

[11]In him you were also circumcised, not with a circumcision done by the hands of men but in the putting off of the sinful flesh. This is a circumcision done by Christ. [12]Having been buried with him in baptism, you have also been raised with him through your faith in the power of God, who raised him from the dead.

NIV, 1984

[11]In him you were also circumcised, in the putting off of the sinful nature, not with a circumcision done by the hand of men but with the circumcision done by Christ, [12]having been buried with Him in baptism and raised with him through your faith in the power of God, who raised him from the dead.

Notes

What does it mean to have Christ in us? First, it means that we are full of life in Christ. Second, it means that we are freed from sin. Paul now speaks of that forgiveness and the means by which we are forgiven.

V. 11. In Christ, we have put off sin. This is one aspect of what it means to have Christ in us.

How did we put off sin? This was accomplished through spiritual circumcision. The Judaizers (Jewish Christians who believed that Gentile Christians needed to obey the Law of Moses, including the ceremonial rite of circumcision, in order to be good Christians) continually pressed Gentile Christians to get circumcised and obey the Jewish customs. Paul adamantly opposed the Judaizers. Here Paul's argument against Jewish circumcision is simple and straightforward: Why should you get circumcised when you have already been circumcised? Paul saw baptism as a spiritual circumcision. This spiritual circumcision of baptism was superior to Jewish circumcision. Jewish circumcision was done by the hands of men; spiritual circumcision was performed by Christ. Jewish circumcision cut off flesh; spiritual circumcision put off sin.

Hendriksen notes the differences between the spiritual circumcision of baptism and the physical circumcision of the Jews in the following chart:[174]

Your circumcision was:	The other was:
(1) the work of the Holy Spirit ("made without hands")	(1) a manual operation (minor surgery!)
(2) inward, of the heart (see Romans 2:28, 29; also N.T.C. on Phil. 3:2, 3)	(2) outward
(3) the putting off and casting away (note double prefix in $\dot{\alpha}\pi\epsilon\kappa\delta\acute{u}\sigma\epsilon\iota$) of your entire evil nature ("the body of the flesh"), in its sanctifying aspect to be progressively realized	(3) removal of excess foreskin
(4) Christian ("the circumcision of Christ" that is, the circumcision which is yours because of your vital union with Christ)	(4) Abrahamic and Mosaic

V. 12. Baptism is a burial. This is the proper mode of baptism (see Romans 6:1–6). Burial is significant because it connects us to the death, burial, and resurrection of Jesus. Burial represents the death of the person; it happens when people die. Baptism is our death to our old life and our resurrection to our new life. Before we rise, we must first die. This is what happens in baptism. Dunnam and Ogilvie write:

> Giacomo Manzu, the artist friend of Pope John XXIII, sculpted the newest doors of St. Peter's in Rome. One door depicts a series of death scenes, "Death by falling," "Death in war," and others. "Death by water" is there, and that is the reason for the sculptor's theme. We are welcomed into the church by *death*. This is the way we enter—the only way. Baptism, our acted out entrance into the church, is by water. So, death by water is a challenging and authentic understanding of baptism. The early church often built its baptismal fonts in the shape of tombs to make the meaning sensually graphic.[175]

I like this image of "death by water." Through baptism, we die to our old life of sin, we are buried in water, and we rise to live a new life in Christ.

The burial precedes the resurrection to a new life. We can be raised only after burial. First we are buried, then the resurrection. Melick writes:

> The term "burial" is appropriate because of what it pictures. The Christian's baptism is a burial. It pictures placing the believer in an environment incapable of sustaining life. For Christ, that meant the grave. For the believer, water symbolizes the grave. It also pictures the resurrection to a new environment of life. The reference to baptism, therefore, calls to mind the practice of immersion because immersion best pictures these truths.[176]

In baptism, we aren't doing anything to earn salvation. Salvation is a gift. In baptism, we aren't performing a work for salvation. In baptism, we are buried so that we might be raised, *"with him through your faith in the power of God."* Baptism is a matter of faith and not of works. Baptism connects us to the saving power of God. The same power that brought Jesus back from the dead is operative in baptism. Melick writes:

> The believer's burial with Christ is affected at his spiritual baptism, and his resurrection with Christ depends on God's power ('the working of God,' NIV). Specifically, through faith in 'the working of God' a spiritual resurrection occurs. God alone produces life after death.[177]

Today, many evangelicals downplay the importance of baptism. Many see baptism as just a sign or a symbol of a salvation that has already been received. But Paul describes baptism as more integral to the salvation process than many teach today. Baptism isn't the whole of the salvation process, but it is an integral part of it. Yes, we must come to faith. Yes, we must repent of our sins. Yes, we must start the walk of discipleship. And, yes, we must also be baptized into the death, burial, and resurrection of Jesus. Douglas Moo writes, "Baptism does not symbolize what happened when we were converted; it somehow is integrally involved in that conversion itself."[178]

Moo goes on to write this interesting note:

> The New Testament connects our coming to Christ (being converted and initiated into the new covenant community) to faith, to repentance, to the gift of the Spirit and to water baptism, in various combinations. Any of these, in a kind of metonymy, could be used to connote the whole experience—implying, of course, in each instance, the presence of all the others. Water baptism, then, as a critical New Testament rite intimately connected to our conversion experience, could be used as shorthand for the whole experience.[179]

Baptism doesn't have to be written into the text for it to be there in thought, just like repentance before baptism doesn't have to be written into the text for it to be there in thought. Baptism is part of the conversion process. Paul saw it as an integral part of that process in that it connected the convert to the death, burial, and resurrection of Jesus.

Hendriksen notes:

> The meaning, then, of Col. 2:11, 12 would seem to be as follows (in summary): "You, believers, have no need of external circumcision. You have received a far better circumcision, that of heart and life. That circumcision is yours by virtue of your union with Christ. When he was buried you—that is, your former, wicked selves—were buried with him. When he was raised you—as new creatures—were raised with him. In the experience of baptism you received the sign and seal of this marvelous Spirit-wrought transformation.[180]

Lest we think that it is only in Colossians 2 that Paul speaks of baptism with this emphasis, compare Colossians 2:11–12 and Romans 6:3–8. Paul uses the same image of baptism as a burial to connect the disciple with the death, burial, and resurrection of Jesus and the new life that follow the resurrection. Consider this chart from Martin's book:[181]

Colossians 2	Romans 6
[11]In him also you were circumcised with a spiritual circumcision, by putting off the body of the flesh in the circumcision of Christ;	[3]Do you not know that all of us who have been baptized into Christ Jesus were baptized into his death?
[12]When you were **buried with him** in baptism, you were also **raised with him** through faith in the power of God, who raised him from the dead.	[4]Therefore we have been **buried with him** by baptism into death, so that, just as Christ was raised from the dead by the glory of the Father, so we too might walk in newness of life.
[13]And when you were dead in trespasses and the uncircumcision of your flesh, God made you **alive together with him**, when he forgave us all our trespasses.	[5]For if we have been **united with him** in a death like his, we will certainly be **united with him** in a resurrection like his. [6]We know that our old self was **crucified with him**....[8]But if we have **died with Christ,** we believe that we will also **live with him**.

The relegating of baptism to a peripheral (or, worse yet, to little or no) role in the salvation process is a recent phenomenon in the church. It has really only been in the past 200 years that preachers and scholars have subjected the role of baptism to a mere symbol of salvation. It is only within the last fifty years that this has become the prominent practice in evangelical Christianity.

You won't find this in the teachings of Paul. Paul states that baptism is central to the conversion process in that it connects us to the death, burial, and resurrection of Jesus. Through it, we have faith in the power of God who raised Jesus from the dead. Through baptism, we begin our new life in Jesus. Let's allow Paul and not evangelical preachers to define the meaning of baptism. When we do, we will see that baptism is a central tenet of Paul's writings and of New Testament Christianity.

3. 2:13–15 Forgiven

[13]καὶ ὑμᾶς νεκροὺς ὄντας [ἐν] τοῖς παραπτώμασιν καὶ τῇ ἀκροβυστίᾳ τῆς σαρκὸς ὑμῶν, συνεζωοποίησεν ὑμᾶς σὺν αὐτῷ, χαρισάμενος ἡμῖν πάντα τὰ παραπτώματα. [14]ἐξαλείψας τὸ καθ' ἡμῶν χειρόγραφον τοῖς δόγμασιν ὃ ἦν ὑπεναντίον ἡμῖν, καὶ αὐτὸ ἦρκεν ἐκ τοῦ μέσου προσηλώσας αὐτὸ τῷ σταυρῷ· [15]ἀπεκδυσάμενος τὰς ἀρχὰς καὶ τὰς ἐξουσίας ἐδειγμάτισεν ἐν παρρησίᾳ, θριαμβεύσας αὐτοὺς ἐν αὐτῷ.

My Translation

[13]And you who were dead in your trespasses and in the uncircumcision of your flesh, God made you alive with Christ when he forgave us all our trespasses. [14]God has erased the handwritten document that stood against us with its legal

demands. God took it away, nailing it to the cross. ¹⁵God disarmed the powers and authorities; he made a public disgrace of them, triumphing over them in him.

NIV, 1984

¹³When you were dead in your sins and in the uncircumcision of your sinful nature, God made you alive with Christ. He forgave us all our sins, ¹⁴having canceled the written code, with its regulations, that was against us and that stood opposed to us; he took it away, nailing it to the cross. ¹⁵And having disarmed the powers and authorities, he made a public spectacle of them, triumphing over them by the cross.

Notes

What does it mean to have Christ in us? First, it means that we are full of life in Christ. Second, it means that we are freed from sin. Third, it means that we are forgiven.

God makes us alive in Christ. God forgives us of our sins. Paul expresses this through three participles:

1. having forgiven us all our trespasses (v. 13)

2. having blotted out the handwritten document that was against us (v. 14)

3. having stripped the principalities and the authorities of their power (v. 15)

V. 13. The first act of God that makes us alive in Christ is the forgiveness of sin. We were dead in our trespasses (sins), and now we are alive in Christ. How? God forgave us.

God has given us a do-over. I love new beginnings. I love to be able to start over. Ever started something that wasn't going the way you hoped it would? I tried to build some shelves once. I like working with wood, but on this occasion, I began the project and realized that it wasn't going to turn out the way I had hoped. So I started over. It's nice to be able to start over. Amateur golfers often give each other a mulligan, an extra shot that isn't scored on the scorecard. You usually save it for when you shank a shot off the tee. It's a do-over. That's what God does for us: He gives us a do-over. He says, "Try again." That's the nature of forgiveness. God doesn't hold any sin or transgression against us. He says, "Start over; try again."

V. 14. The second act of God that makes us alive in Christ is the blotting out of our debt to the law. Verse 14 is key in Paul's argument against the Judaizers (again, these are Jewish Christians who believed Gentile Christians must follow the Jewish law in order to be Christians). Paul says, *"God has erased the handwritten document that stood against us with its legal demands. God took it away, nailing it to the cross."* Many scholars believe that "the handwritten document that stood against us with its legal demands" is a euphemism for the law. Others feel that it is doubtful that Paul would take such a negative view of the law. Some believe this "handwritten document" refers to an actual account that God records in heaven of every debt that each person owes him (an official sin list). A third option is similar to the second; this is a document where God records each time a person breaks the law.

Some scholars do believe that Paul is speaking about the law here. Hendriksen writes:

> But, in making us alive (see on verse 13), not only has God in mercy pardoned our transgressions against his holy law, he has even blotted out the law itself viewed in its demanding and curse-pronouncing character, that law which, because of its many rigid requirements and regulations, condemned us all. As a way of salvation and as a curse suspended above our heads God by means of his Son's substitutionary sacrifice abolished it.[182]

It is difficult to know exactly what Paul meant in this passage. It seems most likely that he was speaking about the debt people owed because they had broken the law (option three). Having said that, it is still true that when Jesus died on the cross a new covenant came into existence that superseded the old covenant and the law (option one).

The Judaizers were still working under the old, pre-cross system. They were still taking count of men's debts against the law. In fact, they had created a legalist system that went beyond the law. Paul spoke directly against this. He did not want disciples of Christ to be burdened by any legalistic, man-made system.

But, we so quickly and easily fall into legalistic practices. That is our nature. It is easier to cross off a checklist of things done for Jesus regardless of the heart than to make sure the heart is engaged in everything we do for him. Thus, it is easy to slide into legalism.

I've been a legalist most of my life. Earlier on, I went to a legalistic church and was trained in the ways of legalism at an early age. I went to a legalistic college and studied the ways of legalism in the college classroom. After college, I became a part of a legalistic movement and learned more thoroughly the ways of legalism. Legalism is easy to embrace. I know; I've embraced it. But legalism is not the way of Christ. It's not the way of the heart. We have to fight against it just as Paul combats legalism in this letter.

What can we do to make sure that we don't become legalists? We can ask the simple question: "Why?" We can step outside of the action and look at the motivation behind it. We can look at our feelings and emotions, and we can see if our heart is engaged in the action. Henri Nouwen observed, "Reflection is essential for growth, development, and change. It is the unique power of the human person."[183] Our unique power as human beings is that we can stop and reflect on what we are doing and ask why we are doing it. When we give up that power, we give up part of our humanity.

In writing about this "unique power of the human person" called refection, Nouwen goes on to write:

> Just living life is not enough. We must know what we are living. A life that is not reflected upon isn't worth living. It belongs to the essence of being human that we contemplate our life, think about it, discuss it, evaluate it, and form opinions about it. Half of living is reflecting on what is being lived. Is it worth it? Is it good? Is it bad? Is it old? Is it new? What is it all about? The greatest joy as well as the greatest pain of living come not only from what we live but even more from how we think and feel about what we are living.[184]

I would add that we should not only apply what Nouwen wrote to the totality of life, but we should apply it to each and every small, daily action that makes up the totality of life. We should step out of the action and reflect on why we are doing what we are doing. Why am I sitting here reading this book? Why do I pray? Why do I talk to strangers about Jesus? Why do I do the little things that I do every single day? Why? Why? Why?

"Why?" is a good question. Reflection is good.

For every action that we do for God, we need to know the reason behind it. So ask, "Why?" Why am I meeting this brother for coffee? Why am I giving to the contribution today? Why am I inviting this person to church? Why am I staying up late to talk to this struggling Christian? Reflect on why you are doing what you are doing. This will keep you from legalism. It will also help you to embrace the unique power of what makes you human: The power of reflection.

V. 15. The third act of God that makes us alive in Christ is the stripping of principalities and authorities of their power. God disarmed the authorities and principalities. Some see these authorities and principalities as angelic beings, but they don't have to be. They can be any authority which sets itself as opposed to God. If these powers are angelic beings, then they must be fallen angels since God publicly disgraces them. There would be no reason to disgrace an angel who was glorifying God.

God triumphed over them, making a public spectacle of them. This image comes from the Roman army who would parade into Rome after a victory on the field with the spoils of war in their arms and with their captives in tow.

There is a carving on an arch in Rome with the Romans hoisting up treasures from the temple in Jerusalem after they conquered that city in AD 70. This is the image that Paul gives us here. God hoists up the principalities, authorities, and powers of this world after the victory of Jesus on the cross to show that these worldly authorities have no real power.

Jesus was victorious on the cross. Satan has been defeated. He still fights, but the war has been won. Anyone who is smart will choose to fight with Jesus because he has already won the war.

When I was in elementary school, we use to have battles on the playground. One of the stronger, more mature boys would put a smaller, younger boy on his shoulders; and they would battle other teams of boys. I always wanted to be on Bill Cramer's shoulders. I was small for my age, but Bill was a giant. I knew that if I were on Bill's shoulders that we would win the battle. And we did.

Wouldn't it be smart to sit on the shoulders of Jesus when you entered battle with Satan? Choose to fight with Jesus. That is the only smart choice, because to choose not to fight with Jesus is to decide to fight against him. That's not a wise choice.

2:16–23. The Doctrine of Sanctification

Paul now moves from the doctrine of salvation (soteriology) to the doctrine of sanctification. Sanctification is the process by which the disciple matures in Christ. It is the idea of how a disciple stays saved and becomes fruitful. It was a favorite topic of Paul and a favorite topic in his letter to the Colossians.

> **Practical Exercise:** List the ways that you struggle with legalism. Are there ways that your legalist rules cause you to belittle other disciples who don't do things exactly the way you do them? How can you root legalistic attitudes and practices out of your life?

F. Free In Christ. 2:16–23.

1. 2:16–19 Let No One Disqualify You.

[16]Μὴ οὖν τις ὑμᾶς κρινέτω ἐν βρώσει καὶ ἐν πόσει ἢ ἐν μέρει ἑορτῆς ἢ νεομηνίας ἢ σαββάτων· [17]ἅ ἐστιν σκιὰ τῶν μελλόντων, τὸ δὲ σῶμα τοῦ Χριστοῦ. [18]μηδεὶς ὑμᾶς καταβραβευέτω θέλων ἐν ταπεινοφροσύνῃ καὶ θρησκείᾳ τῶν ἀγγέλων, ἃ ἑόρακεν ἐμβατεύων, εἰκῇ φυσιούμενος ὑπὸ τοῦ νοὸς τῆς σαρκὸς αὐτοῦ, [19]καὶ οὐ κρατῶν τὴν κεφαλήν, ἐξ οὗ πᾶν τὸ σῶμα διὰ τῶν ἁφῶν καὶ συνδέσμων ἐπιχορηγούμενον καὶ συμβιβαζόμενον αὔξει τὴν αὔξησιν τοῦ θεοῦ.

My Translation

[16]Therefore do not let anyone judge you by what you eat or drink, or in regard to a religious festival, a New Moon celebration, or a Sabbath day. [17]These are the shadow of the things to come; but the reality is in Christ. [18]Do not let anyone who delights in humility and the worship of angels disqualify you for the prize. Such a person goes into great detail about what he has seen, and his unspiritual mind puffs him up with idle notions. [19]He has lost connection with the Head, from whom the whole body, supported and held together by its ligaments and sinews, grows as God causes it to grow.

NIV, 1984

[16]Therefore do not let anyone judge you by what you eat or drink, or with regard to a religious festival, a New Moon celebration or a Sabbath day. [17]These are a shadow of the things that were to come; the reality, however, is found in Christ. [18]Do not let anyone who delights in false humility and the worship of angels disqualify you for the prize. Such a person goes into great detail about what he has seen, and his unspiritual mind puffs him up with idle notions. [19]He has lost connection with the Head, from whom the whole body, supported and held together by its ligaments and sinews, grows as God causes it to grow.

Notes

Paul elaborates more on this theme he has just introduced—freedom in Christ. It is typical of Paul to introduce a topic with a short sentence or two about it, then to come back and explore the topic in a fuller way. Having spoken of the freedom we have in Christ, Paul continues the discussion mentioning specific traditions and regulations that work to steal our freedom in Christ.

V. 16. Paul continues his word of warning here. Ernest Martin writes, "The way the warning is expressed strongly suggests how it is to be understood: 'Stop letting them do this to you.'"[185]

The freedom in Christ of the disciples at Colossae was being challenged by harsh critics who wanted to judge them by what they ate and drank and by their keeping of religious festivals, New Moon celebrations, and the Sabbath. Diet and days—these were the two topics of concern of the ascetics. But Paul says, "No." Don't let anyone judge you based on such legalistic terms.

To understand how serious the topic of diet was to the early disciples, just think about how difficult it was for Peter to change his way of thinking on this topic. God had to address Peter in a vision to help him overcome his food restrictions (see Acts 10). Even after that, it was difficult for Peter to overcome his feeling of prejudice against the Gentiles. Paul had to rebuke him to his face for it (see Galatians 2:11–22).

The pressure to keep the religious festivals of the Jews was also intense in the early church. In Galatians 4:8–11 Paul wrote:

Formerly, when you did not know God, you were slaves to those who by nature are not gods. ⁹But now that you know God—or rather are known by God—how is it that you are turning back to those weak and miserable principles? Do you wish to be enslaved by them all over again? ¹⁰You are observing special days and months and seasons and years! ¹¹I fear for you, that somehow I have wasted my efforts on you.

We begin to see Paul speak directly against the Judaizers. Hendriksen mentions that this direct confrontation began in verse 11, writing:

> In verses 1–10 the warning against the Colossian Heresy was couched in general terms. With verse 11, however, right in the middle of the sentence, it begins to assume specific form. We now learn that the error that was being propagated at Colosse was basically of a Judaistic character.[186]

In 16–19, Paul continues to speak against the heresy in Colossae, mentioning specifics about it and pointing out ways the heresy is contrary to the truth.

V. 17. Verse 17 is one of my favorite verses in Colossians: *"These are the shadow of the things to come; but the reality is in Christ."* What does this verse mean to you? To me, it means that in Christ, I have the real thing.

Paul lets the disciples know that keeping the law is just a shadow of the reality in Christ. There is no real substance in the shadow. The real substance is found in Jesus. The reality is the body that casts the shadow.

Would you rather have a picture of an ice cream cone or a real ice cream cone? Angie, our sister from church, sent around on Facebook a picture of her chocolate macaroons. They looked amazing. But what good is the picture? It just makes your mouth water. Give me the real thing.

If you are married, would you rather hold hands with your wife or with her shadow? Would you rather cuddle up next to a warm fire with her shadow or with her? The shadow has no substance. Reality is found in the person.

Legalism steals the substance from the reality. Max Anders writes:

> Legalism—measuring your own or someone else's spirituality by the ability to keep man-made rules—is a rigid, confining, and life-less way to live. It is easy because all it requires is a list of rules coupled with dutiful compliance. Wisdom or the skillful application of biblical principles to life's situations is unnecessary. Just comply. Legalism is not only rigid and lifeless, but it also fosters hypocritical pride.[187]

I really like Anders' assessment. Legalism is easier in the short term because it is a checklist and the heart doesn't need to be involved. But in the long term it is harder because it is a shadow and the reality is Christ.

The shadow is just a shadow; the substance is the reality. Paul is telling his readers that what they have found in Christ is the real stuff. Therefore, they should let go of the shadow (dietary rules, religious festivals, Jewish rites) and cling to Jesus. Douglas J. Moo writes:

> According to the fundamental salvation-historical perspective of the New Testament writers, the Old Testament, and especially the law, belonged to the time of promise, to the time when God was preparing his people and the world for salvation in Christ. With the coming of Christ, the new era of fulfillment has dawned. The old era and the law have now been brought to their "culmination" (Rom. 10:4). Believers who belong to the new era through their incorporation into Christ therefore experience the reality to which the Old Testament and its law pointed. And they are no longer compelled to follow the laws of that earlier era.[188]

V. 18. Paul continues to warn the disciples of Colossae about the false teachers. He says, "Don't let them disqualify you for the prize." The consequences of following false teachers is dire; therefore, Paul strongly opposed false teaching.

Paul warns against anyone who *"delights in humility."* This is a literal translation of the Greek. But humility is a godly virtue. How could Paul oppose it? These people were delighting in their humility; therefore their humility was not genuine. They feigned humility as a mask to appear as if they were approachable and teachable. But they were salesmen selling a bill of goods. One item on their list of wares was angel worship. How humble it would appear to worship angels along with God the creator. The only problem is that God had expressly stated that he and he alone was to be worshipped. The expression of true humility would be to obey his will and worship no one but him.

Another possible way to interpret "humility" is by connecting it with ascetic practices. This fits the context of this passage. Elite spiritualists often practice fasting and other ascetic customs to prepare for visions. Paul opposes the use of fasting in this way.

Paul moves on to talk about the worship of angels. What was this angel worship? Max Anders writes:

> Scholars debate whether the worship of angels referred to the angels being the objects of worship (the worship given to angels) or to the worship that the angels perform. Either is possible, but the former seems most likely. The mystical experience began with initiation into ascetic rituals (possibly referred to in Col. 2:21) which

led to supernatural visions in which the individual was ushered into the heavenly realms to worship the angels who emanated from God or to join with the angels in the worship of God.[189]

As Anders states, Paul could mean the worship of angels here. That would fit in with a gnostic, pagan setting.

But there is an alternative interpretation. Anders calls it, "worship that the angels perform." This would fit a Jewish context. In esoteric corners of Judaism, there was a belief that the super-spiritual could enter into worship with angels and that type of worship was a superior worship. The Essenes, a first-century Jewish sect from the Qumran community along the Dead Sea, mention this in their literature. Melick writes about this "worship with the angels" stating:

This...describes a commitment to what was perceived as a higher form of worship. Consistent with the Jewish traditions that the angels were higher than humans and that they worshiped and served God, the false teachers seem to have developed a procedure to induce a higher spiritual experience equivalent to the angels' experience. To affect it, however, required severity to the flesh. Through ascetic practices, they taught that the mind and spirit could be sensitized to higher spiritual realities. These became an evidence of spiritual superiority.[190]

But perhaps this interpretation of the phrase is too esoteric. Perhaps this type of worship with the angels was located only around the Dead Sea and had not travelled all the way west to the region of Colossae.

Douglas Moo prefers the first alternative—worship of angels is the worship of angelic beings and not worship with angels. He gives four reasons why he feels that this is the best reading of this phrase.

First, from a purely linguistic point of view, the phrase is more likely to mean "worship offered to angels" than "worship offered by angels." Second, while many Jewish apocalyptic texts refer to angelic worship, and some refer to humans observing or imitating that worship, very few speak of humans joining with angels in such worship.... Third, as we have noted, a key concern of Colossians has been to accentuate the superiority of Christ over spiritual beings (1:16, 20; 2:10, 15). Such a concern to minimize the significance of the angels would make very good sense if, indeed, the false teachers were worshiping them. Fourth, Clinton Arnold has suggested a plausible background for Paul's accusation that the false teachers were worshiping angels. He notes the importance of invoking angels as a means to ward off evil in the ancient world in general and the geographic region of Colossae in particular. Paul would be characterizing this calling on angels for protection as tantamount to the worship of angels.[191]

However you view the worship of angels, Paul is writing against a group of false teachers who have set themselves up as spiritual elitists within the church in Colossae. They go into great detail about what they have seen. They love to talk about their spiritual visions, and they do so in a puffed-up manner. Paul warns the Colossians about these false teachers and directs them not to follow these teachings. If they do, they will be disqualified for the prize.

V. 19. I like the way William Hendriksen in his commentary describes the false teacher in Colossae as a "philosopher-ritualist-angel worshiper-ascetic-visionary."[192] Paul warns against these teachers because they cause the disciple to lose connection with Jesus. If we have lost connection with Jesus, then we are adrift on an endless sea of ritualism, formulaic worship, and legalism. Obviously, this is not a good place to be. The whole church owes its health, growth, and maturity to the head, that is, Jesus.

What happens to a body without a head? First, it withers and dies. It will not survive. Second, if it could survive, it would be directionless. The church that does not have Christ as its head will not survive. If it were to survive, then it would a purposeless, directionless mess.

What is true of the church is true of each disciple. We must make sure that we always stay connected to Jesus. Melick writes:

> Any suggestion of spiritual growth apart from Christ is a false spirituality. The Christian is to be energized and empowered by Christ the head so that genuine spiritual growth can take place. This means, of course, that spiritual experiences like those advocated by the false teachers in Colosse have no lasting value and do not promote real spiritual growth. Thus it is a serious matter for the body to be dislocated from the Head.[193]

I like Melick's subtle understatement in his concluding sentence, "Thus it is a serious matter for the body to be dislocated from the Head." Yes, it's a serious matter. Call the ambulance, get the OR ready, and page the chief of surgery. A body can't exist without a head. If you notice that you are disconnected from Jesus, be urgent. Sound the alarms and call for help. Get reconnected as soon as possible. We have to stay connected to Jesus to grow spiritually.

Practical Exercise: List the things that cause you to lose connection with Jesus. List the things that cause you to connect with him. What can you do to make sure you don't lose connection with Jesus?

2. 2:20–23. Do Not Submit to Human Regulations.

²⁰Εἰ ἀπεθάνετε σὺν Χριστῷ ἀπὸ τῶν στοιχείων τοῦ κόσμου, τί ὡς ζῶντες ἐν κόσμῳ δογματίζεσθε; ²¹Μὴ ἅψῃ μηδὲ γεύσῃ μηδὲ θίγῃς, ²²ἅ ἐστιν πάντα εἰς φθορὰν τῇ ἀποχρήσει, κατὰ τὰ ἐντάλματα καὶ διδασκαλίας τῶν ἀνθρώπων, ²³ἅτινά ἐστιν λόγον μὲν ἔχοντα σοφίας ἐν ἐθελοθρησκίᾳ καὶ ταπεινοφροσύνῃ [καὶ] ἀφειδίᾳ σώματος, οὐκ ἐν τιμῇ τινι πρὸς πλησμονὴν τῆς σαρκός.

My Translation

²⁰Since you died with Christ to the elemental principles of the world, why, as though you still live in it, do you submit to its regulations: ²¹"Do not handle! Do not taste! Do not touch!"? ²²These all refer to things destined to perish with use, because they are based on human precepts and teachings. ²³Indeed such regulations have an appearance of wisdom, with their self-imposed worship, their false humility, and their harsh treatment of the body, but they are of no value in restraining indulgence of the flesh.

NIV, 1984

²⁰Since you died with Christ to the basic principles of this world, why, as though you still belonged to it, do you submit to its rules: ²¹"Do not handle! Do not taste! Do not touch!"? ²²These are all destined to perish with use, because they are based on human commands and teachings ²³Such regulations indeed have an appearance of wisdom, with their self-imposed worship, their false humility and their harsh treatment of the body, but they lack any value in restraining sensual indulgence.

Notes

Paul moves on to speak directly against asceticism. Asceticism is the practice of denying the desires of life in order to achieve a greater level of spirituality.

V. 20. Since the disciples in Colossae have died to the elemental principles of the world in baptism, they should not be controlled by these worldly principles. Paul is asking the question: "Why do you live as though you were controlled by the principles of the world?" The verb "were controlled" is the word δογματίζεσθε, *dogmatidzesthe*. You probably see the word *dogma* there. Paul is asking the disciples why they come under the dogma of the world. This is as good a question for us today as it was for the church of the first century. Too often we are influenced by the world. We might be influenced to become like the world, which can lead to licentiousness, libertarianism, lust, and greed. Or, we can lean to the other side and want to appear so different from the world that we become cultic in our extremism and asceticism. Thus we establish a new Puritanism. Paul is speaking more directly to the second response here.

In the first century, some people believed the "elemental principles" of the world held power over their lives. The ascetics taught that the way to overcome the power of these "elemental principles" was through ascetic practices. Douglas Moo writes:

> Many people in Paul's day lived in fear of these "forces" and sought ways to live in harmony with them. The sense of bondage to these powers appears to have been what made the false teachers' program especially seductive. Paul is therefore at pains to show that Christ's victory over the spiritual beings that are included in the "elemental forces" was complete and final (vv. 14–15) and that people who are in union with Christ share in that victory. In this and the following verses it becomes clear that the main "remedy" for appeasement of the "elemental forces" being suggested by the false teachers was a set of rules focusing on an ascetic lifestyle.[194]

How does a person overcome these "elemental forces"? The false teachers teach that the victory comes through asceticism. Paul, however, clearly states that the victory is in Christ and him alone.

Who is in control of your life? You say, "I am in control." But are you really? People are controlled by greed, lust, the desire to please others, the love of success, and many other cravings.

I'm sure you've seen toy cars that are remotely controlled. There are also helicopters and hovercraft with remote controls. I've seen them at kiosks in our mall. The salesperson stands at the kiosk playing with these toys hoping to entice someone to buy them. With these toys, whoever holds the controller, controls the toy. Who holds the controller of your life? If you say, "I do," then that's the wrong answer. It should be, "Christ does." He is the only one who is going to lead us down the right path. Give him the controller to your life.

V. 21. Paul directly mentions three ascetic rules in this passage: Don't handle, don't taste, and don't touch. The second rule, "Don't taste," has to do with prohibitions of food and drink. What Paul means by the first and third rules, "Don't handle" and "Don't touch," is more difficult to discern. He could have in mind ascetic proscriptions toward sexual abstinence. However, he could be referring to matters of ritual purity here. Whatever the case, Paul is using the false teachers' own words against them.

Following these three rules will not make a person spiritual nor provide victory over the "elemental powers of the world." Hendriksen writes, "He [Paul] says, as it were, why submit to a series of Don'ts, as if by adding enough negatives you would ever obtain a positive, or as if victory over sin and progress in sanctification would ever be achieved by basing all your confidence in sheer *avoidance*."[195]

V. 22. Paul opposes these ascetic practices for many reasons. First he mentions that they perish with use. They are a temporary fix, but they do not provide long-term spiritual fulfillment. Second, they are based on human teaching. This is why they will break down in time. They aren't based on God's eternal principles. Moo writes, "Paul's point…is that the false teachers have been making far too big a deal of matters that do not get to the essence of true Christian spirituality: the change of heart and mind that leads to true holiness."[196]

V. 23. Third, they are a sham. They have some value, but they won't keep you from sin. They have no value in keeping you from indulging in the flesh.

What will work? Paul has already stated it. Christ is the answer. Only Christ can help us win over the flesh.

These practices do have an appearance of wisdom.[197] Paul mentions three areas where asceticism seems to have some benefit, writing, *"with their self-imposed worship, their false humility, and their harsh treatment of the body."*

First, Paul mentions *"self-imposed worship."* The ascetics set their own stringent standards of worship that set them apart. They might stop and pray every hour on the hour. They might practice strict and rigorous cleansing practices before worship. God has not established these requirements. They are "self-imposed" by the false teachers.

Second, Paul mentions *"false humility."* This word, ταπεινοφροσύνη, *tapeinophrosuna,* can mean true modesty and humility or a false form of humility. The context determines the meaning of the word. Paul must mean false humility in this passage. The false teachers' devotion to ascetic practices makes them appear as if they are genuinely humble. However, they flaunt their asceticism as a badge of honor to declare that they are more spiritual than others who don't practice asceticism in the same manner as they do.

Third, Paul mentions *"harsh treatment of the body."* This describes more specific ascetic practices performed to keep fleshly urges at bay. Ascetics sometimes beat their bodies in order to make the flesh surrender to their will. The battle of the flesh is real. But we can't conquer the urges of the flesh unless our hearts are engaged in the battle. Ascetic practices without the heart involved and the right attitude in place have little value. Melick writes:

Asceticism only changed the environment. The flesh could not be conquered through such practices. Therefore, the entire system was flawed. The teachers devoted themselves to ascetic practices and physical torture, hoping to produce a higher spiritual state. In the end, their approach was misguided at three points. It was only a product of this world. It focused on perishable (earthly) objects, and it did not offer a means of conquering the desires of the flesh. What, then, did Paul offer in its place?[198]

What did Paul offer in its place? The answer of course is Christ. Throughout the book Paul continues to drive home this point—Christ is supreme.

Paul has shown how once we have found Jesus, we must not trade him for anything. If we swap Jesus for anything (angel worship or asceticism), then we've made a bad trade. In Christ we are lavished with a spiritual treasure.

Max Anders illustrates this idea with the following story:

> Imagine for a moment that you are poor and needy. You are desperate. Ragged, shabby clothes. You haven't eaten in several days. You are cold, and you are tired because you have been walking all day. Darkness advances swiftly. You notice some lights in the distance through the trees. Your aching stomach urges your throbbing feet to keep going just a little farther. As you draw closer, you see the lights are a blaze of white against the night. It's a huge house. Curtains are drawn back to reveal activity inside. You inch closer for a better look, until your face presses against the window. You stand there for a few moments without being noticed—shocked at what you see. It's a feast. A huge table is covered from end to end with more food than you've seen in months—green vegetables, steaming meat, cold drinks, warm bread. Your stomach rumbles; your mouth waters. You feel faint from hunger. As a butler is serving the guests, the master of the house glances over and notices your face pressed against the window. He thinks to himself, *Here is a needy person.* He motions for the butler to go out and speak to you. Your first instinct is to try to get away fast, because you think they want to punish you for trespassing. The butler calls out to you, "Please, the master would like you to come in and dine at the table." So you go in—and eat. Your great need has been met by the fullness of the table.
>
> In a similar way, our great spiritual need has been met by the fullness of the table of blessings in Christ. Jesus Christ is the fullness of deity, and from his fullness he has given us spiritual fullness. Why look elsewhere? Why look for treasure we already have? As believers we have the awesome opportunity to feed at the table of spiritual blessing in Christ.[199]

As disciples of Jesus, there is no need to look beyond Jesus for our spiritual satisfaction. Jesus provides everything we need to grow spiritually and to fill our every spiritual longing. He invites us to a wonderful banquet. We need to pull up a chair and dine at the table that he has furnished with food. Pull up a chair and feast.

Practical Exercise: List all the spiritual blessings that you enjoy at the banquet that Jesus provides. Take time and think of every blessing that you enjoy in life. Realize every one of these blessing comes from Jesus.

Exposition of Colossians
Chapter Three

II. 3:1-4:18. Ethical Teaching

Paul has established the theological foundation of the letter. What is the main theme of Colossians? Christ is supreme.

Now Paul moves to matters of practical Christian living: Since Christ is supreme and we live/walk in him, this is how we ought to live/walk. That's not to say that he didn't mention matters of practical spiritual living in the first half of the letter; he did. Remember 2:6–7, the thematic verses of the book? But Paul does change his tone in the latter half of the book. He speaks directly to what it means to live/walk as a disciple of Jesus.

In his commentary on Colossians, Max Anders tells this story:

> Dan Jansen is an Olympic Gold Medal speed skater. You may remember him as the man whose sister, Jane, died of leukemia just before the 1988 Winter Games in Calgary. He desperately wanted to win the gold medal in honor of his sister. He failed in Calgary. In the 1992 games in Albertville, France, he again came away empty. Four years later, in Lillihammer, Norway, he won the gold in the one thousand meters and set a world record. It was an emotional moment when he skated his victory lap holding his nine-month-old daughter in his arms. Her name was Jane.
>
> After the Olympics, Jansen was asked how he had overcome so much adversity and kept going. He reflected back to a time when he was twelve years old and had lost a meet. His father drove him home, and Dan pouted all the way. His father was silent until they arrived home. Then, as Dan was going to bed, his dad came into his room and said, "Son, life is more than skating in circles," and walked out. Jansen said that one comment changed his whole perspective on life.
>
> Dan Jansen didn't quit skating in circles. He just had a

bigger picture. His father's words gave him a higher perspective on life, and his skating took on new significance. Jansen will be remembered for doing something ordinary in an extraordinary way.

Ever feel like your life is just skating in circles? The drudgery of the same old routines can make life seem like that. With an earth-bound perspective, life really is little more than skating in circles. The repetitive cycles of infancy, adolescence, and old age; work, rest, and more work; marriage, children, and grandchildren; diapers and dishes; progress and regress can seem awfully ordinary and terribly tedious.[200]

Life can be extremely ordinary. But then Christ enters the picture. Jesus is the most extraordinary person to ever walk the face of the earth. His resurrection is the most extraordinary event to ever happen in the history of humanity. When we are lost in the drudgery of life, Jesus enters the picture and shows us what extraordinary living is all about. Even if we are skating in circles, Jesus shows us how to make skating in circles an extraordinary event.

Perhaps you have heard of Brother Lawrence, a seventeenth-century monk who wrote a book entitled, *The Practice of the Presence of God*. Lawrence was washing dishes in the monastery when he realized that washing dishes could be a holy act if he kept thinking of Jesus as he did it. By practicing the presence of God in an ordinary task, Lawrence made the ordinary become a sacred event. We can do this in our lives today as well.

Paul moves from writing about grand theological themes to speaking about practical matters of Christian living. You might think he moves from the sublime to the ordinary. However, the ordinary becomes the sublime in the hands of Paul. For Paul, theology must be practiced. Thus in this letter, as in many of Paul's epistles, he moves from teaching profound theological lessons to directing the everyday lives of the disciples. Let's see what Paul can teach us about practical Christian living through this letter.

Practical Exercise: Before you read any farther in this commentary, go through chapters 3 and 4 of Colossians and underscore every direct, practical teaching that Paul gives the disciples in Colossae. See how these practical teachings tie in to the great theological themes discussed in the first two chapters.

A. The Foundation of Christian Living; The New Self. 3:1–4

Spirituality involves the whole of human life; nothing is nonspiritual.... In fact, spirituality is to be expressed primarily in the ordinary everyday affairs and relationships of our lives.[201]
—Ranald Macaulay and Jerram Barrs

Paul now gets down to where we live our lives. In doing so, he makes the common, ordinary acts of daily life sacred. Every bit of our lives, no matter how small or mundane, falls under the lordship of Christ. Therefore, we set our eyes above, on things that are not seen. We live life differently than the world around us. We live life with hope: hope for another life, a great life, that will be filled with glory.

Some see verses 1–4 as concluding the discussion of chapters one and two. Others see these verses as beginning a new, practical section. Max Anders writes, "Colossians 3:1–4 is a hinge between the primarily doctrinal section of chapters 1–2 and the primarily practical section of chapters 3–4."[202] I think it is best to see these verses as a transition to a new section in Paul's letter. This section focuses on how to live the life of discipleship under the supremacy of Christ. It is a very important section of the letter, chock full of theological themes and practical advice. It serves as a perfect transition between chapters 1–2, which were theologically centered, and chapters 3–4, which are practically oriented. Moo writes:

> Colossians 3:1–4 occupies a transitional place in the argument of the letter. It applies the key theological concept of union with Christ, which Paul develops negatively in vv. 16–23 to counter the false teaching, in a positive direction, calling on believers to recognize the basic implications of their status as "dead" to the "elements of the world," "alive" with Christ in heaven, and destined for glory.[203]

Ernest D. Martin speaks to the difference between the tone of chapters 1–2 and chapters 3–4. He writes:

> The gospel is normally stated in indicatives (e.g., Christ died for our sins; he was raised from the dead). But the gospel also contains imperatives (e.g., be reconciled; be holy). The imperatives of the gospel of Christ grow out of the indicatives. Exhortations about life spring from the foundation of Christology. In Colossians we hear the call to become in daily experience what we are in Christ.[204]

This is an important concept to recognize: Imperatives are built on indicatives. Before a mountain climber begins the ascent, he or she first makes sure the rope is grounded to the mountain. The same is true of the Christian life/walk. We obey the commands of God because we are sure of who God is and who we are in Christ. Without that surety, the commands can become legalistic demands. Without that surety, we lack the confidence to follow through with the commands.

Ernest Martin has given six observations concerning the use of indicatives and imperatives in Colossians. He writes:

1. The indicatives review the acts of God, with primary focus on what God has done in Christ.

2. The imperatives do not hold up abstract virtues as ideals (as Greek philosophy does), but have to do with attitudes and actions, works and fruits (yet without falling into Jewish legalism).

3. No clean-cut division exists between the indicative and imperative sections....

4. The order is crucial. Never are the imperatives a prerequisite for receiving God's grace in Christ. Grace and salvation come before the demands. This is always God's way....

5. The imperatives are not of the nature of legal demands. Instead, they are characterized by an appeal: Do what is fitting in light of what you have experienced in Christ.

6. The imperatives, as well as the indicatives, are a form of the gospel. The fact that they are there at all implies that believers are set free and enabled to do God's will, and that is good news. Rather than think of the imperatives as the dark side of the gospel, we should see them as open gateways into the potentials of life in Christ.[205]

Martin doesn't stop there. He goes on to summarize his findings in these words:

The biblical integration of the indicative and the imperative is profoundly important. The indicatives of theology and Christology may not be proclaimed or discussed as if they have nothing to do with the issues of behavior. Likewise, ethical imperatives may not be separated from the message of what God has done in Christ. The gospel call is to *be* in daily practice what we *are* potentially in Christ.[206]

We need to understand why we do what we do. God wants us to know why we need to obey him. Paul is careful to let his readers see the superiority of Christ in the letter, then he goes on to tell them how to live. The "why" needs to precede the "how." After all, the answer to the question "Why?" is the key to proper motivation. Paul gives the readers motivation before he directs them in how they should live. We need to understand this. It is important for our own growth and maturity and for the growth of others.

3:1–4. The New Self

¹Εἰ οὖν συνηγέρθητε τῷ Χριστῷ, τὰ ἄνω ζητεῖτε, οὗ ὁ Χριστός ἐστιν ἐν δεξιᾷ τοῦ θεοῦ καθήμενος· ²τὰ ἄνω φρονεῖτε μὴ τὰ ἐπὶ τῆς γῆς. ³ἀπεθάνετε γὰρ καὶ ἡ ζωὴ ὑμῶν κέκρυπται σὺν τῷ Χριστῷ ἐν τῷ θεῷ· ⁴ὅταν ὁ Χριστὸς φανερωθῇ, ἡ ζωὴ ὑμῶν, τότε καὶ ὑμεῖς σὺν αὐτῷ φανερωθήσεσθε ἐν δόξῃ.

My Translation

¹Since, then, you have been raised with Christ seek the things that are above, where Christ is seated at the right hand of God. ²Set your minds on things that are above, not on earthly things. ³For you died, and your life is now hidden with Christ in God. ⁴When Christ who is your life appears, then you also will appear with him in glory.

NIV, 1984

¹Since, then, you have been raised with Christ, set your hearts on things above, where Christ is seated at the right hand of God. ²Set your minds on things above, not on earthly things. ³For you died, and your life is now hidden with Christ in God. ⁴When Christ, who is your life appears, then you also will appear with him in glory.

Notes

V. 1. The phrase *"since, then, you have been raised with Christ,"* harkens back to verses 11–12 where the disciple experiences the power of the resurrection baptism. When that happens we are a new creation. The old life is past and the new life begins.

Therefore, we look at things differently. We now seek the things that are above. This is an imperative. God isn't just telling us that it's a good idea to set our hearts on things above; he's commanding that we focus on what is above. Christian living begins with a mind-change. We focus on heaven, where Christ is seated at the right hand of God. The image of Christ seated at the right hand of God expresses both power and privilege.

What we focus on in life, we get. Focus on heaven; get heaven.

At one of the darkest moments of my life I began to study Kung Fu with Sifu Karl Romain.[207] When you enter Sifu Romain's school, you are to leave all your cares and concerns at the door and come ready to train. You step through the door, bow, and greet everyone with a hearty, "Hello, sir; hello, ma'am." When you enter and exit the training mat, you say, "Yes, I can." This sets your mind for work. It also keeps a positive affirmation in your mind. The repetition of that phrase, "Yes, I can," over and over hundreds of times has helped me to become a more positive person. How? Because what we focus on in life, we get. What we focus on in life, we become.

Paul tells us here to focus on what is above. Keep your focus on Jesus, eternity, and heaven. Anders writes:

> The reality of our resurrection with Jesus should produce in us new motivations and new minds. Paul tells us that since we have been raised we are to set [our] hearts on things above. Believers are being urged literally to seek, pursue with diligence things above.[208]

The NIV translates the phrase "τὰ ἄνω ζητεῖτε, *ta ano dzateite*" as "set your hearts on things above." The word "ζητεῖτε, *dzateite*" is the word "seek." It is the same word in Matthew 6:33 where Jesus says, *"Seek first his kingdom and his righteousness."* I translate this phrase more literally, "seek the things that are above." Just as we are to seek the Kingdom first in our lives by making the rule and reign of God a constant priority, we must also seek the things above, meaning that we make the future reality of heaven a present reality in our lives by keeping our minds focused on heavenly things throughout the day. Douglas Moo makes an insightful comment here, writing:

> For Paul is not saying so much that believers should seek to *possess* "the things above" as that they are to seek to orient themselves totally to these heavenly realities…. Rather, we are to make that heavenly status the guidepost for all our thinking and acting. And, by using the present tense, Paul indicates that believers should be constantly occupied in striving for this orientation…. Believers "seek the things above" by deliberately and daily committing ourselves to the values of the heavenly kingdom and living out of those values.[209]

V. 2. Where is your mind? What do you think about during the day? Again, what we focus on in life we become. Therefore, we must set our minds on things above.

Martin Luther once challenged one of his students by saying, "I'll get you a new horse and carriage if you can pray the Lord's Prayer and concentrate on every phrase without losing your train of thought." The young man thought, "No problem." After he had prayed the prayer, however, he confessed to Luther, "All I could think about was the horse and carriage." As much as he tried to concentrate on the Lord's Prayer, his mind was drawn elsewhere.

"Things above" is contrasted with negative things that often drag us down: "not on earthly things." Paul isn't just saying "set your sights on heaven," but "above" refers to a higher moral ground. Ernest Martin writes:

> The *above* metaphor, set over against *earth* in Colossians 3:2, is sometimes contrasted with *below*. These terms do not usually have a literal *up* and *down* meaning. They do not refer to locations

in the universe, but rather have a religious or mor
translates the word *anō*, found also in Jesus' word
"You are from below, I am from above" (see also
3:14). As usage indicates, *above* also points to the
kingdom of Christ.[210]

Our minds can't be two places at one time. Either we are focused on things above or on earthly things. Since Jesus is Lord of our lives, we must strive to keep our focus on things above.

We can either set our mind on earthly things or on things above/heavenly things. Earthly things will weigh us down to the things of this world. Heavenly things will cause us to soar above the world so that we become spiritual people. It all begins with our mindset, our focus.

This is a great verse to help us grow or mature in Christ. We have to set our minds on things above/on heavenly things. If we will do that, then we will become more like Christ.

What you allow your mind to think about will have an impact on your life. If you allow the world into your mind, then worldly thoughts will take over your mind.

I live fairly close to the Hudson River, one of America's most beautiful rivers. I love walking the Palisades in New York and looking down on the majestic Hudson. But a few decades ago, the Hudson wasn't as majestic as it is today.

Just thirty years ago, the Hudson was one of the most polluted rivers in the US. Why? Companies and industry upriver dumped their waste into the river. They contaminated it. Fish died, and birds that ate the fish died. Animals that ate the birds that ate the fish died. The river became so filthy that people didn't want to have anything to do with it.

Then the environmentalists got involved. They told the polluters to "Stop!" Many companies changed their practices. Now, instead of receiving waste and contaminated garbage, the river receives cleansing, purifying rain. The snow in the mountains of the Adirondacks melts in the spring and runs into the Hudson. It is cleaner than it has been in decades; now it is one of the cleanest rivers in the US. It's true; I read it in the *New York Times*. I'm not making this up.

When we allow filth into our minds, it pollutes our minds. When we keep the garbage out and put spiritual thoughts in, then we become more spiritual people.

Helen Lemmel, a songwriter, put it this way:

> Turn your eyes upon Jesus,
>> Look full in his wonderful face,
> And the things of earth will grow strangely dim
>> In the light of his glory and grace.[211]

—4. Why focus on things above? Because you have already been resurrect-once to a new life in Christ and you will be resurrected a second time when Christ comes in glory.

Paul goes back to the idea of our death to our old life through baptism. He says, "You died. Remember we had a burial. The old you was left in the tomb of baptism. Your life is now hidden with Christ." To be "hidden with Christ" means that the new source of our life comes through Christ. Christ is our life. Everything we are should be about Jesus. Every step we take should be in his footprints. In Philippians 1:21, Paul writes, *"For to me, to live is Christ and to die is gain."* Galatians 2:20 states, *"I have been crucified with Christ and I no longer live, but Christ lives in me. The life I live in the body, I live by faith in the Son of God, who loved me and gave himself for me."* Paul is clear—the life we now live is life in Christ.

Moo demonstrates how central death, burial, and resurrection in Christ is to the life of a disciple. He writes:

> As we have noted, the believer's union "with" Christ in death (v. 20), burial (v. 12a), and resurrection (v. 12b; cf. 13) provides the Colossians with the spiritual security that they were craving, including especially forgiveness and protection from evil spiritual powers (vv. 13–15). Christ's death, burial, and resurrection are the essential moments of the climactic salvation-historical drama (1 Cor. 15:3–5), and they mark the transition from the old era to the new.[212]

Sometimes when scientists make a new discovery they say, "This changes everything." When we take on Christ in baptism, it changes everything. Now we no longer live, but Christ lives in us. Christ becomes the reason for life. All of our goals, dreams, and aspirations in life are filtered through the Christ filter. Jesus becomes the reason we live.

How Can You Set Your Mind on Things Above?

(1) **By choosing Jesus: "Since, then, you have been raised with Christ."**

We aren't able to do this on our own. We need the power of Christ to be able to think spiritually, so Christ gives us a fresh start so that we can begin thinking spiritually and learn to focus our minds on heavenly things.

Galatians 3:26–27 tells us, *"You are all sons of God through faith in Christ Jesus, for all of you who were baptized into Christ have clothed yourselves with Christ."*

We need to cloth ourselves with Christ. Another word for clothe here is to wrap or envelop. We need to wrap ourselves up in Christ.

For those of you who are parents, when you first have your baby the nurses take the newborn and wrap him or her in a fresh cloth. The baby is packed into that cloth. I was like, "How did you do that? How did you get the baby tucked into that cloth so nice and tight?" That provides security for the baby.

Are you enveloped in Jesus? Is he your security? If so, then you'll get your self-esteem from Jesus. You will know you are of value because you are wrapped in him. No need for pride. No need to talk so much about yourself.

Being clothed in Jesus means we have a fresh start in life. And that fresh start can begin any time. And that fresh start can be every day.

(2) By preparing your mind: *"Set your minds."*

As I'm working on this section, the Summer Olympics of 2012 have been taking place in London, England. I love the Olympics. I love watching the best athletes in the world competing for their countries. This summer, I've really enjoyed the track events and the swimming events.

In both those contests, before the athlete runs or swims, they have to get in the starting block. They get set. Then the starter starts the race.

Before you race, you have to get set for the race.

On Friday night, I was watching the BMX bike racing. I'm not sure why this is an Olympic event, but it is. I was watching the American athlete when the race was about to begin. This was the race for the gold metal. The starter said, "Set," and the American leaned back. I thought, "Why are you leaning back instead of forward?" I said to the TV, "Lean forward, get set, lean forward." It was too late. The race started and the athlete came out of the blocks last. He had lost the race before it even began because he wasn't set.

We have to set our minds. Every day we have to set our minds for the day ahead of us. Some days you have to set your mind more than on other days. If you go through the day without setting your mind, you are asking for trouble.

Before Jesus began his day, we see him up early in the morning having time with God. Before Jesus went to the cross, he first went to Gethsemane to prepare his mind

1 Peter 1:13–16 reads:

Therefore, prepare your minds for action; be self-controlled; set your hope fully on the grace to be given you when Jesus Christ is revealed. As obedient children, do not conform to the evil desires you had when you lived in ignorance. But just as he who called you is holy, so be holy in all you do; for it is written: 'Be holy, because I am holy.'

Peter says, *"Prepare your minds for action."* Get set.

One great way to get set is to think about Jesus all through the day. The more we focus on Jesus, the more we will become like him. Max Anders states:

Four times in four verses, Paul mentioned Christ. Jesus is central and supreme. Paul doesn't want believers to forget that. Jesus is seated above in the position of honor. Believers are identified with him. With this solid foundation, the lives of believers can be transformed.[213]

Jesus can transform our lives. Let's set our minds on Jesus. Let's picture him walking beside us throughout the day. We can call this the "with Jesus" life.

Practical Exercise: Take a moment and think about your day. Envision taking Jesus with you wherever you go and in whatever you do on this day. Would that change the day in any way? Now go live out this day as if Jesus were beside you at each and every moment (because in reality he is beside you every moment of every day).

B. 3:5–17. The Transformation of Christian Living

1. 3:5–11. Put Off.

⁵Νεκρώσατε οὖν τὰ μέλη τὰ ἐπὶ τῆς γῆς, πορνείαν ἀκαθαρσίαν πάθος ἐπιθυμίαν κακήν, καὶ τὴν πλεονεξίαν, ἥτις ἐστὶν εἰδωλολατρία, ⁶δι᾽ ἃ ἔρχεται ἡ ὀργὴ τοῦ θεοῦ [ἐπὶ τοὺς υἱοὺς τῆς ἀπειθείας]. ⁷ἐν οἷς καὶ ὑμεῖς περιεπατήσατέ ποτε, ὅτε ἐζῆτε ἐν τούτοις· ⁸νυνὶ δὲ ἀπόθεσθε καὶ ὑμεῖς τὰ πάντα, ὀργήν, θυμόν. κακίαν, βλασφημίαν, αἰσχρολογίαν ἐκ τοῦ στόματος ὑμῶν· ⁹μὴ ψεύδεσθε εἰς ἀλλήλους, ἀπεκδυσάμενοι τὸν παλαιὸν ἄνθρωπον σὺν ταῖς πράξεσιν αὐτοῦ ¹⁰καὶ ἐνδυσάμενοι τὸν νέον τὸν ἀνακαινούμενον εἰς ἐπίγνωσιν κατ᾽ εἰκόνα τοῦ κτίσαντος αὐτόν, ¹¹ὅπου οὐκ ἔνι Ἕλλην καὶ

Ἰουδαῖος, περιτομὴ καὶ ἀκροβυστία, βάρβαρος, Σκύθης, δοῦλος, ἐλεύθερος, ἀλλὰ [τὰ] πάντα καὶ ἐν πᾶσιν Χριστός.

My Translation

[5]Therefore put to death the earthly members: sexual immorality, impurity, lust, evil desires and greed, which is idolatry. [6]Through these comes the wrath of God [upon the children of disobedience]. [7]You yourselves used to walk in these ways, when you lived in them. [8]But now you must rid yourselves of all these things: anger, rage, malice, blasphemy, and filthy language out of your mouth. [9]Do not lie to each other, since you have put off the old man with its practices [10]and have put on the new man, renewed in knowledge in the image of its Creator. [11]Here there is no Greek or Jew, circumcised or uncircumcised, barbarian, Scythian, slave or free, but Christ is all and in all.

NIV, 1984

[5]Put to death, therefore, whatever belongs to your earthly nature: sexual immorality, impurity, lust, evil desires and greed, which is idolatry. [6]Because of these, the wrath of God is coming. [7]You used to walk in these ways, in the life you once lived. [8]But now you must rid yourselves of all such things as these: anger, rage, malice, slander, and filthy language from your lips. [9]Do not lie to each other, since you have taken off your old self with its practices [10]and have put on the new self, which is being renewed in knowledge in the image of its Creator. [11]Here there is no Greek or Jew, circumcised or uncircumcised, barbarian, Scythian, slave or free, but Christ is all, and is in all.

Melick points out that in this section of the letter from 3:5 to 4:6 Paul gives a series of commands to the church community. He writes:

> The command section contains at least fifteen commands. Four of these, based on the grammatical constructions of the passages, urged the Colossians to stop practices which were ongoing (3:5; 3:8; 3:9; 3:21), and eleven encouraged the cultivation of Christian attitudes in the individual or community.[214]

> **Practical Exercise:** Before you read any further in the commentary, read Colossians 3:5 to 4:6 and see if you can find at least fifteen commands that Paul directs to the disciples in Colossae.

Melick divides these commands into four sections. He writes:

> First, some encourage personal spiritual growth. These are: "put to death" (3:5), "put off" (KJV) or "you must rid yourselves" (3:8),

"do not lie" (3:9), and "put on" (KJV) or "clothe yourselves" (3:12), "bear with each other and forgive whatever grievances you may have against one another" (3:13), "forgive" (3:13), and "put on love" (3:14). Paul used two pictures to organize these commands: death to life, and changing clothes.

The second group of commands is directed to the church (3:15–17). Twice Paul referred to characteristics that should always be present. In v. 15 Paul said, *"Let the peace of Christ rule in your hearts"*; and in v. 16 he said, *"Let the word of Christ dwell in you richly."* This smaller section describes the order God desires in the church.

The third group of commands concerns the family (3:18–4:1). These commands inform and encourage church members to submit to God's order in their homes. Ephesians 5:22–6:1 is similar to Col 3:18–4:1 and helps explain the Colossians passage.

Finally, a fourth group of commands relates to the ministry of the gospel (4:2–6). Although this group begins with Paul's desire that the church pray for him, it clearly stresses the collective witness in the world. Paul would have his opportunities for service; so would they. Although the format is the same, the subject changes from their *being* what was proper in God's economy to their *doing* what was proper in Christian witness. For that reason, 4:2–6 has a distinct place of its own.[215]

Paul begins with an imperative, *"Put to death."* If we have "died in Christ," then why do we need to continue to "put to death" these evil deeds in our lives? Because evil deeds are like zombies. Once dead, they keep coming back to life. We have to keep putting them to death over and over again.

Specifically, Paul urges us to put to death whatever belongs to our earthly nature. Literally, this is "Put to death the earthly members." Paul is not saying the body is inherently evil. The body is neutral, but it is drawn to sensual practices and must be tamed and controlled by the spiritual mind. These practices of the earthly members include: sexual immorality, impurity, lust, evil desires, and greed, which is idolatry. We don't live/walk in these things any longer. Why? Because we died and were raised in Christ. We now live in Christ.

We also must get rid of anger, rage, malice, slander, filthy language and lies. They aren't a part of our new self. We now recognize that we have the stamp of the Creator in our lives. This frees us to be a new person. It frees us to live in a new community, a community without racial or class distinction. In Christ there is no Greek or Jew, circumcised or uncircumcised, barbarian, Scythian, slave or free. We are all one in Christ. That being the case, we are more alike than we are different. You see, because we have found Christ, this single event changes everything.

V. 5. Since we now have a new focus in life, we need to put practices that characterized our past life. These are things that earthly nature. Anders writes:

> In telling believers to put to death certain behaviors, Paul is calling for complete extermination, not careful regulation. What must go? Paul gives us an 'outside in' perspective He starts with external actions and then moves to the internal drives which cause the conduct. In his "vice lists" Paul mentions three categories of behavior: (1) perverted passions, (2) hot tempers, (3) sharp tongues.[216]

Four of the first five are sexual temptations. Again, Paul is not saying the body is evil, but it is drawn toward sexual sin. With God's help, we must tame these passions. Paul then moves to greed, which he considers idolatry. Then comes a list of three sins that fall under self-control of our temper. Finally, Paul list three sins of the tongue.

What are we to put to death? This first list of five vices includes four in the sexual category plus greed. Of the two in the sexual category, the first two, sexual immorality and impurity, are very closely related; and the second two, lust and evil desires, are very closely related. All five were considered to be sins of the Gentiles.

(A) Sexual immorality.

In the Greek, πορνεία, *porneia*, refers to any illicit sexual activity. It is also translated as "sexual immorality" and, less accurately as "fornication." This is a general term for all sexual sin. It includes any type of sexual activity outside of the marriage relationship.

The Bible does not teach that sex is wrong. It does teach that a person should remain celibate before marriage. The Bible teaches that sexual activity should be confined within the marriage relationship. In that context, sex is to be enjoyed, and God created it for our enjoyment within that context. Ernest D. Martin writes:

> A distinction between sexuality and sex is helpful. Sexuality refers to all that makes us either male or female. Every person is always a sexual being. Sexuality is an integral part of personhood in all dimensions, emotional and psychic as well as biological. To deny sexuality is to deny humanness. Sex refers to sexual expressions, mental and physical, having to do with genital activity. Humans can do without sex, but they cannot cease to be sexual. Morality enters the picture because sexuality comes with certain specifications as to what are healthy and what are sick sexual expressions. The Creator has set boundaries that require control over sexual feelings and drives. Genital sex, in God's design, is right and good, but only

within the covenant marriage of one man and one woman.[217]

Martin makes an important distinction here. We are all sexual beings. God created us to be sexual beings. As sexual beings, we are to monitor and control our sexual expression. Paul goes on to list certain categories where we need to monitor our sexual expression.

(B) Impurity (ἀκαθαρσία, *akatharsia*)

Arndt, Danker, and Bauer's *Greek-English Lexicon* (ADBGL) defines this as (a) "any substance that is filthy or dirty," and (b) "a state of moral corruption."[218] The first definition would include unwholesome or impure thoughts, whereas the second would comprise illicit sexual activity.

(C) Lust (πάθος *pathos*)

Closely associated with the following phrase, *epithymian kakan*, lust is a desire that when left unchecked grows into a more passionate, evil desire.

(D) Evil desires (ἐπιθυμίαν κακήν, *epithymian kakan*); also translated as "passions."

"Desires" is a neutral word. We have good desires and bad desires. However, Paul here is describing a desire that has turned evil, especially sexual desires that have gone bad. This same word is used in James 1:14–15 where temptation is described as an evil desire that entices a person to sin. James writes, "...*but each one is tempted when, by his own evil desire, he is dragged away and enticed. Then, after desire has conceived, it gives birth to sin; and sin, when it is full-grown, gives birth to death.*" Hendriksen writes:

> Evil desire is the inordinate craving for sexual satisfaction, or for other things, such as idol-worship, material possessions, renown, etc. The *emphasis*, in the present context, is, however, on illicit sex relationships, but not to the exclusion of other wicked yearnings.[219]

(E) Greed, which is idolatry.

The Greek word for greed is πλεονεξία, *pleonexia*. It is also translated as "covetousness." ADBGL defines it as "the state of desiring to have more than one's due, *greediness, insatiableness, avarice, covetousness*."[220] How is greed idolatry? In that it causes us to place someone or something before God.

Greed has become an accepted part of the Western way of life, but the Bible has much to say about it. Consider these verses:

Ephesians 5:5

[5]For of this you can be sure: No immoral, impure or greedy person—such a man is an idolater—has any inheritance in the kingdom of Christ and of God.

Mark 7:21–23

[21]"For from within, out of men's hearts, come evil thoughts, sexual immorality, theft, murder, adultery, [22]greed, malice, deceit, lewdness, envy, slander, arrogance and folly. [23]All these evils come from inside and make a man 'unclean.'"

Luke 12:15

[15]Then he said to them, "Watch out! Be on your guard against all kinds of greed; a man's life does not consist in the abundance of his possessions."

1 Corinthians 5:11

[11]But now I am writing you that you must not associate with anyone who calls himself a brother but is sexually immoral or greedy, an idolater or a slanderer, a drunkard or a swindler. With such a man do not even eat.

1 Corinthians 6:9–11

[9]Do you not know that the wicked will not inherit the kingdom of God? Do not be deceived: Neither the sexually immoral nor idolaters nor adulterers nor male prostitutes nor homosexual offenders [10]nor thieves nor the greedy nor drunkards nor slanderers nor swindlers will inherit the kingdom of God. [11]And that is what some of you were. But you were washed, you were sanctified, you were justified in the name of the Lord Jesus Christ and by the Spirit of our God.

Ephesians 5:3

[3]But among you there must not be even a hint of sexual immorality, or of any kind of impurity, or of greed, because these are improper for God's holy people.

Why Stay Away from Earthly Practices?

V. 6. The first reason is that the wrath of God will come upon those who practice such things. The Bible does not shy away from the idea of God's wrath. God isn't swayed by human emotion like the Greek gods, but the God of the Bible does take covenant loyalty seriously. When a person breaks covenant loyalty with God, he or she will face God's wrath. This is one reason why we should make a solid conviction to live pure and righteous lives.

The phrase, *"upon the children of disobedience,"* is found in the earliest and best Greek manuscripts, yet it is left out of many modern translations (or is relegated to their footnotes). Some translations leave it out of the text because they feel it was placed in the text to match Ephesians 5:6. I place it in brackets in my translation to indicate that it is in many important Greek manuscripts, but there is a problem with the Greek text at this point and the translator needs to make a decision upon inclusion or exclusion of the phrase.

V. 7. A second reason to stay away from these earthly practices is that these acts are a part of your old life and should not be included in the new life in Christ. These sins were a part of the life you used to live. They should not appear in the life you now live.

Paul, however, is a realist. He knows how weak we can be. He knows the pull of temptation and desire on our lives. He knows the flesh is weak. He doesn't teach "Christian perfectionism."[221] He calls the disciples in Colossae to live a holy life. He continues to tell the Colossians what must change in their lives. He reminds the disciples of God's wrath and their past lives in order to motivate them to keep sin out of their lives. He gives a second list of practices that must die in the next verse.

V. 8. Here Paul gives a second list of "vices" that the disciple must abandon. These are more along the social realm. Although the list applies to everyone, Paul has in mind the Christian community and how we need to treat each other. *"You must rid yourselves"* is another imperative. The sins that follow have to do with speech, but also the heart behind what we say and sin that leads to hurtful words. The first three vices are attitudes behind abusive speech: anger, rage, and malice. Moo writes, "Paul's purpose is not to single out three specific sins but to use the three words together to connote the attitude of anger and ill will toward others that so often leads to hasty and nasty speech."[222] The last two have to do with the act of abusive or evil speech: blasphemy and filthy language. The list of five vices is as follows:

(1) Anger
From the Greek ὀργήν, *orgēn*, this word and the next are synonyms. Both are attitudes of the heart that give rise to hurtful and harmful speech.

(2) Rage
This word is from the Greek Θυμόν, *thumon*, meaning, "a state of intense displeasure, *anger, wrath, rage, indignation*."[223]

(3) Malice
The Greek word κακίαν, *kakian*, is a general word for wickedness or baseness. Considering the context here: It is often given the tenor of malice or

hatred, thus it is where blasphemy, slander, and filthy language have their root.

(4) Blasphemy

This is also translated as "slander." The Greek βλασφημίαν, *blasphamian* is usually translated "blasphemy," which is slander toward God, but in the context this word could also be used in reference to people, thus the translation, "slander."

(5) Filthy language from your mouth

Also translated as "abusive language from your mouth," the Greek is αἰσχρολογίαν, *aischrologian*, and it means, "speech of a kind that is generally considered in poor taste, *obscene speech, dirty talk.*"[224]

Paul uses the image of taking off clothing here. These are clothes we should have taken off when we were baptized. They are clothes that we must not wear any longer. We need to strip off anger, rage, malice, blasphemy, and filthy language.

Paul is making a radical statement here. Don't let the image of a change of clothing fool you; Paul is speaking of no less than changing our basic character. Dunnam and Ogilvie write, "Paul is calling for radical surgery. He is saying that we are to put to death every part of our being which is against God, and which prevents us from doing God's will."[225] This type of change is only possible because of Jesus.

V. 9. Paul singles out the sin of lying on its own. The present tense indicates that Paul is saying, "Stop your lying." This direct command demonstrates that the people of Colossae struggled in this area. But don't all people everywhere struggle with lying? We want to look good; therefore, we shade the truth. But God's community should be built on truth. In order to trust, relationships have to be built on honesty. So Paul singles out this area for a directive: "Stop lying."

V. 10. We strip off the old clothes, but we put on the new clothes. Moo writes:

> The verb behind *have taken off* (*apekdyomai*) is the same verb that Paul used in 2:15 to describe God's "stripping" of the power of the powers and authorities, and, significantly, is cognate to the noun that Paul uses in 2:11 to refer to the "stripping off" (*apekdysei*) of the "sinful nature" that takes place in "Christian circumcision."[226]

We strip off old habits, but we replace them with some new habits. Science teaches that nature abhors a vacuum. This is true in our spiritual lives as well. When we put off the old practice/habit, we replace it with a new practice/habit.

If not, the old habit has the tendency to come back.

But Paul isn't just talking about habits; he is also talking about character. Martin writes:

> The terms *old self* and *new self* call for further exploration. What is put off and what is put on? The exchange goes deeper than quitting a few bad habits and trying harder to be nice. It involves a change of character, not only a change in status before God. This implies an inner regeneration that is then to result in changed outward behaviors.[227]

Yet it is going too far to say that we strip off our old nature and put on a new nature, as if we are born in sin and tainted by our human flesh. Paul does not say the flesh is evil. The Gnostics and neo-Platonists taught that the flesh was evil; Paul didn't. Paul says our *choices* are good or evil. Melick writes:

> The definition of the old self and the new self is crucial to a proper understanding of Christian experience. Sometimes interpreters understand them as synonymous with an old nature and a new nature. Actually, there is little in Scripture about the "natures" of a Christian person, though there are many descriptions about the Christian's new actions, desires, and values.[228]

As disciples, we can't blame sin in our lives on the old self. When we sin, we choose to go against God.

Life is all about the choices we make.

We put off the old man and are renewed in knowledge in the image of our Creator. To put off the old man, we must renew our lives in the knowledge of God. Knowledge is important to Paul. It was also important to the Gnostics and other false teachers that Paul opposed. For the Christian to grow, he or she must grow in knowledge. Not a special *gnosis* (knowledge) of the Gnostics (or of today's new-age groups), but knowledge of God as revealed in Scripture and knowledge of God's image as revealed in Christ. Growing in knowledge is a process. It takes desire, effort, and time to grow in knowledge. But the results are worth the effort. Knowledge leads to maturity. It allows us to become more like Christ, to be remade in the image of God. Desire the knowledge of God.

We must also understand that we are made in the image of God, and when we become disciples, we are remade in the image of God. Martin writes:

> By designating the actualized renewal process as a re-creation, recalling the original work of the creator, the writer emphasizes how radical the transformation needs to be. It also becomes clear that this renewing after the image of God is God's work in

the believers, with their cooperation, and not a matter of self-reformation or self-actualization.[229]

V. 11. Jesus not only gives us new individual lives in him, he also placed us in a new community. The renewal comes not just to the individual, but to the whole of the community. In Christ's community, there are no divisions according to nation, race, or culture. Paul spells this out very specifically, stating, "Here there is no," and states it in:

Nationalist terms
1. Greek: the Gentiles.
2. Jew: the covenant community.

This was a way of distinguishing between the ethnic or national differences between the Gentiles and the Jews.

Religious terms
3. Circumcised: repetition of Jews but with a religious connotation added, most likely repeated because of the Judaizers who were demanding the Gentile Christians receive Jewish circumcision.
4. Uncircumcised: a way to say the Gentiles were not a part of God's covenant community.

The first four terms are two ways of differentiating between Jews and Gentiles. The unity of the early church was always fragile, and the line of division was often caused because of the differences between the Jews and the Gentiles.

Cultural terms
5. Barbarian: any foreign person; based on the word "babble" because their language could not be understood.
6. Scythian: considered an uncivilized group of people.
   Scythian was a cultural term that was used to speak of uncivilized people. The Scythians rose to power near the Caucasus about 630 BC. Herodotus records the invasion of the Fertile Crescent by the Scythian people. They pressed as far as Egypt putting pressure on Pscammetichus I, king of Egypt, who paid them tribute to hold off their advance. On their return they plundered the temple of Venus in Ashkelon. Records reveal that they joined forces with the Medes and Persians in the conquest of Nineveh. Later, the Medes, a hearty group of people who lived in the territory that is present day Iran, defeated them. Their dominance in Asia lasted for a short 28 years. Theodore H. Robinson identifies them by writing:

> Miscellaneous and heterogeneous bands of people, collected by the hope of plunder and following no single leader, poured one after another over western Asia during this period. From time to time, it is true, these bands would unite into larger bodies which could meet and even defeat the armies of the more settled peoples in the open field, but there seems to be no instance on record of their having prosecuted a successful siege of any duration.[230]

We can relate the Scythians to the Vikings of Europe. The Scythian horror was so impressionable that centuries later Paul used the word "Scythian" as a synonym for barbarian in Colossians 3:11. These bands of Scythians are known to have swept into Syria-Palestine in the second half of the seventh century, but they seem to have kept free of Judah.

Class or economic terms

7. Slave: Paul refers to class distinction here. Slave had no rights as citizens.
8. Free: Citizens of the Roman Empire who enjoyed all the right of legal citizens.

In saying there are no slaves or free, Paul declares that everyone is equal in Christ. In Christ, there are no class and economic distinctions.

Instead of thinking in terms of race, religion, culture, economic, or class distinctions, disciples are to see each other as Christians and Christians only. Why? Because *"Christ is all and in all."*

The church should represent a cross-segment of society. Unfortunately, this has not always been the case. In fact, churches have often been known for creating and upholding barriers between people.

The late Dr. Martin Luther King, Jr. made this point in several of his speeches. He said, "The Sunday church hour is the most segregated hour of the week." This was true for many churches in the 50s and 60s in the United States. I know it was true of the church in which I grew up in Tennessee in the 60s. It was a racially segregated church. Whites and blacks did not worship together. How great it would be to say that all that has now changed. There has been some change, but not enough. Many churches across the US are still racially segregated today.

True New Testament Christianity ought to be different. Race and class should have no distinction at church. But prejudice dies hard. How do we fight against racial and class division in the church) Paul writes, *"Christ is all and in all."* If we recognize that Christ is "in all" (in every person) and if Christ truly "is all" in our lives, then we see everyone as our brother and sister in Christ. Christ is the key. Paul again echoes a very high Christology in this verse, and his high Christology is the answer to divisions within the church.

Practical Exercise: Do you see any divisions within your local ministry today? If so, what can be done to eradicate divisions in your ministry? How can we free our hearts of all prejudice?

2. 3:12–17 Put On.

¹²Ἐνδύσασθε οὖν, ὡς ἐκλεκτοὶ τοῦ θεοῦ ἅγιοι καὶ ἠγαπημένοι, σπλάγχνα οἰκτιρμοῦ χρηστότητα ταπεινοφροσύνην πραΰτητα μακροθυμίαν, ¹³ἀνεχόμενοι ἀλλήλων καὶ χαριζόμενοι ἑαυτοῖς ἐάν τις πρός τινα ἔχῃ μομφήν· καθὼς καὶ ὁ κύριος ἐχαρίσατο ὑμῖν, οὕτως καὶ ὑμεῖς· ¹⁴ἐπὶ πᾶσιν δὲ τούτοις τὴν ἀγάπην, ὅ ἐστιν σύνδεσμος τῆς τελειότητος. ¹⁵καὶ ἡ εἰρήνη τοῦ Χριστοῦ βραβευέτω ἐν ταῖς καρδίαις ὑμῶν, εἰς ἣν καὶ ἐκλήθητε ἐν ἑνὶ σώματι· καὶ εὐχάριστοι γίνεσθε. ¹⁶ὁ λόγος τοῦ Χριστοῦ ἐνοικείτω ἐν ὑμῖν πλουσίως, ἐν πάσῃ σοφίᾳ διδάσκοντες καὶ νουθετοῦντες ἑαυτούς, ψαλμοῖς ὕμνοις ᾠδαῖς πνευματικαῖς ἐν [τῇ] χάριτι ᾄδοντες ἐν ταῖς καρδίαις ὑμῶν τῷ θεῷ· ¹⁷καὶ πᾶν ὅ τι ἐὰν ποιῆτε ἐν λόγῳ ἢ ἐν ἔργῳ, πάντα ἐν ὀνόματι κυρίου Ἰησοῦ, εὐχαριστοῦντες τῷ θεῷ πατρὶ δι' αὐτοῦ.

My Translation

¹²Therefore, as the elect of God, holy and beloved, put on bowels of compassion, kindness, humility, gentleness, and patience, ¹³bearing with one other and forgiving each other, if anyone has a grievance against another. Even as the Lord forgave you, just also should you forgive. ¹⁴But over all these things put on love, which is the bond of perfection.

¹⁵Let the peace of Christ rule in your hearts, in which you were called in one body. And be thankful. ¹⁶Let the word of Christ dwell in you richly in all wisdom, as you teach and admonish one another singing psalms, hymns, and spiritual songs with gratitude in your hearts to God. ¹⁷And whatever you do, whether in word or deed, do it all in the name of the Lord Jesus, giving thanks to God the Father through him.

NIV, 1984

¹²Therefore, as God's chosen people, holy and dearly loved, clothe yourselves with compassion, kindness, humility, gentleness and patience. ¹³Bear with each other and forgive whatever grievances you may have against one another. Forgive as the Lord forgave you. ¹⁴And over all these virtues put on love, which binds them all together in perfect unity.

¹⁵Let the peace of Christ rule in your hearts, since as members of one body you were called to peace. And be thankful. ¹⁶Let the word of Christ dwell in you richly as you teach and admonish one another with all wisdom, and as you sing psalms, hymns and spiritual songs with gratitude in your hearts to God. ¹⁷And whatever you do, whether in word or deed, do it all in the name of the Lord Jesus, giving thanks to God the Father through him.

(A) 12–14. Relationships within the Christian Community

Paul begins by addressing the disciples as the elect or called of God, holy and beloved. This is their new community. Moo describes this community, writing:

> The Christian community formed by and in Christ, transcends the boundaries of religious background, ethnicity, and social status—and any other "boundary" drawn from this world that we might like to draw. Whatever our worldly background or status, we all now have our fundamental identity determined by Christ and the people of Christ to whom we belong.[231]

Paul lets the disciples know who they are before he tells them what to do. What we do should flow out of who we are before God.

What are the new clothes we are to wear now that we live/walk in Christ? They are virtues which characterize the community of Christ. They are how we are to treat each other and live with each other. William Barclay writes:

> It is most significant to note that every one of the virtues and graces listed has to do with personal relationships between man and man. There is no mention of virtues like efficiency, cleverness, even diligence and industry—not that these things are not important. But the great basic Christian virtues are the virtues which govern and set the tone of human relationships. Christianity is community.[232]

Melick sees movement in Paul's thought in these verses from the individual to the community. He writes:

> Every social group has its problems, and the church is no exception. Paul, therefore, called the Colossians individually first and then collectively to be characterized by Christian graces which enhance their relationships. He began with individual qualities (3:12), moved to interpersonal qualities (3:13), and concluded with one indispensable quality (3:14).[233]

Individual Qualities

(1) Compassion, bowels of

In the Greek the words are σπλάγχνα, *splagchna* (bowels, inner organs) οἰκτιρμός, *oiktirmos* (compassion). σπλάγχνα, *splagchna* identifies the inner organs of the body and is often equated with the seat of the emotions. It can also be translated as "tenderness of heart" or "merciful of heart." "Compassion" is a good translation. Behind the English word "compassion" is the idea of suffering with someone. Compassion moves us to act for someone else's good. Jesus exemplified this in his ministry.

(2) Kindness

This word is χρηστότης, *chrēstotēs* in the Greek. It can also be translated as "good," "useful," or "gracious." It is the same word used to describe the yoke of Jesus in the Gospels.

(3) Humility

In the Greek this word is ταπεινοφροσύνη, *tapeinophrosuna*, and can also be translated, "modesty." Martin writes, "Humility connotes modesty, and it is the opposite of arrogance and conceit. Among the parallel concepts in Philippians 2:3–4 is the capacity to look to the interests of others rather than the wishes of the ingrown self."[234]

(4) Gentleness

The word in the Greek is πραΰτης, *prautēs*. It can also be translated as "meekness." Meekness is characterized as strength under control. We learn meekness by following Jesus, who had all the strength of the universe but exhibited control in his every response and action.

(5) Patience

This is μακροθυμία, *makrothumia* in the Greek, and according to the ADBGL means "the state of remaining tranquil while awaiting an outcome, *patience, steadfastness, endurance*…the state of being able to bear up under provocation, *forbearance, patience* toward others."[235] It also can be translated as "longsuffering" and "tolerance." Martin writes, "Said another way, patience is the capacity to put up with aggravating behaviors in others without resorting to retaliation."[236]

Interpersonal Qualities

(6) Forbearance: *"Bear with each other."*

In the Greek, ἀνέχω, *anecho* means forbearance. ADBGL defines it as, "to regard with tolerance, *endure, bear with, put up with*."[237] Dunnam and Ogilvie write:

> Paul urged us to be *forebearing* with one another. To forebear has the negative meaning, "to refrain or abstain," or "to control oneself." But it also has the positive meaning of *bearing* one, or carrying. Thus one translator substitutes "affirming" for fore-bearing in this text. We are forebearing when we affirm, when we value and respect another.[238]

In the church, we are going to have our differences. We all have different personalities and pasts, different likes and dislikes, and different cultures and backgrounds. At times, we might offend each other. Being in a church doesn't mean that we will never have bumps with others within the church, but when we do bump, we are willing to work things out. We are willing to bear with each other's differences. The introvert learns to forebear what he or she considers the lack of tact of the extrovert. The type-A, driven individual learns to accept the deliberative nature of a more passive person. We learn to accept one another in spite of our differences. That is the community of Christ.

We must learn to bear with each other even when offended. Richard Melick writes:

> Enduring speaks to the practice of other Christian characteristics. Some believers in the church were being offended by the actions of others. The terms called the believers to a high standard of personal action when offended. "Enduring" is putting up with others even when they fail or act differently from what is expected.[239]

(7) Forgiveness

In the Greek this is χαρίζομαι, *charidzomai,* which according to ADBGL, means "to cancel a sum of money that is owed, *cancel…*to show oneself gracious by forgiving wrongdoing, *forgive, pardon.*"[240] Dunnam and Ogilvie write, "*Charizomai,* the Greek word used in this verse, is from the root word *charis,* which means grace; thus to 'forgive' is to 'give graciously.' This forgiveness is gift, not accomplishment."[241]

Forgiveness must be a hallmark of the Christian community. We must bear with each other's differences, and if there comes a time where a brother or sister offends us, we must be willing to forgive. The onus is on the offended person.

This is a tough teaching. I know because I have experienced it in my own life. A brother offended me. He hurt me deeply, and I had a very difficult time forgiving him. It was only after another brother approached me and said that my lack of forgiveness was hindering my prayers that I understood how much my lack of forgiveness was hurting God, the church, my family, and me. Once I realized that, I reached out to the brother I needed to forgive and started the process of forgiveness.

Is there anyone whom you haven't forgiven? The onus is on you to get the ball rolling. You might need help. I did. If so, talk to a brother or sister you trust about the situation. Forgiveness should characterize the Christian community. God has forgiven us; therefore, we should forgive others.

One Indispensable Quality

(8) Love: *"But over all these virtues put on love, which is the bond of perfection."*

Love is ἀγάπη, *agape*. We often think of agape love as the unconditional love of God for his people. It is that, but this same type of love must characterize the community of Christ: We must have agape love for one another. When outsiders enter our community, they should note that something is different in the way we treat each other. This is the virtue that ties everything else together; it is the virtue that gives us unity.

Paul once again uses the clothing image when he speaks of love. Love is like an overcoat that we put on top of all our other clothing. Thus I translate, *"But over all these things put on love."* Moo writes:

> The clothing imagery that is picked up from v. 12 suggests rather that love is being pictured as a garment that is to be put on "on top of" the other items of dress that Paul has enumerated in v. 12. In this case, the implication would be that love is not just another virtue to be added but the supreme virtue.[242]

Love is not only our topcoat, it is also the glue that holds us together as a community. The text literally reads, "love, which is the bond of perfection." "Perfection" could also be translated "maturity." I usually choose maturity over perfection. But in this instance, the context seems to call for the word "perfection." Paul is speaking of the community, the church, and not the individual disciple. Love is the glue that will bind the community of Christ together so that it will shine like a beacon in a world filled with darkness.

Vv. 15–17. After Paul lists the "new clothes" that are to adorn Christians in Christ, he turns to the Christian community and describes a few characteristics that must be a part of that community. There are five of these: (1) peace, (2) thanksgiving, (3) the word of Christ, (4) performing every action in the name of the Lord Jesus, and (5) gratitude.

V. 15. (1) Peace

Paul writes, *"Let the peace of Christ rule in your hearts, in which you were called in one body."*

Peace (εἰρήνη, *eirana*) is not just the cessation of conflict; it also conveys the idea of wholeness. It is the OT concept of *Shalom*, an integrated life where God gives one security, confidence, satisfaction, and fulfillment. Moo writes, "The peace established through Christ is *shalōm*, the eschatological state of cosmic restoration that the Old Testament prophets anticipated."[243] Picture a little baby who has just been fed and is now ready for a nap. The baby has a silly grin on its face because he or she is satisfied. God wants his peace to rule in our hearts.

The word for "rule" (βραβεύω, *brabeuo*) is used of an arbitrator who makes a ruling in a legal matter or of an umpire who controls an athletic event.

The ADBGL defines this word as to "be in control of someone's activity by making a *decision, be judge, decide, control, rule*."[244] The peace of Christ is to be the arbitrator of our hearts so that God's wholeness flows through our lives.

This is to be a hallmark of the community of Christ. Instead of conflict and division, the community of Christ should reflect wholeness. After all, we are members of one body. In the natural body, do members wage war against each other? Or course not. The body works as a whole for the good of the person. In the church, each member works together with the other members in peace for the good of the body of Christ. After all, we were called to peace. And we were called to peace in one body. The call is both individual and corporate. Moo writes:

> The gospel is inescapably individual in its focus: each of us, on our own, is "called" by God and responds in faith on our own. Yet, at the same time, the gospel is inescapably corporate: we are called along with other people, with whom we make up "one body.[245]

As we as individuals allow peace to rule in our hearts, we bring that same peace into a community which allows peace to reign in our one another relationships. This become a beacon to the world of the wonders of God's community.

(2) Thanksgiving: *"And be thankful."*

Peace flows into thanksgiving. The word here is εὐχάριστος, *eucharistos*. In this word you might see the ecclesiastical word for the Lord's Supper, eucharist. The word means, "thankful" or "grateful." Paul will repeat this sentiment three times in verses 15–17. Gratitude was an important concept in his teaching. Paul was grateful for his salvation and for what he had discovered in Christ. He wanted the community of Christ to be known for its gratitude.

V. 16. (3) The word of Christ

Paul now directs the Christian community, *"Let the word of Christ dwell in you richly."* The community of Christ is to be known as a group that feasts on the word of Christ. Hendriksen writes, "The objective, special revelation that proceeds from (and concerns) Christ—"the Christ-word"—should govern every thought, word, and deed."[246] What is the word of Christ? Melick writes:

> The Colossians were to look back to the words of Christ, not within or ahead to the words Christ would speak. This phrase is best understood as the word *about Christ*. The community was constantly to recognize the reason for its existence by a continual concern for the gospel message and its implications in the congregation.[247]

Please notice Paul is speaking of the church here. Although the word of

Christ must dwell richly in the hearts of each member, Paul directs his attention to the community and the assembly of the church. He says to the community, "You are to let the word of Christ dwell in you richly." I like to remind my local ministry from time to time that we are to be "a people of the Book." The word of Christ should be front and center in our assemblies. It should be a main component in our conversations in fellowship. When a visitor walks into our fellowship, he or she should notice right away that we are committed to preaching, teaching, and living the word of Christ.

How is the word of Christ to dwell richly in the assembly of the church? Paul gives us some help here by writing, *"...in all wisdom, as you teach and admonish one another singing psalms, hymns and spiritual songs with gratitude in your hearts to God."* It happens in three areas: (a) in all wisdom, (b) teaching and admonishing, and (c) singing.

(a) In all wisdom

Our teaching and admonishing must be within the realm of the wisdom of God. Melick writes, "Paul encouraged them to express their corporate worship in real wisdom, which centers in and promotes Christ. Thus as they grew in their understanding of spiritual truth, they were to encourage others in the context of real wisdom."[248]

(b) Teaching and admonishing

We've mentioned this before (1:28), but it should be repeated. Teaching has to do with instruction and giving information. It can be theological and theoretical, but not exclusively so. Admonishing is more about encouragement and correction. It has to do with practical matters of how to live the life. In the assembly of the church, both are important.

(c) Singing

One mechanism for teaching and admonishing the church in wisdom is song. Isn't that interesting? Singing isn't just about praising God; it is about teaching and admonishing the church. We sing: (i) psalms, (ii) hymns, and (iii) spiritual songs. Singing isn't just vertical worship. Singing should also be horizontal as we encourage one another in song. The fact is, our singing should be 360° worship.

Paul mentions singing psalms, hymns, and spiritual songs.

(i) Psalms (ψαλμός, *psalmos*) are the psalms of the Hebrew Bible. Moo writes, "'Psalm' refers generally in Greek to a song that is sung to the 'plucking' (Gk. *psallō*) of the strings of an instrument (esp. a harp). In the New Testament, following the LXX, the word is usually applied to the Old Testament Psalms."[249] One way we can allow the word of Christ to dwell in the Christian community is by literally singing the word of God in our services. The OT

Psalms were Jesus' hymnal. As we sing the psalms we sing the words with which Jesus worshipped in the temple.

(ii) Hymns are usually thought of as hymns of praise. The word ὕμνος, *'hymnos* may be translated as "a song with religious content, *hymn/song of praise* especially in honor of a deity."[250] A major goal of our worship should be to praise and honor God. Hymns help us direct our attention to the object of worship—our God whom we adore.

(iii) Spiritual songs (ᾠδαῖς πνευματικαῖς, *'odais pneumatikais*) include whatever doesn't fit into the category of psalms and hymns. But note: They are spiritual songs and not secular songs.

Singing is to occur with gratitude in our hearts. Here is the second time Paul mentions gratitude in verses 15–17. Gratitude is linked to grace. Singing should fill us with grace. James says it this way, *"Is anyone happy? Let him [or her] sing."*[251]

Singing is about the heart. The heart in the Old Testament was the seat of the emotions. It was also synonymous with the whole person. When we sing, we sing with emotion and we put our whole self into the act of worship. Melick writes, "Paul encouraged them to express their corporate worship in real wisdom, which centers in and promotes Christ. Thus as they grew in their understanding of spiritual truth, they were to encourage others in the context of real wisdom."[252]

V. 17. (4) Performing every action in the name of the Lord Jesus

Paul writes, *"And whatever you do, whether in word or deed, do it all in the name of the Lord Jesus, giving thanks to God the Father through him."*

Time for a short review. Paul is listing five ways the Christian community should be adorned in Christ. So far he has listed three ways: through 1) peace, 2) thanksgiving, and 3) the word of Christ. Now come the fourth and fifth ways: through 4) performing every action in the name of the Lord Jesus and 5) gratitude.

Everything we do should be done in the name of the Lord. Two points here: First, Paul assumes we will be doing something. The community of Christ should be an active community. We ought to be doing some good in the world around us. We don't have to all do the same thing, but we have to do something. Jesus was active in his ministry. He went "teaching,…preaching,…and healing." That would be a good place for your local ministry to start.

Second, every action should be done *"in the name of the Lord."* The phrase, "the name of the Lord," is synonymous with "the authority of the Lord." If we are performing an action in Jesus' name, we are performing it with his authority. This should give us confidence as a community. Christians aren't to be weak and insecure. We are to walk around with confidence that comes from Christ.

(5) Gratitude: *"…giving thanks to God the Father through him."*

This is now the third time in three verses (vv. 15–17) that Paul mentions thanksgiving and/or gratitude. It is a theme that runs throughout this letter. Verse 15: *"And be grateful."* Verse 16: *"With gratitude in your hearts."* Verse 17 *"Giving thanks to God the Father through him.'* He rings this bell three times. Listen to it ring.

> Ring: Grateful.
> Ring: Gratitude.
> Ring: Giving Thanks.

How often do you sound the bell of gratitude in your life during the day? Gratitude should naturally flow from the life of a disciple. Paul makes this abundantly clear in his writings. To Paul, there was no such thing as a sour, dour, bitter, ungrateful Christian. The life of a disciple can be distinguished by gratitude. The community of Christ is a grateful community. When people enter our community they should be overwhelmed by our gratitude. We should ring the bell of thanksgiving.

> Ring: Grateful.
> Ring: Gratitude.
> Ring: Giving Thanks.

Practical Exercise: Ring the bell of thanksgiving. List all the ways that you as a disciple of Jesus are grateful. List all the reasons the community of Christ (your local ministry) has to be grateful. Ring that bell of thanksgiving today and every day.

C. Relational Matters; Household Conduct. 3:18–4:1

Christ is supreme. We have died with Christ and our former selves are now gone. We now live/walk in Christ and in the power of his resurrection.

These are all powerful and moving statements, but how do they stand in the real world where we live? Paul now moves into that arena. His model for addressing these matters comes right from the Greco-Roman world. Aristotle considered the home the basic unit of state. He spoke of the management of the home as οἰκονομία, *oikonomia*, "household management." Paul uses this well-known model to address the households within the church in Colossae. He speaks to husbands, wives, parents, children, slaves, and masters. Can Christianity be lived out in the real world? Paul says, "Yes," and then he gives some practical ideas of how to make this happen.

Notice that Paul begins with what would be considered the subordinate roles in first-century culture: wives, children, and slaves. For Paul to single them out at all, much less to mention them first, was radical. Christianity turned social convention upside-down.

Notice that Paul is a single man speaking about marriage and parenting. He is able to speak authoritatively on this topic because he is revealing God's will for marriage.

Other ancient writers give an overview of households and household duties, but Paul's list is different in three ways. Hendriksen lists these ways in which Paul's list differs from other lists:

> (1) Christianity, as proclaimed by Paul, etc., supplied the *power* to carry out the commands, that power being the grace of God.... All other moral philosophies, the very best of them, are trains lacking engines!

> (2) Christianity also presented a new *purpose*. That purpose was *not* simply "to try to live in agreement with Nature," but "to do everything to the glory of God."...

> (3) Christianity, as originating in Christ, supplied the only true *pattern* for God-glorifying conduct on the part of the very groups here discussed, namely, wives and their husbands, children and their fathers, servants and their masters. Christ himself, as the bridegroom, in his matchless love for the church, his bride, furnished the standard for the love of *Christian marriage* (Eph. 5:25, 32).[253]

Paul lets Christian households know that they live/walk with 1) God's power, 2) a new purpose, 3) and a true pattern. This distinguishes the Christian household from the pagan one.

Colossians 3:18-4:1

[18]Αἱ γυναῖκες, ὑποτάσσεσθε τοῖς ἀνδράσιν ὡς ἀνῆκεν ἐν κυρίῳ. [19]Οἱ ἄνδρες, ἀγαπᾶτε τὰς γυναῖκας καὶ μὴ πικραίνεσθε πρὸς αὐτάς.

[20]Τὰ τέκνα, ὑπακούετε τοῖς γονεῦσιν κατὰ πάντα, τοῦτο γὰρ εὐάρεστόν ἐστιν ἐν κυρίῳ. [21]Οἱ πατέρες, μὴ ἐρεθίζετε τὰ τέκνα ὑμῶν, ἵνα μὴ ἀθυμῶσιν. [22]Οἱ δοῦλοι, ὑπακούετε κατὰ πάντα τοῖς κατὰ σάρκα κυρίοις, μὴ ἐν ὀφθαλμοδουλίᾳ ὡς ἀνθρωπάρεσκοι, ἀλλ᾿ ἐν ἁπλότητι καρδίας φοβούμενοι τὸν κύριον. [23]ὃ ἐὰν ποιῆτε, ἐκ ψυχῆς ἐργάζεσθε ὡς τῷ κυρίῳ καὶ οὐκ ἀνθρώποις, [24]εἰδότες ὅτι ἀπὸ κυρίου ἀπολήμψεσθε τὴν ἀνταπόδοσιν τῆς κληρονομίας. τῷ κυρίῳ Χριστῷ δουλεύετε· [25]ὁ γὰρ ἀδικῶν κομίσεται ὃ ἠδίκησεν, καὶ οὐκ ἔστιν προσωπολημψία.

[4:1]Οἱ κύριοι, τὸ δίκαιον καὶ τὴν ἰσότητα τοῖς δούλοις παρέχεσθε, εἰδότες ὅτι καὶ ὑμεῖς ἔχετε κύριον ἐν οὐρανῷ.

My Translation

[18]The wives, you must submit to your husbands, as is fitting in the Lord.
[19]The husbands, you must love your wives and do not embitter them.

[20]The children, you must obey your parents in all things, for this is well pleasing to the Lord. [21]The fathers (parents), do not exasperate your children, or they will lose heart. [22]The slaves, in all things you must obey your masters on the earth; and do it, not only when their eye is on you and to win their favor, but with sincerity of heart fearing the Lord. [23]Whatever you do, work at it with all your soul, as for the Lord, not for men, [24]knowing that you will receive a reward of an inheritance from the Lord. You serve the Lord Christ. [25]The one who does wrong will receive the consequence for his wrong, and there is no partiality.

[4:1]The Masters, provide your slaves with what is right and fair, knowing that you also have a Lord in heaven.

NIV, 1984

[18]Wives, submit to your husbands, as is fitting in the Lord. [19]Husbands, love your wives and do not be harsh with them. [20]Children, obey your parents in everything, for this pleases the Lord. [21]Fathers, do not embitter your children, or they will become discouraged. [22]Slaves, obey your earthly masters in everything; and do it, not only when their eye is on you and to win their favor, but with sincerity of heart and reverence for the Lord. [23]Whatever you do, work at it with all your heart, as working for the Lord, not for men, [24]since you know that you will receive an inheritance from the Lord as a reward. It is the Lord Christ you are serving. [25]Anyone who does wrong will be repaid for his wrong, and there is no favoritism.

[4:1]Masters, provide your slaves with what is just and fair, because you know that you also have a Master in heaven.

1. Marriage. 3:18–19

(A) 3:18 Wives: *"The wives, you must submit to your husbands, as is fitting in the Lord."*

Paul begins by speaking of marriage. As he speaks of marriage, he begins with the wives. Earnest Martin writes, "Wives, who had few if any rights in the male-dominated social order of that time, are addressed as free, responsible persons. It is not up to the husbands to keep their wives in line!"[254] Dunnam and Ogilvie state:

> Paul has often been criticized as being down on women. The truth is, he presented a radically new view of marriage and family which elevated women and children to a hitherto unthinkable level of equality. The Hebrew and Greek understanding of marriage reduced women to "things" to be used and enjoyed, not loved and cherished. Women were seen as totally subservient to men, not

only in society but in the home. It was a man's world in every way.[255]

The wives are called upon to act a certain way toward their husbands. They are to submit to their husbands. This is the imperative voice (a command). Different translations look for various ways to get across the idea expressed in this verb ὑποτάσσεσθε, *hupotassesthe*. The verb can mean to submit to, to subordinate, to place under, to surrender one's will. The NIV has, "submit to." The NEB,[256] NRSV,[257] and NASB have, "be subject to." Others have, "submit yourselves to" or "be subordinate to." All are trying to communicate the idea of submission. Melick writes, "The term does not suggest slavery or servitude, and certainly never calls for the husband to make his wife submit. If he could, her heart would not be in it. Besides, Paul addressed wives here, not husbands."[258]

Having worked in the ministry for four decades and counseled dozens of married people (as well as having been happily married for over thirty years), I would say that in marriage there are two primary areas of concern for the wives. I am speaking from my own personal observations. The first area of concern is respect. Does the wife respect her husband? The second area of concern is submission. Not subservience, but submission. Is the wife willing to follow the leadership of her husband?

Submission does not mean the wife has to be a doormat. She can express her views and concerns in a respectful way. But the husband has to have the freedom to lead. After receiving input from his wife, the husband has to be able to make decisions for the good of the marriage and the good of the family. From my years of working with married couples, I have seen what happens when a wife isn't willing to follow her husband's lead. The husband either retires in hurt, or he rebels in anger. Either way, it's not a pretty picture.

Also, it should be said that just because Paul commands the wives to submit to their husbands doesn't mean that husbands do not need to submit to their wives. According to Ephesians 5:21 we are to submit to one another out of reverence to Christ.

Notice the reason *why* wives are to submit to their husbands. It's not because they are second-class citizens. It's not because wives are inferior to their husbands. It's because this "is fitting in the Lord." "Fitting" means "proper" or "appropriate." Melick writes:

> The motivation for voluntary submission is that it is a proper Christian attitude. The phrase "as is fitting in the Lord" identifies these concerns. The word "fitting" has the idea of proper as a duty. By employing the statement, Paul made it clear that such submission is an outworking of the lordship of Christ. It is part of the Christian order.... Submission is a matter of Christian commitment. It comes with salvation. Voluntarily taking a position of submission

is a matter of a wife's relationship to the Lord, not to her husband. It is "fitting in the Lord."[259]

The prime example of submission for wives and husbands is Jesus himself. Jesus became a slave for all of us (Philippians 2:1–8).

> **Practical Exercise:** Wives, think about the areas where it is difficult for you to submit to your husband. Now pray to Jesus for your heart to change in these areas.

(B) 3:19 Husbands: *"Husbands, you must love your wives and do not be harsh with them."*

Husbands are given two directives here, one positive and one negative.
The positive: Husbands, love your wives.
The negative: Husbands, don't be harsh with them.
Both are commands.
This command, *"Husbands, love your wives,"* was a uniquely Christian command. Moo writes:

Requiring wives to submit to husbands, as we have noted, matches widespread Greek and Jewish teaching about marriage. Requiring husbands to love their wives does not. The concern in the secular codes was usually effective household management—especially since the household was typically viewed as a key building block of society and of the state. Accordingly, the focus of the codes was on the *paterfamilias*—the "head of the household"—and what he should do to maintain order and decorum in his household. Referring to a husband's love for his wife would not fit this purpose—and, indeed, no other code we have discovered from the ancient world requires husbands to love their wives. Moreover, the word for "love" here is *agapaō*, the distinctly (though certainly not uniquely) Christian word for the kind of sacrificial, self-giving love whose model is Christ himself.[260]

In my forty years of marriage counseling and thirty years of marriage, I have learned that the number one area that comes up in marriage counseling from the wives is that they want and need to feel love from their husbands. Paul uses the word *agape* here. Melick writes, "The term *agapē*, used here, never occurred in secular household tables. The command, therefore, appears to be a distinctively Christian element of the marriage relationship."[261] It is a selfless love that looks out for the needs of the person. It is an unconditional love, the same type of love that Christ has for the church.

Paul also says, *"Husbands,...do not embitter [your wives.]"* Another way of saying this is, "Never treat them harshly." The word is πικραίνω, *pikraino,* meaning "to embitter" or "to make bitter." It is an imperative: Never embitter your wife.

There is never a time and never a reason for harshness. A harsh word or a harsh tone can drive love right out of a marriage. Have you ever said something hurtful to your wife? Something like: "You are just like your mother." "I wish I had never married you." "I wish I could find a biblical reason to divorce you." There is no room in the marriage for hurtful jabs.

But just as harmful as words can be your tone and your attitude. The raised voice, the disgusted look, the belittling tone, or the angry stare can hurt as much as words.

Dunn makes an interesting point about πικραίνω, *pikraino,* "embitter." He notes that the verb is in the middle voice and points back to the subject, the husband. Most translations do not translate it this way.[262] They translate the verb as applying to how the husband is treating his wife (*"Husbands,…do not embitter [your wife]"*). If we take the verb to reflect back on the subject, then we could translate it as, "Husband don't embitter yourself against your wife." What would this mean? Dunn suggests:

> But the passive voice here presumably implies that the bitterness is experienced by the husbands. What is in view, therefore, is probably the feeling of the dominant partner who can legally enforce his will on his wife but who will not thereby win her love and respect and can thus feel cheated and embittered at not receiving what he regards as his due.… This is the likely outcome for anyone who stands on his rights alone and who knows and exercises little of the love called for in the first half of the verse.[263]

That's deep. If the husband doesn't love the wife as he should, then the wife will not respect the husband. Thus the husband will become bitter because his wife doesn't respect him. But it is his own fault. His lack of love breeds a lack of respect from his wife, which flies back in his own face. When you fail to love your wife as you should, you hurt yourself. As I said before, so say I now again: That's deep.

> **Practical Exercise:** Husbands, go ask your wife if she feels loved. If your wife doesn't answer in the way you hoped, don't react. Work on loving her unconditionally for a week. Then ask her the same question, "Do you feel loved?" If you still don't get the answer you hoped, don't react. Practice and repeat.

2. Family: 3:20–21

(A) 3:20 Children: *"The children, you must obey your parents in all things, for this is well pleasing to the Lord."*

Children in the Roman culture were looked upon as property. The father, not the mother, owned the child. The mother had primary influence over the child until seven years of age. After that, the father took over instruction of the child. Thus, the next verse (21) is directed to the fathers.

Paul moves from marriage to speak to families. He begins with children. Children must obey their parents in everything. Some commentators note that "children" includes children of all ages. We must continue to show our parents proper respect after we are grown. Just because you are grown doesn't mean you aren't someone's child. However, Melick writes, "The term 'children' primarily describes children in relation to their parents, so the assumption is that they were at home and under the parents' supervision."[264] Paul seems to be talking to children with Christian parents. Since he says obey "in all things/in everything," it seems to imply that the parents are disciples. He is writing to children in the community of faith.

If we see the context here as saying that children are to obey their parents regardless of whether they are Christians or not, then how does the child respond when the parent asks him or her to go against the will of God? Then we take this verse and put it in the larger context of the entire Bible. Jesus is our Lord; we must obey him first. Remember, we must interpret Scripture by using Scripture.

Paul again answers the question "Why?" in this passage. It's always a good question to ask. The "Why?" behind our actions is our motivation. So "Why?" must children obey their parents? Paul writes, *'Because this is well pleasing to the Lord."* The word for well pleasing is εὐάρεστος, *euarestos*, and can also mean "acceptable." We obey are parents to please our Father in heaven. We obey our parents because it is what our heavenly Parent expects of us. This should be our motivation for everything that we do—we should want to please the Lord.

> **Practical Exercise:** Children, take a moment and ask your parents how they feel you are doing in the area of obedience. Also, think about how you are doing at making your parents happy. Is there any place where you can make improvements in your relationship with your parents? However, be aware that you can't change anyone but yourself. Always work on you, regardless of the reaction you might receive from any other person.

(B) 3:21 Fathers/Parents: *"The fathers (parents), do not exasperate your children, or they will lose heart."*

Paul addresses this next line to the fathers, but since he was writing to a patriarchal society in which the father had legal rights over children (and the mother didn't) it is possible to widen the application of this address in our day to include both parents. How patriarchal was first-century society? The father had the legal right to sell the children even if the mother went against the sale.

The word used for fathers (πατέρες, *pateres*) was sometimes used to refer to fathers and mothers or parents. Moo writes, "The Greek word for fathers (*pateres*) can sometimes refer to both parents, as in Hebrews 11:23: 'By faith Moses' parents (*pateres*) hid him for three months after he was born, because they saw he was no ordinary child, and they were not afraid of the king's edict.'"[265]

Having said that, I do believe that it is more common for fathers than for mothers to exasperate and provoke their children. Mothers tend to be nurturers. Fathers tend to be protectors. Part of that protector role is to toughen up the children. I'm speaking in generalities here (so please don't get upset with me), but these are tendencies that I've noticed in my thirty years of ministry.

To provoke/exasperate/embitter/irritate/rouse to anger/drive to resentment (ἐρεθίζω, *erethizō*) is to criticize or nag the child until he or she becomes angry. The child loses spirit and becomes discouraged. This is what Paul means when he says, *"or they will lose heart"* (ἀθυμῶσιν, *athumōsin*). θυμός, *thumos*, is "courage," "spirit," or "strong spirit." Fathers/parents who exasperate their children steal their spirit and make them timid, sullen, and discouraged. The opposite of this is to encourage our children. Positive words of encouragement and affirmation build up the hearts of our children.

I want to recommend an excellent book on parenting by John and Karen Louis entitled, *Good Enough Parenting*.[266] The second chapter of this book is called "Frustration of Core Emotional Needs." In this chapter, John and Karen write about Colossians 3:21 and describe what happens when a parent "frustrates" or "embitters" a child, and the harm that comes from such action.

John and Karen list and define the "core emotional needs" that every person has. When a parent fails to meet these core emotional needs, the child becomes exasperated. When these core emotional needs aren't met over a long period of time, a child may develop schemas or lifetraps. John and Karen write, "Parents that cause repeated frustrative and traumatic experiences by not meeting the core emotional needs will actually facilitate the development of maladaptive schemas/lifetraps and unhealthy coping styles."[267] The book differentiates between the occasional mistakes that all parents make verses repeated frustrations that cause schemas.

It is extremely important that parents meet the core emotional needs of their children. It is also vital that parents do not repeatedly frustrate their children. Again, this is especially true of fathers who tend to be less nurturing than mothers. John and Karen write:

> Please do not buy into the philosophy that depriving children of the core emotional needs will make them become tough and more resilient adults. In fact, the outcome of this kind of twisted logic is

that often the children turn out to be just the opposite; they are insecure, fearful, not trusting, and with a low sense of self. Such children will grow up not knowing how to handle disappointments and frustration because of their insecurity and fear. They may be tense and constantly on guard. The stakes are high because causing frustrative and traumatic experiences (i.e., exasperation), even accidentally, brings much harm to children.[268]

Everything that John and Karen write about in their book is supported by scientific research. It is interesting to note (and John and Karen point this out in their work) that long before science demonstrated how prolonged frustrative experiences cause emotional schemas, Paul through the Holy Spirit warned fathers, *"Do not exasperate your children."* I marvel at the wisdom of the Scriptures. Truly the Word is a *"lamp to my feet and a light for my path."*

> **Practical Exercise:** Parents, think for a minute. Are there any ways that you exasperate your children? Are there any things that you say or do that cause them to get angry to the point that they distance themselves from you? If you aren't sure, then ask other parents who know you and your children what they see. Ask the youth worker in your ministry what he or she sees.

3. Slavery. 3:22–4:1

(A) 3:22 Slaves: *"The slaves, in all things you must obey your masters on the earth; and do it, not only when their eye is on you and to win their favor, but with sincerity of heart fearing the Lord."*

Slavery was an accepted institution in the Bible. That is not to say that it was a divinely appointed institution or a biblically endorsed institution like government, marriage, and the church. God has an ideal will and a permissible will. Marriage for life is God's ideal will. Divorce fits within God's permissible will. Slavery was part of God's permissible will. It was not ideal. Paul, by writing about slavery, does not endorse it. He recognized slavery as a part of the social fabric of his day. Since it was, he had a few words to say to slaves and to masters.

Why did Paul not call for slaves to rebel against their masters? Paul, and all the early Christians, operated within the governments where they lived. Biblical Christianity was very apolitical by nature. It was not the point of the church to change government and society through rebellion. It was the point of the church to change the world one heart at a time.

It is estimated that one third of the Roman world was made up of slaves. Some say that slavery in the Roman world was different than in modern times, that it was more humane and less cruel. That's debatable. I find the notion extremely suspect. It seems to me that slavery is always slavery. Slavery dictates that people are bought and sold like cattle. They are used and abused. They are considered property. Melick writes:

> Most slaves (*douloi*, sometimes translated "servants") found themselves in situations of hopelessness. Slaves were, generally speaking, victims of war. The slavery was political and economic, not racial. Similarly, virtually every class of person lived with the realization that war could cause them to lose everything and be sold into slavery.[269]

Based on what Melick states, it doesn't sound like slavery in the first century was much different from slavery in the eighteenth century. If you wish to say biblical writers didn't oppose slavery because it was more humane than slavery in early US history, you are on shaky ground.

Paul understood that the institution of slavery was not God's ideal law, but he also understood that an attempt to overthrow the institution would have brought the wrath of the Roman Empire upon the church. For Paul, the purpose of the church was not to overthrow government institutions. The purpose of the church was to overthrow Satan by spreading the news of the glorious kingdom of Jesus. Melick writes:

> It seems that Paul should have written to undermine the institution of slavery or at least to encourage the revolt of the slaves. On the one hand, to do so, would have caused significant difficulty in the first-century setting, and undue persecution would result. Besides, Christians could do little by force. On the other hand, the teaching of the apostle here and elsewhere clearly sowed the seed for the emancipation of slaves and the end of the institution. Paul did what he could in the best way possible.[270]

Paul and the early church made a choice. They chose not to oppose slavery on the political/governmental level. Dunn writes:

> In the choice between revolution and transformation from within, Christianity chose the second; though we always need to bear in mind the political powerlessness of such small groups within the pervasiveness of Hellenistic culture and under the imperial might of Rome.... Instead Christianity recognized that it had perforce to live within an inevitably flawed and imperfect society and sought to live and witness within that society by combining that society's proven wisdom with commitment to its own Lord and the transforming power of the love which he had embodied."[271]

In Colossians, Paul is talking to slaves within the church. According to church historians, many slaves became a part of the early church. Earnest Martin writes, "Much more is said to slaves than to masters. This may reflect the relative numbers in the church or, more likely, the intensity of the questions being raised as slaves become fellow believers in Christ."[272] These slaves were grateful for the freedom and equality that they experienced in the church. But they had to be careful that they didn't take the freedom found within the church as a license to leave their masters or to disregard their wishes.

Paul begins with the same command he gave children in regard to their parents, *"obey...in everything."* He must mean to obey in everything whether they liked it or not. Paul would not have commanded the slaves to obey in areas of sin. He is speaking more to the attitude of the slave than to the type of command given by the master.

Paul distinguishes that he is commanding them to obey their earthly masters. If Paul had just said, "Obey your master," then there could have been confusion because Jesus is our Lord and Master. The word, *kurios*, means both "lord" and "master." But Paul is clear here. He is speaking of obedience in relation to their "earthly" masters (κατὰ σάρκα, *kata sarka, according to the flesh*).

The Christian slave must obey with the right heart. Motivation is important here. They must obey because they fear the Lord. They must not only obey when they are being watched or in order to curry favor from the master, but they must obey with sincerity of heart whether the master notices them or not.

Ὀφθαλμοδουλία (*'ophthalmoodoulia*) is a compound word (eye and servant) meaning "eye-servant." The slave is not to obey as an eye-servant, only when the master is watching. Paul uses another compound word, ἀνθρωπάρεσκος (*'anthropareskos*), human-pleaser, to help Christian slaves understand that their primary focus is to please God.

Slaves must obey their masters with sincerity (ἁπλότης, *'aplotas,* "simplicity" or "singleness") of heart. "Simplicty of heart" can also be translated as "singleness of heart." This emphasized focus and consistency. The slave is to focus on pleasing God and on making him happy. The slave obeys because he or she has a healthy respect/fear of God. Because the slave respects God, he will serve his earthly master in a consistent, godly manner. This is a good directive for every disciple of Jesus (after all, we are all slaves of Jesus).

(B) 3:23–25 Slaves specifically and everyone in general: *"Whatever you do, work at it with all your soul, as for the Lord, not for men, knowing that you will receive a reward of an inheritance from the Lord. You serve the Lord Christ. The one who does wrong will receive the consequence for his wrong, and there is no partiality."*

V. 23. The next section continues with directives to the Christian slave but can also be applied to a broader audience because we all serve the Lord.

Practical Exercise: Before you read more commentary, ask yourself: "What do I see in this passage that might apply to a broader audience than just Christian slaves?

Paul repeats what he has just said in the sentence before, but with different words this time; therefore what he just said needed repeating. Dunn writes:

> The implication is that one of the chief dangers of the slave status was a lack of personal motivation which made all work a drudgery provided grudgingly, with lack of effort and always with a view to doing as little as one could get away with. Such an attitude can be sustained only at tremendous personal cost, with other aspects of the personality "switched off," withdrawn, or suppressed, or with a calculating motivation fed by resentment and bitterness.[273]

When we work, we should put our whole soul into what we are doing. I translate the phrase ἐκ ψυχῆς ἐργάζεσθε, *'ek psuchas 'ergadzesthe* as "work from the soul" or "soul work." "Soul" (ψυχή, *psucha*) is the vital life force of our personality or personhood. "Soul" is our whole person or who we are as a person. We put our souls into our work because we are doing it for the Lord and not for men. Paul addresses motivation again. What is the reason we work? Do we work only to get a paycheck? Do we work because it is expected of us by society? Or, do we work for the Lord?

V. 24. If you work with your soul, you will receive a reward of an inheritance from the Lord. Slaves never expected any compensation. To hear this idea of a reward of an inheritance would be music to their ears. Earnest Martin writes, "According to Roman law, slaves could not inherit anything and had no reason to expect any compensation. Thus it must boggle the minds of Christian slaves to hear that they will receive an inheritance as a reward from the Lord."[274]

Paul again repeats the motivation, *"You serve the Lord Christ."* This is the third verse in a row where Paul repeats this idea. He wanted to imprint it on their minds. One of my best friends and the man who trained me to be an evangelist, Mike Taliaferro, used to say to me, "Steve, a person doesn't really remember something until you repeat it three times." For Paul to repeat this three times demonstrates its importance. Dunn writes, "The triple repetition suggests that slaves would need to keep reminding themselves that their loyalty to Christ transcended their loyalty to their masters, thus making it easier to bear the harsher features of their enslavement."[275]

Another way of translating this is, "You are slaves to the Master Christ." Christian slaves needed to understand that they served two masters—the Master Christ and their earthly master. Soul work or service of the heart was done for the Master Christ. Hendriksen writes, "The anointed Lord is the slave's employer. What a privilege and honor."[276]

Lord (*kyrios*) emphasizes the Sovereignty of Jesus. Christ (*Christos*) emphasizes his saving work as the Messiah. Both would encourage the slave to accept his lot in this life realizing that Jesus oversees and rules the totality of his life (along with the whole of the universe) and if he or she would remain faithful to Jesus as Lord, then Jesus as the Christ would save him or her for all eternity. Again, this is realized eschatology. There is more to the here and now than the here and now.

V. 25. The person who does wrong will receive retribution from God who administers justice without partiality. The Jerusalem Bible translates this as "Anyone who does wrong will be repaid in kind." This verse can point backward to slaves or forward to what will be said next about the master. It applies to both slave and master. Our #1 deterrent against doing wrong should be our respect for God.

God is impartial. This could be a reminder to Christian slave owners that they should be impartial (Ephesians 6:9). It could also remind the slaves of the reality of their situation. They will not receive justice on this earth, but God will distribute justice impartially in the next life. Melick believes the phrase applies more to the slaves than the masters. He writes, "However, the connective 'for' (*gar*) makes this statement dependent on what preceded, and the flow of thought continues well without changing subject. On the whole, it seems that Paul comforted and motivated the slaves by appealing to God's justice."[277] I see this verse as a nice transitional verse summarizing what Paul has just written to the slaves and moving toward what he will say to the masters.

Exposition of Colossians
Chapter Four

(C) 4:1 Masters: *"The Masters, provide your slaves with what is right and fair, knowing that you also have a Lord in heaven."*

Paul turns his attention to masters. He doesn't have much to say to them, but what he does say is important. Moo writes, "Paul's admonition is remarkable, in comparison with secular parallels, for its concern with the kindness and 'other-regard' with which the duties of household management are to be carried out."[278]

Perhaps the brevity of the admonition to the masters can be explained by understanding the social background of the church. Many scholars believe that the church had far more slaves in its membership than masters. Perhaps the brevity comes from a particular situation in Colossae where slaves were facing more hardship than the masters and thus needed more words of encouragement.

Masters are commanded to provide what is just and fair for their slaves. τὸ δίκαιον (*to dikaion*) is literally, "the just." It also means "the rightness. " τὴν ἰσότητα (*tan 'isotata*) is literally, "the fair." It has to do with equity. Some say it means equality, but that presses the word too far and goes beyond what Paul is saying here. Paul impresses on the minds of the masters just and fair treatment of their slaves.

History is replete with stories of the harsh treatment of slaves by their masters. Paul lets Christian masters know that their treatment of slaves must be different: It must be characterized by fairness, justice, and rightness.

In saying such, Paul is calling for the ethical treatment of slaves and opens the door for the consideration of slaves being equal with their masters. Paul doesn't call for the abolition of slavery because to do so might hinder the advancement of the gospel. Paul's main concern was the spread of the gospel across the Roman world and not the change of political policies of the Roman government. Again, early Christianity was apolitical. It could exist in any political environment. The goal of the early church was to change the world one heart at a time.

Paul again speaks to motivation. Why treat slaves fairly? Because you know that you also have a Master in heaven. Don't you expect Jesus to treat you with fairness and justice?

Note: Some commentators want to extend the application of this section on slaves and masters to the employee/employer relationship. It is difficult to do this because the relationships are very different. But there are some applications that seem to carry over to our work relationships. For example:

- We should work hard whether the boss is looking or not.
- We should work with sincerity of heart fearing the Lord.
- Employers should provide their worker what is just and fair.

Ernest Martin comments on this point, writing:

Can we simply replace the words 'slaves' and 'masters' in the Domestic Codes with the words 'employee' and 'employer'? In some respects this seems like a natural way to contemporize these texts. If both employees and employers function as if Christ is their Employer, they would effectively apply the gospel to the workplace relationships. Working honestly and wholeheartedly and treating workers as persons in ways that are right and fair—this is consistent with naming Jesus as Lord.[279]

Richard Melick proposes that Paul is speaking of a theology of hard work in this passage. He writes, "A theology of work emerges. Genuine service in honest vocation brings honor to God. God watches the stewardship of energy, time, and life. This passage teaches that work is honorable even if the profits do not accrue to the worker."[280]

I think the key idea here *is found back in verse 23, "Whatever you do, work at it with all your soul."* This idea of "soul work" should help us keep our work in the proper perspective. We aren't just working for an employer, but we are working to serve God. We don't just give our all when our boss is watching. To a disciple of Jesus, we give the same effort whether no one is watching or the whole company is watching. Why? We do our best because we know that God is always watching. If we view our work as "soul work," then it keeps work from staying in the realm of the secular and ordinary, it translates work into a spiritual discipline.

D. Further Instructions. 4:2–6.

Two of my favorite sections in Paul's letters are at the end of Colossians and the end of Romans when he begins naming people in his ministry and in the church. I love this because it shows the depth of relationships Paul had in the church. Paul was a minister who touched people's lives. You see this near the end of the book of Acts when he is making his way toward Rome because he is a prisoner for the cause. When brothers and sisters around Rome catch word that Paul is on the road toward the Imperial City, they come out to greet him. They want to see him and be around him.

Paul had family wherever he travelled. You get the sense that he loved people and loved being around people. He cared for them; he visited with them in their homes; he knew people by name. Paul was a people person.

This church, in Colossae, is a church that Paul had never visited, yet he knew people there. He was connected across churches through people in other churches. For Paul, the church was a network of communities. Just as he loved people, he loved the church.

It is easy to skip over this section of Colossians thinking that all this personal information was important to the church in Colossae but not important to us today, but that would be a mistake. In this closing section we see the heart of Paul and his love for people. The instructions that he gives here are as applicable in our relationships today as they were to Paul's first-century audience. Please take time to read these verses, learn from them, reflect on what is written, and apply what you learn to your life.

1. 4:2–4. Instructions on Prayer

²Τῇ προσευχῇ προσκαρτερεῖτε, γρηγοροῦντες ἐν αὐτῇ ἐν εὐχαριστίᾳ, ³προσευχόμενοι ἅμα καὶ περὶ ἡμῶν, ἵνα ὁ θεὸς ἀνοίξῃ ἡμῖν θύραν τοῦ λόγου λαλῆσαι τὸ μυστήριον τοῦ Χριστοῦ, δι' ὃ καὶ δέδεμαι, ⁴ἵνα φανερώσω αὐτὸ ὡς δεῖ με λαλῆσαι.

My Translation

²Be continually devoted to prayer; be alert and thankful in it. ³At the same time pray for us, also, that God may open a door for the word so that we may speak the mystery of Christ, on account of which I am in prison. ⁴Pray that I may reveal it clearly, as I should.

NIV, 1984

²Devote yourselves to prayer, being watchful and thankful. ³And pray for us, too, that God may open a door for our message, so that we may proclaim the mystery of Christ, for which I am in chains. ⁴Pray that I may proclaim it clearly, as I should.

V. 2. Paul begins to close his epistle. He ends like he began—with prayer. He encourages the disciples to pray with (A) devotion, (B) alertness, and (C) thankfulness.

(A) To *"be devoted to prayer"* means to be actively and fully engaged in prayer. Προσκαρτερέω (*proskartereo*) means to "be persistent in," "be consistent in," "remain with, "attach oneself to," "be busily engaged in," "hold fast to," "continue in," "persevere in", or "be devoted to."[281] O'Brien writes:

> The verb προσκαρτερέω, which means to "adhere to," or "persist in," came to be used of a boat that always stands ready for someone (Mark 3:9), or an activity that one was devoted to or busily engaged in. It was in this latter sense that it came to be employed to denote continuance in prayer.[282]

Paul is saying, "Don't get sidetracked from prayer." Prayer is an essential. It is not a peripheral matter.

When you are devoted to something, you invest time and energy to it. Most of us know what it means to be devoted to a relationship with someone. You put thought and energy into making the other person happy and staying connected with the person. This same type of energy should be devoted to our relationship with God. Devotion to prayer demonstrates devotion to God.

Prayer is not something we pull out only in times of emergency. It's not like Commissioner Gordon in the Batman comics. When Gotham City is in trouble, Commissioner Gordon uses the Bat Signal to ask Batman to save the day. Prayer should not be used like a God signal: "God, I need you. Come running and save the day."

Prayer needs to be a daily conversation with God. Think of what a privilege we have that the Creator of the universe wants to hear our prayers. If we think of it in that way, we should be devoted to it.

We should begin our day in prayer, end it in prayer, and pray throughout the day. C. S. Lewis writes:

> No one in his senses, if he has any power of ordering his own day, would reserve his chief prayers for bedtime—obviously the worst possible hour for any action which needs concentration.... My own plan, when hard pressed, is to seize any time, and place, however unsuitable, in preference to the last waking moment.... The body ought to pray as well as the head.[283]

Lewis makes a great point. We shouldn't push prayer off to the moment of the day when we are the most tired. We should prioritize prayer in our lives. One writer talks about making prayer a scheduled event in the day. When we make prayer a scheduled event, we are more likely to be devoted to it.

(B) We should also be "alert" in our prayers. Another word for alert is "watchful." The word is γρηγορέω, *gragopeo* (the Gregorian chant comes from this word). It literally means, "Stay awake." It is an attitude of alertness and is associated with mental toughness. It comes from the imagery of guard duty in the military. When the guard is on duty, he or she must stay alert. In this context, Paul is asking the disciples to be prayer warriors concerning his ministry. Dunn writes, "At the very least the sense of an impending threat requiring constant alertness is retained, and prayer functions as the vital channel of communication with the commander in chief."[284]

When you think of staying alert in prayer, it is difficult not to reflect on Jesus in the Garden of Gethsemane with his disciples. The disciples could not stay awake with Jesus. Would you have been alert in prayer in the Garden? If you want to know the answer, ask yourself how alert you were in prayer in your spiritual life today.

In Kung Fu, we had a circle drill where one person had to stand in the middle of a circle and Sifu Romain (our instructor) would signal for someone to attack. The person in the middle never knew who was going to attack next, so you had to keep your head on a swivel. You had to look right and left to see who was going to come at you next. You had to be alert. If not, you would get hit. We are in a spiritual circle drill every day. Satan is firing temptation at us from all directions. Prayer helps us keep our head on a swivel so that we can overcome temptation.

(C) Prayer should be filled with thanksgiving—once again Paul speaks of being thankful. He fills this epistle with appeals for thanksgiving. This time, he mentions it in connection with prayer. How much time in prayer do you spend expressing thanks to God? If we are thankful to God in prayer, it will make us a more thankful person when we aren't praying. Paul keeps ringing this bell—be thankful, be grateful, be appreciative.

Vv. 3–4. Paul isn't hesitant about asking for prayers. He does this at the beginning and end of the book. Paul believes in the power of intercessory prayer, so he asks for prayer. O'Brien writes:

> Clearly Paul attached great importance to the mutual intercession of himself and his converts. Not only does he constantly pray for them all, but also he begs them to assume wider responsibilities in supporting him in petitionary prayer.... When they interceded for him it was not the completing of some formality, but an actual cooperating with him, an assisting of him in prayer.[285]

Paul sees intercessory prayer as a way of cooperating with him in his ministry.

But notice Paul's request. He doesn't ask to be set free of his chains. He asks that he can boldly profess his faith while in chains. He asks for a door of opportunity to come his way so that he can share his message with others. He is truly content in every situation. He is focused on the mission. His focus is outward and not inward.

He wants to reveal (make manifest/to reveal what is hidden) the message (literally, "the word," τοῦ λόγου, *tou logou*). "To reveal" φανερόω, *phaneroo* can also be translated as to "cause to become visible, expose publicly, reveal a message with clarity, disclose, show, or make known."[286] Paul wanted to make sure that he clearly communicated the message of God to people. He wanted to make sure that people understood what he was saying. What was his message? Jesus. Paul reveals the mystery that is Christ. Paul knew he was commissioned by God to reveal this wonderful mystery to the Gentiles. His commission drove him to keep revealing the mystery while he was in chains.

We learn from the book of Philippians that while Paul was in prison in Rome, he had an effective ministry there. His prayers were answered. Philippians 1:12–13 reads, *"Now I want you to know, brothers, that what has happened to me has really served to advance the gospel. As a result, it has become clear throughout the whole palace guard and to everyone else that I am in chains for Christ."* In Philippians 4:22, Paul writes, *"All the saints send you greetings, especially those who belong to Caesar's household."* Also, Acts 28:30–31 reads, *"For two whole years Paul stayed there in his own rented house and welcomed all who came to see him. Boldly and without hindrance he preached the kingdom of God and taught about the Lord Jesus Christ."* Paul knew his mission—reveal the mystery, which is Christ, to the Gentiles. He was committed to actualizing this mission. Prayer helped.

> **Practical Exercise:** Take a moment to pray for God to open doors of opportunity for you to reveal the mystery, which is Christ, to others. Now walk through those doors.

2. 4:5–6. Instructions on How Work With Outsiders

Paul moves on to talk about how the disciples in Colossae should be with "the ones on the outside." Paul uses this phrase to refer to those outside the church or those outside the circle of faith—non-Christians. Let's see what we can learn from Paul on this important topic.

⁵Ἐν σοφίᾳ περιπατεῖτε πρὸς τοὺς ἔξω τὸν καιρὸν ἐξαγοραζόμενοι. ⁶ὁ λόγος ὑμῶν πάντοτε ἐν χάριτι, ἅλατι ἠρτυμένος, εἰδέναι πῶς δεῖ ὑμᾶς ἑνὶ ἑκάστῳ ἀποκρίνεσθαι.

My Translation

[5]Walk/live in wisdom toward those outside, buying up the time. [6]Let your conversation/speech be always full of grace, seasoned with salt, knowing how you might answer everyone.

NIV, 1984

[5]Be wise in the way you act toward outsiders; make the most of every opportunity. [6]Let your conversation be always full of grace, seasoned with salt, so that you may know how you ought to answer everyone.

Notes

V. 5. Paul encourages the disciples to be wise in their dealings with outsiders (πρὸς τοὺς ἔξω, *pros tous echo*, literally, "to the ones outside"). O'Brien comments, "The expression 'outsiders' corresponds to the rabbinic *ha-ḥîṣônîm*, 'those who are outside,' that is, either heretics or 'the people of the land';…carries a semi-technical meaning and refers to non-Christians generally, especially pagans."[287] Paul delineates that the nature of evangelism implies we must leave the comfort of the fellowship within the church to speak to those outside the fellowship. When we go outside our fold, we are to be prudent and wise.

We are to "redeem the time;" literally, "to buy back" or "to purchase back" the time (τὸν καιρὸν ἐξαγοραζόμενοι, *ton kairon exagoradzomenoi*). O'Brien writes, "The verb ἐξαγοράζω, *exagoradzo* ('buy,' 'buy up,' 'redeem') is drawn from the commercial language of the market place (ἀγορά, *agora*), and its prefix, the preposition ἐκ, *ek*, denotes an intensive activity, a buying which exhausts the possibilities available."[288] Be aware that time is a precious commodity. We must be good stewards of time; it is a gift from God and must not be wasted. καιρός (*kaipos*) in the New Testament often signifies a special or significant time (compare the use of *kronos*, which is chronological time). Dunn believes the use of καιρός (*kaipos*), "helps focus the thought on the present time as an unique climactic period in which every minute is precious."[289]

Being wise toward outsiders and buying back the time are an interesting combination. Ernest Martin writes:

> What connection is there between wise conduct toward outsiders and *making the most of the time?* A tension exists between wisdom (acting at the right time and in the right way) and urgency (seizing the moment because time and opportunities are not unlimited). Caution and enthusiasm need each other. So much is at stake that Christ's witnesses dare not slide off the road on either side.[290]

I think this is an important point. Time and wisdom must be considered. As Martin said, "Caution and enthusiasm need each other." When we reach out to someone, we must be aware of our timing. Too much, too soon and it might overwhelm someone. How many times have freshly baptized disciples gone back to share everything they just learned about Jesus with a parent or a friend, but the young disciple forgets that it took them months to learn what they now know? To share with someone in a single sitting everything you've learned in a month is like trying to give someone a drink of water from a fire hose. The right timing and much wisdom are essential in reaching out to people.

V. 6. As we reach out to people, our conversation must be filled with grace.[291] There are a few ways to take this. (1) Our conversation must be gracious or charming. (2) Our conversation should be filled with thanksgiving. But Paul usually portrays grace with deeper meaning: (3) Our conversation must dispense grace to the unbeliever. It should be conversation that offers the grace of God to people. I believe that Paul had the third meaning in mind because it fits better with his consistent portrayal of God offering grace to humanity, which we see throughout his letters.

Our conversation should also be *"seasoned with salt."* In the first century, salt was used as a preservative, a fertilizer, and a seasoning. Here Paul references salt as seasoning. A pinch of salt makes everything taste a little better. I'm sure those of you from the southern part of the US would agree. We must add a pinch of salt to our conversations with those on the outside.

How can conversation be seasoned with salt? Some believe Paul is talking about adding wit to our conversations. But most likely, Paul is paralleling the statement he just made about wisdom; wisdom is the salt we need to add to our conversations.

We have to learn how to talk to people so that they are drawn into our conversations. Here are two ideas of how to add salt to your conversations: (1) Say the person's name. Studies have shown the number one word a person wants to hear is his or her name. (2) Here is an adage that I learned from Sifu Karl Romain, my Kung Fu instructor: "To be interesting, be interested." In other words, ask people about their lives and actively listen to their response. People love to talk about themselves. To draw a person into a conversation, switch the conversation to something they would like to talk about.

Finally, Paul says we ought to know how to answer everyone. The apostle Peter admonishes us to *"always be prepared to give an answer to everyone who asks you a reason for the hope that you have"* (1 Peter 3:15). We need to learn how to answer people. When we are asked about our faith, we need to know how to give people good answers. Part of this is practice. The more we converse with people about spiritual matters, the better we will become at answering their questions. The more Bible we know, the better equipped we will be to answer people's questions about God's word.

Practical Exercise: Go out today and be with outsiders. While you are with them, practice Paul's practical guidelines from Colossians: (1) Be wise, (2) make the most of every opportunity, (3) let your conversation be full of grace, (4) let your conversation be seasoned with salt, and (5) know how to answer everyone. Practice these guidelines as you are with people. The more you practice them, the better you will get.

E. Final Greetings and Messages; Farewell. 4:7–18

As Paul begins to close his epistle, he sends personal greetings to various people in Colossae and mentions people in his ministry. As mentioned above, we see here a glimpse into the relational nature of Paul's ministry. He depended on others to help him in his ministry; he was not a "one horse" show. As we mentioned in the first chapter, Paul had a team ministry. This becomes evident in the list of people he mentions at the end of his letter.

Paul believed in staying in close contact with his churches. He didn't start the ministry and then pull back. He wanted to know what was happening in the church, and he wanted the church to be aware of what was going on in his life. Thus, we have the epistles.

The relationships that Paul had built over the years helped him stay in contact with churches. Without a network of people to help him deliver news back and forth, it would have been almost impossible for him to have stayed connected with all the churches in his care. Paul cared greatly for the churches. As he is going through his list of hardships in 2 Corinthians, he mentions, *"Besides everything else, I face daily the pressure of my concern for all the churches"* (2 Corinthians 11:28).

As we get a glimpse of Paul's ministry here, it should cause each of us to reflect on our life and ask, "How am I doing at building relationships with other people?" Paul's letters are filled with "one another" passages. In this section, we see how he put those "one another" passages into practice in his ministry. Perhaps by seeing how Paul did this, it will prompt us to do it as well.

1. 4:7–9 Travel Plans; Tychicus and Onesimus

⁷Τὰ κατ᾽ ἐμὲ πάντα γνωρίσει ὑμῖν Τυχικὸς ὁ ἀγαπητὸς ἀδελφὸς καὶ πιστὸς διάκονος καὶ σύνδουλος ἐν κυρίῳ, ⁸ὃν ἔπεμψα πρὸς ὑμᾶς εἰς αὐτὸ τοῦτο, ἵνα γνῶτε τὰ περὶ ἡμῶν καὶ παρακαλέσῃ τὰς καρδίας ὑμῶν, ⁹σὺν Ὀνησίμῳ τῷ πιστῷ καὶ ἀγαπητῷ ἀδελφῷ, ὅς ἐστιν ἐξ ὑμῶν· πάντα ὑμῖν γνωρίσουσιν τὰ ὧδε.

My Translation

⁷Tychicus, the beloved brother and a faithful servant/minister and fellow slave in the Lord, will let you know everything about me. ⁸I have sent him to you

for this very reason that you may know everything about us and that he may encourage your hearts. ⁹With him is Onesimus, faithful and beloved brother, who is one of you. They will let you know everything that is happening here.

NIV, 1984

⁷Tychicus will tell you all the news about me. He is a dear brother, a faithful minister and fellow servant in the Lord. ⁸I am sending him to you for the express purpose that you may know about our circumstances and that he may encourage your hearts. ⁹He is coming with Onesimus, our faithful and dear brother, who is one of you. They will tell you everything that is happening here.

Notes

Vv. 7–8. Paul begins with Tychicus, a name not very common in the Greco-Roman world, but common in Paul's ministry. After Timothy and Titus, Paul mentions Silvanus (Silas) and Tychicus more than any other men in his circle of ministers. We can deduce that Tychicus was a very close associate of Paul.

Paul describes him as a beloved (dear) brother, faithful servant/minister, and a fellow slave/servant. He was the type of person that Paul could depend on to perform any task that was required. We need people like this in the church. These are loyal, trusted, faithful, dependable people who get things done.

Paul sent Tychicus to Colossae to give the disciples news of "our" circumstances and to encourage their hearts. The plural "our" underscores Paul's team ministry. He isn't a "Lone Ranger" evangelist, off working on his own. He isn't trying to make everyone dependent on him. Paul built a network of people that would go in and out of churches to meet whatever needs arose. Tychicus was one of his evangelists whom Paul could send into places to meet needs. This seems to have been the role of the evangelist in the first century church. The local leadership of a church was made up of elders. The evangelists served as (for lack of a better term) circuit preachers that Paul sent from place to place as the need dictated.

Tychicus probably carried the epistle to the church in Colossae. It is also highly probable that he delivered the letter to the church in Ephesus (Ephesians 6:21). Later on, Tychicus would relieve Titus in his ministry in Ephesus (Titus 3:12), and as Paul was nearing his death, Tychicus ministered to the church in Ephesus (2 Tim. 4:12).

Paul mentions that the express purpose for sending Tychicus to Colossae was so that the church could know about the circumstances of him and his team in Rome. James Dunn writes:

> Here again we see how strong were the personal bonds which linked the members of these various churches, particularly with the mission teams which had founded them and their fellow

churches elsewhere. It mattered to them how Paul and Timothy were faring.[292]

V. 9. Onesimus, a slave who had run away from Colossae, comes back to Colossae with Tychicus. This story is told in the book of Philemon. The two letters, Colossians and Philemon, were probably delivered at the same time. In the epistle to Philemon, Paul asks Philemon, a disciple in Colossae, to receive back Onesimus, not as a slave, but as a brother in Christ. In Philemon 10–16, Paul writes:

> *[10]I appeal to you for my son Onesimus, who became my son while I was in chains. [11]Formerly he was useless to you, but now he has become useful both to you and to me.*
>
> *[12]I am sending him—who is my very heart—back to you. [13]I would have liked to keep him with me so that he could take your place in helping me while I am in chains for the gospel. [14]But I did not want to do anything without your consent, so that any favor you do will be spontaneous and not forced. [15]Perhaps the reason he was separated from you for a little while was that you might have him back for good—[16]no longer as a slave, but better than a slave, as a dear brother. He is very dear to me but even dearer to you, both as a man and as a brother in the Lord.*

In Colossians, Paul does not mention Onesimus as a fellow servant/slave in the ministry. That seems to distinguish him from Tychicus. He wasn't a part of Paul's circle of evangelists, but from Paul's letter to Philemon, it seems that Paul wanted to add Onesimus to that circle. He said that Onesimus was "useful" to him. Before Paul could use Onesimus in the ministry, he needed Philemon's permission. He was not going to overstep the master/servant relationship. Paul did not consider himself above the law. He honored the civil laws and civil authorities as being ordained by God. Here we see an example of Paul's attitude toward civil law. As was mentioned before, Paul did not want to start a social revolution. Paul was out to change the world one person at a time.

2. 4:10–15. Greetings

(A) 4:10–11 Aristarchus, John Mark, and Jesus/Justus

[10]Ἀσπάζεται ὑμᾶς Ἀρίσταρχος ὁ συναιχμάλωτός μου καὶ Μᾶρκος ὁ ἀνεψιὸς Βαρναβᾶ (περὶ οὗ ἐλάβετε ἐντολάς, ἐὰν ἔλθῃ πρὸς ὑμᾶς, δέξασθε αὐτόν) [11]καὶ Ἰησοῦς ὁ λεγόμενος Ἰοῦστος, οἱ ὄντες ἐκ περιτομῆς, οὗτοι μόνοι συνεργοὶ εἰς τὴν βασιλείαν τοῦ θεοῦ, οἵτινες ἐγενήθησάν μοι παρηγορία.

My Translation

[10]Aristarchus, my fellow prisoner, sends you his greetings, and Mark, the cousin

of Barnabas, (you have received a command concerning him; if he comes to you, welcome him); [11]and Jesus, the one called Justus, also sends greetings. These are the only ones of the circumcision among my fellow workers for the kingdom of God, and they have become a comfort to me.

NIV, 1984

[10]My fellow prisoner Aristarchus sends you his greetings, as does Mark, the cousin of Barnabas. (You have received instructions about him; if he comes to you, welcome him.) [11]Jesus, who is called Justus, also sends greetings. These are the only Jews among my fellow workers for the kingdom of God, and they have proved a comfort to me.

Notes

V. 10. Aristarchus was from Thessalonica. He seems to have been a constant companion of Paul. He accompanied Paul on his trip to Jerusalem (Acts 20:4). When Paul was in need, Aristarchus was there to give Paul a helping hand. He was with Paul during the riot in Ephesus (Acts 19:29) and he accompanied Paul on his journey by ship to Rome. He was with Paul in the shipwreck on that journey (Acts 27:2). When Colossians was written, Aristarchus was with Paul in prison (συναιχμάλωτος, *sunaichmalotos*, "fellow prisoner or prisoner of war"). We need this type of constant companion in our lives. When the storms come, they are there for us. They weather the storms of life with us.

Mark (John Mark) and Paul had been estranged for some time after the first missionary journey. Paul and Barnabas took John Mark with them on their first journey, but before that journey ended, Mark left to go back home to Jerusalem (Acts 15:38). The text does not give details as to why John Mark returned home. Perhaps he was homesick. Perhaps he was responding to an emergency. Or, perhaps he did not agree with Paul's acceptance of the Gentiles. All we know is that John Mark returned home and Paul felt like John Mark abandoned the mission.

Barnabas, Paul's companion on the first journey, wanted to bring John Mark on the second tour. Barnabas and John Mark were cousins. Paul was against this decision. Barnabas and Paul were at a stalemate and Paul would not acquiesce. Therefore, Paul and Barnabas parted company over this. Acts 15:37–39 reads:

> [37]*Barnabas wanted to take John, also called Mark, with them,* [38]*but Paul did not think it wise to take him, because he had deserted them in Pamphylia and had not continued with them in the work.* [39]*They had such a sharp disagreement that they parted company. Barnabas took Mark and sailed for Cyprus.*

Barnabas is not mentioned again in the text until 1 Corinthians 9:6. John Mark isn't mentioned until the present verse in Colossians.

There is a much-debated issue here. Who was right in the decision concerning John Mark, Paul or Barnabas? Why did Paul not want John Mark on the second journey? Maybe Paul felt like Mark wasn't cut out for mission work. Or, perhaps Paul simply felt that Mark needed to mature a little more.

Some say Barnabas made a mistake leaving Paul for John Mark. He gave up big-time mission work for his cousin. But later, Mark becomes a valuable asset to Paul and his ministry. Perhaps Barnabas saw the future possibilities of Mark and decided to invest in him. Later on we do see that Mark was a capable minister. Paul writes of him, *"Get Mark and bring him with you, because he is helpful to me in my ministry."*[253] Tradition states that John Mark became a disciple of Peter and penned Peter's remembrances of Jesus in the Gospel of Mark. It seems that Barnabas was right not to give up on Mark.

So who was right, Paul or Barnabas? Given the circumstances they could have both been right. I'm not waffling to waffle. I really believe that both could have been right. Paul was right to say that Mark wasn't ready for the next missionary journey. Barnabas was right to stay with John Mark and invest in him. In the end, it all turned out all right.

In Colossians, we learn that John Mark and Barnabas were cousins. That must have played into Barnabas' decision to take John Mark with him to Cyprus instead of accompanying Paul on the second missionary journey. Was Barnabas being sentimental? Perhaps. Sentimentalism isn't necessarily bad. Sometimes it keeps us from giving up on people.

Paul instructs/commands the church in Colossae to receive Mark if he comes to them. The question arises: "Why would Paul need to command the church to receive Mark?" Perhaps the rift between Paul and Mark had become common knowledge in the churches. Perhaps the rift was only recently mended. Perhaps some in the church considered Mark a Judaizer. Or, there might be another reason that we don't have details about. The word Paul uses is a strong word—ἐντολή, 'entola, "command." The context could demand that the word "command" be weakened to "instruction." Moo writes, *"Instructions*, the English word used in most of the translations, captures accurately the sense of the Greek *entolas* here. This word would usually be translated 'commandments,' but there is good reason to think that it has a weaker sense here."[294] Regardless of how the word is translated, Paul wanted to make sure that the church in Colossae warmly received Mark if he came to their town.

V. 11. *"Greet…Jesus Justus."* Jesus was his Jewish name (Joshua in the Hebrew) and Justus his Roman name. This is all we know of this disciple. He was one of the few of the circumcision group who was a fellow worker with Paul, and he (along with John Mark and Aristarchus) brought comfort to Paul. Martin writes of the word "comfort," "It is a medical term for a tonic. The meaning here is consolation or soothing action."[295] Our churches are filled with unsung heroes who comfort other people. Every now and then it would be nice to give them a "shout-out."

Paul distinguishes these three men as the only ones *"of the circumcision"* that were his fellow workers. Paul usually uses this phrase "of the circumcision" in reference to the Judaizers—Jewish Christians who felt that Gentile Christians needed to keep the ceremonies and traditions of the Jews. But here, Paul uses it to let the church know that not everyone from a Jewish background was a Judaizer. Dunn writes:

> The reference presumably is intended to assure the Colossians that there were such Jews, or at any rate other Jews apart from himself, who, as Jews, were fully approving of and cooperative in the Gentile mission ('fellow workers'), despite, presumably, the disapproval of most of their compatriots.[296]

These men were fellow workers for the kingdom of God.

(B) 4:12–13 Epaphras

[12]ἀσπάζεται ὑμᾶς Ἐπαφρᾶς ὁ ἐξ ὑμῶν, δοῦλος Χριστοῦ ['Ιησοῦ], πάντοτε ἀγωνιζόμενος ὑπὲρ ὑμῶν ἐν ταῖς προσευχαῖς, ἵνα σταθῆτε τέλειοι καὶ πεπληροφορημένοι ἐν παντὶ θελήματι τοῦ θεοῦ. [13]μαρτυρῶ γὰρ αὐτῷ ὅτι ἔχει πολὺν πόνον ὑπὲρ ὑμῶν καὶ τῶν ἐν Λαοδικείᾳ καὶ τῶν ἐν Ἱεραπόλει.

My Translation

[12]Epaphras, who is one of you, a servant of Christ Jesus, sends greetings. He is always wrestling/striving for you in his prayer, in order that you may stand mature and fully assured in all the will of God. [13]I testify for him that he has much labor on your behalf and for those at Laodicea and Hierapolis.

NIV, 1984

[12]Epaphras, who is one of you and a servant of Christ Jesus, sends greetings. He is always wrestling in prayer for you, that you may stand firm in all the will of God, mature and fully assured. [13]I vouch for him that he is working hard for you and for those at Laodicea and Hierapolis.

Notes

V. 12. We met Epaphras earlier (1:7). He is from Colossae and is, most likely, the person who started the church there. He is Paul's source of information concerning the church in Colossae. He is with Paul in Rome as Paul writes this letter. Epaphras is a servant of Christ Jesus. He sends his greetings to the church in Colossae.

Epaphras is a prayer warrior. He is always wresting in prayer for the

Colossians. *"Wrestling in prayer"* is an interesting image. Have you ever wrestled? It is one of the most physically tiring of all sports. To wrestle in prayer symbolizes struggling in prayer, pouring out your whole heart to God. The word is ἀγωνιζόμενος, *agonidzomenos*, "striving." A form of this word is used to describe Jesus' prayer in Gethsemane. Luke 22:44 reads, *"And being in anguish* (ἀγωνία, *agonia*) *he prayed more earnestly."* You can see our word "agony" or "to agonize" in this word. Wrestling in prayer is emotionally agonizing. It is draining. Epaphras was continually agonizing in prayer for the disciples in Colossae.

Epaphras prays for the disciples to stand firm in all of God's will. The verb is in the passive, which can convey the idea of the divine passive, meaning that God gives them the strength to stand.

The prayer is for them to be mature and fully assured. Epaphras knew that if the disciples in Colossae were going to survive, they needed to grow up in the Lord. He also knew that prayer would help them in their growth. This is a prayer of discipleship. Dunn writes:

> It is not least in significance that their ambition...was not merely for individuals to be converted, but that they should stand firmly, "mature"..., that there should be an emotional depth and balance to their faith ("fully assured"), and that it should express itself in daily conduct where doing the will of God was the primary objective and yardstick.[297]

Paul and Epaphras weren't interested in just baptizing people and watching them wallow in a pool of mediocrity. They didn't want to create a "revolving door" ministry where people leave the church as quickly as they enter. They wanted disciples to grow and mature in their faith. They expected disciples to stand firm, become strong, and be confident in Christ.

V. 13. Paul vouches for Epaphras, saying he is working hard for the disciples in the tri-city area of Colossae, Laodicea, and Hierapolis. The word for "work" is not the typical work (*ergon*), but a less common word πόνος, *ponos*, that is usually associated with pain. ADBGL defines this word as "work that involves much exertion or trouble, (*hard*) *labor, toil.*"[298] Epaphras isn't just working, he is working hard for the disciples in Colossae. If Paul knew of your work for the disciples in your ministry, could he commend you in the same way he commended Epaphras?

(C) 4:14–15 Others

[14]ἀσπάζεται ὑμᾶς Λουκᾶς ὁ ἰατρὸς ὁ ἀγαπητὸς καὶ Δημᾶς. [15]Ἀσπάσασθε τοὺς ἐν Λαοδικείᾳ ἀδελφοὺς καὶ Νύμφαν καὶ τὴν κατ' οἶκον αὐτῆς ἐκκλησίαν.

My Translation

[14]Luke, the beloved doctor, and Demas send greetings. [15]Give my greetings to the brothers at Laodicea, and to Nympha and the church in her house.

NIV, 1984

[14]Our dear friend Luke, the doctor, and Demas send greetings. [15]Give my greetings to the brothers at Laodicea, and to Nympha and the church in her house.

Notes

V. 14. Two other travelling companions are with Paul in Rome. There is Luke, whom we know as the author of Luke and Acts. It is here that we learn that Luke was a physician. Then there is Demas, who will later abandon the faith. Paul writes of him in 2 Timothy 4:10, *"For Demas, because he loved this world, has deserted me and has gone to Thessalonica."*

V. 15. Nympha. This is the only time she is mentioned in the New Testament. She was a friend of Paul, and the church met in her house. This is, if she was a she. She might have been a he. Anders writes:

> Even the gender of Nympha is debated. The form of the name in the Greek, an unaccented accusative, allows for the reference to be to a man or a woman. This explains the textual variations in gender with reference to the church in either 'her house' (NASB, NIV), 'his house' (KJV), or even 'their house' (RSV). The manuscript evidence can be used to argue for any of the options. In the end the identity of Nympha remains a mystery.[299]

Here we have another mystery to solve when we get to heaven.

Regardless of gender, we do know that Nympha had a house. Some have said that Christians were commanded to give up their property when they became Christians. This wasn't a requirement to be a disciple. There were property owners in the early church; Nympha owned property.

The meeting of disciples in houses was fairly common in the New Testament. Church buildings didn't exist in New Testament times. O'Brien writes:

> On occasion a whole congregation in one city might be small enough to meet in the home of one of its members, and it must be remembered that it was not until about the middle of the third century that early Christianity owned property for purposes of worship.... In other places house-churches appear to have been smaller circles of fellowship within the larger group. In addition to Nympha's house in Laodicea we know that in Colossae Philemon's house was used as a meeting-place (Philemon 2). At Philippi Lydia's

home seems to have been used in this way (Acts 16:15, 40) while at Corinth Gaius is described as "host...to the whole church.... Aquila and Priscilla extended the hospitality of their home to house groups in the successive cities where they lived, e.g., in Ephesus (1 Cor 16:19) and Rome (Rom 16:5). Concerning the details of these house churches we know little.[300]

Some writers note that the church in Nympha's house should be distinguished from the church in Laodicea. They don't believe the whole church met in her house. Instead, small cell groups met within the homes of a number of disciples. Together, these made up the larger church in Laodicea. It is difficult to reconstruct the structure of the church in Laodicea on such sparse evidence.

Even if the church met in smaller groups in Colossae (which is very likely), this doesn't mean this pattern has to be followed exactly today. Some conservative Christian groups believe in "patternism." Patternism is a hermeneutical principle which states that whenever the reader of the text sees a pattern in the ministry of Jesus or the practice of the NT church, the reader must follow the exact details of that pattern in his or her ministry today. The idea is that a biblical example is just as binding as a biblical command. This was prevalent teaching in the churches of Christ throughout most of the twentieth century.

The problem with this hermeneutical principle is that it doesn't allow for social or cultural differences that exist between New Testament times and the current century. For example, it is obvious that Jesus wore sandals on his feet. John the baptizer makes reference to this when he says he (John) is unworthy to untie the laces on Jesus' sandals (Mark 1:7). Jesus set the example of wearing sandals. Is this example binding on Christians today? No. It's not a command; it's a pattern or example from the life of Jesus. If Jesus were to live in our day, in the Northeastern United States in the winter, he probably wouldn't wear sandals. You have to account for social and cultural differences.

Here's another quick example: When Jesus observed his last supper with his disciples, he passed around a single goblet of wine and everyone drank from the same cup. A "patternist" would make this example binding. He or she would say we must use one cup when we participate in communion today. However, the text never commands that we use one cup. To make the example a command is to overstep what is written in the text.

There is a different approach to applying New Testament patterns and examples in the church today: We study the patterns of church polity and practice in the New Testament to learn principles that worked in the first century. We apply those principles to the needs of the church in the twenty-first century, accounting for social and cultural differences. However, when it comes to doctrinal matters, we strictly follow the doctrine of the apostles.

For example, in Jesus' ministry he went throughout the towns and villages of Galilee, "teaching,...preaching,...and healing." These three participles are used to describe his ministry in Matthew 4:23. Jesus sets this example for us. It seems wise and prudent to do ministry the way Jesus did it. After all, no one has ever been more effective in the ministry than Jesus. Therefore, it would be wise to follow the example and pattern of Jesus in the practice of ministry today. In our ministry today, we teach the valuable lessons of Scripture, preach the good news of the gospel, and heal the spiritual and emotional wounds in people's lives. In doing so, we imitate the ministry of Jesus.

3. 4:16–17. Final Instructions

¹⁶καὶ ὅταν ἀναγνωσθῇ παρ' ὑμῖν ἡ ἐπιστολή, ποιήσατε ἵνα καὶ ἐν τῇ Λαοδικέων ἐκκλησίᾳ ἀναγνωσθῇ, καὶ τὴν ἐκ Λαοδικείας ἵνα καὶ ὑμεῖς ἀναγνῶτε. ¹⁷καὶ εἴπατε Ἀρχίππῳ, Βλέπε τὴν διακονίαν ἣν παρέλαβες ἐν κυρίῳ, ἵνα αὐτὴν πληροῖς.

My Translation

¹⁶After this epistle has been read to you, make sure that it is also read in the church of the Laodiceans and that you read the letter from Laodicea.

¹⁷Say to Archippus: "See that you complete the ministry/service you have received in the Lord."

NIV, 1984

¹⁶After this letter has been read to you, see that it is also read in the church of the Laodiceans and that you in turn read the letter from Laodicea.

¹⁷Tell Archippus: "See to it that you complete the work you have received in the Lord."

V. 16. There was a letter from Laodicea, but we don't have a copy of that letter today. We don't know why, but the letter was not preserved for us. Perhaps it was lost. Some believe it to be the letter to Philemon, but that would place Philemon in Laodicea and not Colossae. Others speculate that it is the letter to the Ephesians. But many scholars believe that Ephesians was written after Colossians. It is best to view this letter as a lost letter that is not in our canon. Martin writes, "The conclusion of most commentators is that the letter in question has not survived. One guess about how it was lost is that it perished in the earthquake in the area in AD 60–61."[301]

We do see in this example how Paul's letters were circulated. We also see how the process of canonization began. Dunn writes:

> We see here already the beginnings of that sense of the letters' importance that thereafter developed over the decades into an acknowledgment of their canonical status. Moreover, we begin to see something of the process by which, presumably, Paul's letters gained growing influence as a group; that is, by increasingly

widespread circulation, different letters would not only gain wider recognition but also be put together with other letters.[302]

V. 17. Paul mentions Archippus in the opening of his letter to Philemon. Paul writes, *"To Philemon our dear friend and fellow worker, to Apphia our sister, to Archippus our fellow soldier and to the church that meets in your home"* (Philemon 1b–2). It seems that Archippus was the son of Philemon and Apphia. He is considered a fellow soldier to Paul, which probably means Archippus had an active role in the ministry in Colossae.

Paul wants Archippus to know that he must not give up on the work he was doing in the Lord. Perhaps he was discouraged because of the false teaching he was battling. Paul wants him to stay strong.

What does this section tell us about Paul as a person? Much. Ernest Martin has done an excellent job summarizing what we can learn about Paul from this final section of Colossians. Martin sees Paul as:

1. *A people person.* As in other correspondence, the names of colleagues and acquaintances were important to Paul. So was an exchange of news about personal circumstances. An aroma of personal caring permeates the letter.

2. *An appreciative person.* He had a warm way of identifying persons and he mentioned those who had been a comfort to him. This reveals a person who deeply appreciated the loyalty and kindness of those who stayed with him.

3. *An affirming person.* Many affirmations of character and contribution surround the names of persons mentioned. What he said about Epaphras is a prime example.

4. *A team person.* Although Paul was more of a leader than a follower, he saw his ministry as shared with co-workers and fellow servants in the Lord. These verses indicate that he strongly supported his colleagues.

5. *A church person.* Far from being a free-lance preacher out there doing his own thing, Paul assumed church relationships as integral with the gospel. He worked at both intracongregational and intercongregational relationships.

6. *A spiritually concerned person.* What he affirmed in Epaphras was his own priority as well. His pastoral-care concern about maturity led to warning people, as well as building them up in the faith.

7. *A praying person.* The letter as a whole shows that Paul as well as Epaphras prayed earnestly for the Lycus Valley believers.

8. *A kingdom-oriented person.* When he lauded several associates who stayed with him as co-workers for the kingdom of God (4:11), he revealed his own orientation and priority.

9. *Christ's person.* This obvious characteristic colors all that Paul was and was doing.[303]

4. 4:18 Farewell; Personal Note; Final Statement

[18]Ὁ ἀσπασμὸς τῇ ἐμῇ χειρὶ Παύλου. μνημονεύετέ μου τῶν δεσμῶν. ἡ χάρις μεθ᾽ ὑμῶν.

My Translation

[18]The greeting, in my hand of Paul. Remember my chains. Grace with you.

NIV, 1984

[18]I, Paul, write this greeting in my own hand. Remember my chains. Grace be with you.

Notes

V. 18. Paul closes the letter as simply as he opened it. This simple closing reminds us of three important themes in Paul's writing:

(A) The Personal Touch

He scribbles this last greeting with his own hand. This was a way of authenticating the letter. It was also a personal touch. Paul believed in the importance of relationships.

(B) The Importance of Prayer

He asks the church to remember his chains. Perhaps the chains on his hands were rattling as he attempted to sign the letter. This is a last plea for the prayers of the disciples in Colossae. Paul believed in prayer.

(C) A Grace Note

And he signs off with, *"Grace with you."* χάρις, *charis,* "grace," was a word of greeting or exiting in the Greco-Roman world, but Paul, most likely, means more when he uses the word. Paul closes all of his letters with a grace note.

In music a grace note is an ornamental note placed in the notation that slides into the major note. It is usually printed in a smaller size to distinguish it from the note. The composer allows the musician to add a small flourish to the music. At times, Chopin added a series of grace notes to his works allowing the musician to pick exactly how she or he wanted to play those notes (in terms of speed and dynamics). These notes enhanced the music. That's what grace does to our lives. Our lives should begin with grace. It should slide into every aspect of our lives. Grace enhances our lives.

Paul begins and ends the letter with grace. His life was all about the grace of God. For Paul, grace was more than the grace note; grace was the whole symphony. Thus this is a fitting way for him to close the letter.

This is a great way for me to close this commentary as well.

In the words of Paul: "ἡ χάρις μεθ' ὑμῶν, *a charis meth' 'umon.*"

Grace with you.

—G. Steve Kinnard

Appendix One

The Major Theme of Colossians— Christ Is Supreme

I have spent quite a bit of time during the course of this book pointing out ways in which Paul demonstrates that Christ is supreme. It is arguably the main theme of the book. That being said, it seems prudent for us to review one more time the ways that Paul rings this bell. He rings it loud and he rings it often.

Let's run through Colossians one more time and highlight all the ways that Paul speaks about Christ being supreme.

Practical Exercise: Before you read the following section, first go through Colossians one more time and mark all the passages you can find where Paul highlights the supremacy of Christ.

Now it's my turn. Here we go:

1. 1:13–14, *"For he has rescued us from the dominion of darkness and brought us into the kingdom of the Son he loves, in whom we have redemption, the forgiveness of sins."* What do you see here? What is Paul saying about the supremacy of Christ in these verses?

I see four points. First, Christ rescues us from the dominion of darkness. That's a powerful image of Christ. He is our rescuer. When we were drowning, Christ jumped into the deep end of the pool to save us. You were worth rescuing. You are worth rescuing.

Second, we are brought into the kingdom of the Son. The Kingdom is Christ's kingdom. That means Christ is king. Since he is king, we need to treat him as king and surrender our lives to him.

Third, Jesus is the Son God loves. This is a special designation that God gives only to Jesus. Jesus is the only begotten, one-and-only, unique Son of God. Have you ever bought something that was one-of-a-kind? That tends to make things more valuable. It makes the item pricey. Why? There is only one. Nothing else is like this one. Jesus is that way.

Fourth, in Christ we have redemption, forgiveness of sins. He bought us back with a price. That's redemption. Again, to Jesus, you were worth the sacrifice. He was willing to buy you back.

Four brilliant points in one short verse.

2. 1:15–20, the Hymn of the Supremacy of Christ

This is the longest and most elaborate portrait of the supremacy of Christ in Colossians (and perhaps in the New Testament).

He is the image of the invisible God, the firstborn over all creation. For by him all things were created: things in heaven and on earth, visible and invisible, whether thrones or powers or rulers or authorities; all things were created by him and for him. He is before all things, and in him all things hold together. And he is the head of the body, the church; he is the beginning and the firstborn from among the dead, so that in everything he might have the supremacy. For God was pleased to have all his fullness dwell in him, and through him to reconcile to himself all things, whether things on earth or things in heaven, by making peace through his blood, shed on the cross.

What do you see here? We went through this quite thoroughly in the commentary so we won't spend much time here, but let's list these traits again.

- He is the image of the invisible God.
- He is the firstborn over all creation.
- All things were created by him and for him.
- He is before all things.
- In him all things hold together.
- He is the head of the body, the church.
- He is the beginning and the firstborn from among the dead, so that in everything he might have the supremacy.
- God was pleased to have all his fullness dwell in him.
- All things were reconciled through him.

3. 1:21–22, *"Once you were alienated from God and were enemies in your minds because of your evil behavior. But now he has reconciled you by Christ's physical body through death to present you holy in his sight, without blemish and free from accusation."*

Look at what Christ was able to accomplish through his death. He was able to change our standing with God both in our own minds and in the reality of our situation.

We were enemies of God in our minds because of our evil behavior. We had declared war on God. What do you think of when you hear the word enemy? In our twenty-first century American culture, we might think of Islamic extremists. In their mind, American is the evil empire. How can we change this perception? It's going to take a mind-change. That's not easy. That's what Christ is able to do for us.

But not only were we enemies of God in our mind, we actually stood as enemies against God because of our sin. That was the reality we were living in. We were unholy, blemished, and full of accusation. Christ changed that. And how did he accomplish this feat? Through his death on the cross. He changed our situation with God. We are no longer enemies; now we are holy, without blemish, and free from accusation in God's sight. Only Jesus could accomplish such a feat.

4. 1:27, *"To them God has chosen to make known among the Gentiles the glorious riches of this mystery, which is Christ in you, the hope of glory."*

The glorious mystery among the Gentiles is Christ. He also is our hope of glory.

5. 1:28–29, *"We proclaim him, admonishing and teaching everyone with all wisdom, so that we may present everyone perfect in Christ. To this end I labor, struggling with all his energy, which so powerfully works in me."*

Christ enables us to become mature. Paul labored toward this goal. Christ gave Paul the energy to work hard in the ministry. His energy worked powerfully in Paul. Do we allow Christ's energy to work in our lives or do we try to do it on our own energy?

6. 2:2–3, *"My purpose is that they may be encouraged in heart and united in love, so that they may have the full riches of complete understanding, in order that they may know the mystery of God, namely, Christ, in whom are hidden all the treasures of wisdom and knowledge."*

What does this verse tell us about the supremacy of Christ?

Christ is described here as the mystery of God. What that means is this: If you want to unravel the mystery of God, then go to Christ. Christ reveals who God is to us. That's the beauty of the incarnation. The Gentiles didn't understand much about God because they didn't receive the revelation of God in the Torah. But God made himself known to the Gentiles, not through the Torah, but through Christ.

Also, in Christ are hidden all the treasures of wisdom and knowledge. This is a very grand statement about Christ. Not "some of the treasures"; not "most of the treasures"; but, "all of the treasures."

7. 2:9-10, Here is a majestic statement of the supremacy of Christ: 2:9–10, *"For in Christ all the fullness of the Deity lives in bodily form, and you have been given fullness in Christ, who is the head over every power and authority."*

If you are looking for the most concise statement of the supremacy of Christ in the letter, I believe it is here. In this verse, Paul states in unequivocal language that Christ is divine.

In Christ all the fullness of the Deity lives in bodily form. He is head over every power and authority. This reminds us of John 1:14, *"The Word became flesh and made his dwelling among us"*: Deity lives in bodily form.

Christ is the head over every power and authority. Both the Jews and the Gentiles believed there were spiritual powers that animated the earthly world. Some feared these powers. Well, if you have fullness in Christ, then there is no need to fear these powers because Christ has authority over all of them.

8. 2:11–12

> *In him you were also circumcised, in the putting off of the sinful nature, not with a circumcision done by the hands of men but with the circumcision done by Christ, having been buried with him in baptism and raised with him through your faith in the power of God, who raised him from the dead.*

Christ takes away our sinful nature through baptism.

9. 2:13–15, A grand statement of what Christ was able to accomplish on the cross is found here.

> *When you were dead in your sins and in the uncircumcision of your sinful nature, God made you alive with Christ. He forgave us all our sins, having canceled the written code, with its regulations, that was against us and that stood opposed to us; he took it away, nailing it to the cross. And having disarmed the powers and authorities, he made a public spectacle of them, triumphing over them by the cross.*

What does dead in sin mean? Powerless. We could not overcome sin on our own. It was impossible. But God made us alive in Christ.

He forgave our sins.

What is the written code? It could be a list of all debts (our IOUs) that we owe to God because of our sin. Many people believe it is the law. Perhaps it's not the law, but a list of ways we couldn't live up to the standard of the law. We couldn't live up to the written code, so Jesus nailed it to the cross.

He took all the spiritual powers that were mentioned earlier in the letter, and he triumphed over them on the cross. He made a public spectacle of them.

This is what a conquering emperor did with his captives of war. He would parade them in the street to show the superiority of his military. Christ won the spiritual war. It's over. Done with. Finished on the cross. We need to trust that Christ is the victor. He has already won the war. To side with anyone else is to join the losing side. We need to stick with Christ.

10. 2:17, Next comes one of my favorite phrases in the whole book of Colossians: *"…the reality, however, is found in Christ."*

A few years back there was a Cola war going on. Which Cola was the best? In the battle, there were two major contenders for supremacy—Coke and Pepsi. In this battle, Coca-Cola billed itself as "The Real Thing." There was a jingle, sung by the Fortunes, that went:

> It's the real thing. Coke is.
> That's the way it should be. Coca-Cola.
> What the world wants to see
> Is the real thing.[304]

There was another jingle, sung by a multicultural group of teenagers on the top of a hill, that went:

> I'd like to buy the world a home and furnish it with love.
> Grow apple trees and honeybees and snow white turtle doves.
> I'd like to teach the world to sing in perfect harmony.
> I'd like to by the world a Coke and keep it company.
> It's the real thing. Coke is. What the world wants today
> Is the real thing.[305]

Every other soda, including Pepsi, was an imitation of the "real thing."

In the church in Colossae there was a spiritual war being waged. The main contenders were Judaism, the pagan mystery cults, and Christianity. Paul lets the disciples know that Christ is the real thing. There are many things that can entice us to make us think they are the real thing. But the only real thing is Christ.

If you trade Christ for anything else, then you've made a bad trade. Christ is the real thing.

11. 3:1, *"Since, then, you have been raised with Christ, set your hearts on things above, where Christ is seated at the right hand of God."*

Christ is seated at the right hand of God, the place of honor and authority.

12. 3:4, *"When Christ, who is your life, appears, then you also will appear with him in glory."*

Another incredibly beautiful statement: *"Christ, who is your life."* Christ is our reality. Christ is our life. He is also the future hope of glory. In other words, Christ is everything (check out 3:11).

13. The perfect phrase to end our study of the ways Paul speaks of the supremacy of Christ As if he hasn't said it enough so that it is abundantly clear, he rings the bell one more time.

Paul says in 3:11, *"But Christ is all, and is in all."*

This is a grand statement of the supremacy of Christ. Paul trims down everything he has to say about the supremacy of Christ into this short phrase, literally, "But the all and in all [is] Christ."

Christology

What do all these statements about the supremacy of Christ tell us about Christ? Ernest D. Martin lists eight ways Christ can be viewed through the lens of Colossians. Here are Martin's eight ways of viewing Christ:

1. *The preeminent Christ.* The Christ-hymn, 1:15–20, repeatedly affirms the priority and supremacy of Christ. Echoes are heard in 2:9–10, 17, and 3:1.

2. *The cosmic Christ.* Colossians breaks out of the confines of parochial human thought to reveal the one through whom and for whom all things were created, and who is before all things. This universe with whom Christ has to do includes the principalities and powers and the elements of the universe (1:13, 15–17; 2:15, 20)...

3. *The redeeming Christ.* In addition to the specific affirmation in 1:14, a strong note of freedom can be heard in 2:13–23. Forgiveness and redemption come by way of the cross, Christ's death...

4. *The triumphing Christ.* The key text is 2:15, which presents Christ as the one through whom God has exposed and disempowered the powers and accomplished a decisive victory over them through the cross

5. *The reconciling Christ.* The reconciliation motif stands out in 1:20–22. Alongside the cosmic dimension of God's intent, the relational impact of Christ's death is also put in personal terms...

6. *The revealing Christ.* Christ, as the image of God, reveals who God is (1:15). As the one in whom believers come to fullness, he reveals the human potential (2:9–10). The virtues to be put on (3:12–14) are the qualities found in Jesus.

7. *The nourishing Christ.* Growing, bearing fruit, and going on to sta-
   bility and maturity—these all have their source in Christ. There is
   imagery of Christ as rootage and foundation, of believers being
   attached to Christ the head, and of the word of Christ dwelling in
   the community. All these affirm Christ as the source of life (2:6–7,
   19; 3:3–4, 16).

8. *The adequate Christ.* The repeated appeal in 2:8–23 amounts to
   this: With all that is yours in Jesus Christ, why would you regress to
   inferior and worthless allurements?[306]

William Hendriksen also lists a number of ways that Paul speaks of the
attributes of Christ in Colossians. Hendriksen lists six attributes of Christ. He
writes that Christ is:

- the Architect and Sustainer of the universe;

- the Head of all things, and especially the organic and ruling Head
  of his own Body, the Church, its all-sufficient, one and only Savior;

- the image of the invisible God, the embodiment of all the divine
  fulness;

- the Source of the Christian's life and peace and joy;

- the Rewarder of those who strive to be a blessing to others, regardless of social position; and

- as present within us, our "Hope of glory."[307]

As we read through Colossians, it is evident that the major theme of the
book is the supremacy of Christ. Paul comes at this idea from many different
angles. He wants to make sure the disciples in Colossae don't trade Jesus in for
a cheap imitation. If you have found Jesus, then you've found it all. No need to
search any further. Jesus is the all in all.

Appendix Two

Other Themes from Colossians

I. Christians Ought to Grow

Paul believed that every disciple in the church ought to be growing and becoming more mature. If we aren't growing, then we are going backwards.

Consider these verses:

In 1:10–14, Paul writes:

And we pray this in order that you may live a life worthy of the Lord and may please him in every way: bearing fruit in every good work, growing in the knowledge of God, being strengthened with all power according to his glorious might so that you may have great endurance and patience, and joyfully giving thanks to the Father, who has qualified you to share in the inheritance of the saints in the kingdom of light. For he has rescued us from the dominion of darkness and brought us into the kingdom of the Son he loves, in whom we have redemption, the forgiveness of sins.

A. Paul's Ministry Goal. 1:28–29

We proclaim him, admonishing and <u>teaching everyone with all wisdom</u>, so <u>that we may present everyone perfect in Christ</u>. To this end I labor, struggling with all his energy, which so powerfully works in me.

B. Directives for Holy Living. 3:1–5, 12–14

There are some keys to becoming spiritually mature here. We see three ideas expressed:

Since, then, you have been <u>raised</u> with Christ, set your <u>hearts</u> on things *above, where Christ is seated at the right hand of God. Set your minds on things above, not on earthly things. For you died, and your life is now hidden with Christ in God. When Christ, who is your life, appears, then you also will appear with him in glory.*

Put to death, therefore, whatever belongs to your earthly nature: sexual immorality, impurity, lust, evil desires and greed, which is idolatry.

Therefore, as God's chosen people, holy and dearly loved, clothe yourselves with compassion, kindness, humility, gentleness and patience. Bear with each other and forgive whatever grievances you may have against one another. Forgive as the Lord forgave you. And over all these virtues put on love, which binds them all together in perfect unity.

How can we set our hearts on things above?

1. By being in the Word every day.

2. By praying every day. I recently ran across this quote by Corrie ten Boom: "Don't pray when you feel like it. Have an appointment with the Lord and keep it. A man is powerful on his knees."

3. By having fellowship every day.

4. By saying no to sin every day.

II. False Doctrine Is Dangerous

Paul takes time in his letter to warn the church against heresy and false doctrine. He takes on this heresy beginning in 2:4, writing, *"I tell you this so that no one may deceive you by fine-sounding arguments."*

In 2:8 Paul gives a stern warning: *"See to it that no one takes you captive through hollow and deceptive philosophy, which depends on human tradition and the basic principles of this world rather than on Christ."* The idea of taking captive is literally "take as a booty of war." The arguments of the false teachers were built on human tradition and not on Christ who is superior to any human tradition.

Another warning is in 2:16–17, *"Therefore do not let anyone judge you by what you eat or drink, or with regard to a religious festival, a New Moon celebration or a Sabbath day. These are a shadow of the things that were to come; the reality, however, is found in Christ."*

Paul gives warning: *Don't be deceived; don't be taken captive; don't let anyone judge you.* Paul talked about the harm of false doctrines and false teachers.

We should not take a lackadaisical attitude toward false doctrine. We need to understand how dangerous it is.

Back in February 2012, I went to the skin doctor, and he found a place on my leg that was melanoma. He sent me to a fantastic surgeon in Manhattan named Dr. Shapiro. When I met with Dr. Shapiro, he took this melanoma very seriously. He said, "Steve, we are going to cut deep and we are going to cut wide and we are going to get all of this." That's what I wanted to hear. I wanted him to be serious. He did get it all. He cut deep, and he cut wide. That's the attitude we need to have about false doctrine.

Let's look at 2:8 again: *"See to it that no one takes you captive through hollow and deceptive philosophy, which depends on human tradition and the basic principles of this world rather than on Christ."*

We live in a world filled with hollow and deceptive philosophies. There is atheism that says there is no god. But the Bible says, *"The fools says in his heart, 'There is no God'"* (Psalm 14:1).

There is the existentialism of Camus and Sartre that says there is no meaning to life, which is what Ecclesiastes says until it gets to the end and says: *"Fear God and keep his commandment, for this is the whole duty of man"* (12:13b).

There is post-modernism, which says everything is relative and there is no absolute truth. But when you say there is no absolute truth, you've just stated an absolute truth.

Jesus said, *"I am the way and the truth and the life."*

They say everyone and everything has to be included and accepted. Except they exclude anyone who doesn't say that everyone and everything has to be included and accepted.

There is materialism, which says the person who has the most things wins. But Jesus said of the rich fool who kept building bigger barns, *"But God said to him, 'You fool! This very night your life will be demanded from you. Then who will get what you have prepared for yourself?' This is how it will be with anyone who stores up things for himself but is not rich toward God"* (Luke 12:20).

There is the asceticism of many new-age philosophies which says that things are wrong and we need to rid ourselves of things. Paul handles this in Colossians 2:20–23:

> Since you died with Christ to the basic principles of this world, why, as though you still belonged to it, do you submit to its rules: "Do not handle! Do not taste! Do not touch!"? These are all destined to perish with use, because they are based on human commands and teachings. Such regulations indeed have an appearance of wisdom, with their self-imposed worship, their false humility and their harsh treatment of the body, but they lack any value in restraining sensual indulgence.

These philosophies are all hollow and deceptive. They are like some packaging that you see for food. You see a big bag of potato chips and you open it up and there are only three chips in the package. It's full of air.

But, Christ is Supreme.

III. The Church Is Important

Colossians 1:13 reads, *"For he has rescued us from the dominion of darkness and brought us into the kingdom of the Son he loves, in whom we have redemption, the forgiveness of sins."*

Paul speaks of the church as the body of Christ (1:18, 1:34–25, 4:15–16). In 1:18 he mentions that Jesus *"is the head of the body, the church."*

If the church is the body of Christ, then we are the limbs. He gets his work done through us. Paul calls himself a "servant" and a "minister" of the church.

The church isn't perfect, because we aren't perfect. But because you aren't perfect, you don't give up on yourself, saying, "I'm going to quit me and start another me."

> We are a body. We are stronger together than apart.
> None of us is as smart as all of us are together.
> None of us is as talented as all of us are together.
> None of us is as spiritual as all of us are together.
> None of us can do as much as all of us can together.
> We need to appreciate the church. Paul did.

Conclusion

There is so much more that we could discuss from this rich book. I want to leave you with the main theme of book—Christ is Supreme. If you are in Christ, then you've discovered the best thing in the world, so don't let go of it. If you aren't in Christ, then explore what it means to be a disciple of Jesus and you'll see that it's the best thing going today. Once you find Christ, there is no need to search for anything else. Christ is supreme.

Appendix Three

How to Change a Bad Habit: Colossians 3:1–17

Whatever your present situation, I assure you that you are not your habits. You can replace old patterns of self-defeating behavior with new patterns, new habits of effectiveness, happiness, and trust-based relationship.[308]
—Stephen R. Covey, motivational speaker and author

A habit is what we repeatedly do, so when we change what we repeatedly do, we change our habits. At times, we all develop bad habits. But they can be broken. We don't have to let our habits define us; rather, we can replace bad habits with good ones.

We have different types of habits. Think of the things that you repeatedly do and place them in one of these categories:

- Good habits
- Bad habits
- Neutral habits
- Sin (a bad habit with eternal consequences)

Habits are important because our character is the sum of our habits. Good character comes from practicing good habits. The opposite is also true: Bad character comes from practicing bad habits.

Keep the following leadership maxim in front of you as you read this chapter:

Leadership Maxim
Sow a thought; reap an action.
Sow an action; reap a habit.
Sow a habit; reap a character.
Sow a character; reap a destiny.

Notice the progression here: thought > action > habit > character > destiny. Habits are formed from our thoughts and actions. Our destiny is formed from our habits and character.

Colossians 3:1–17

The scripture that we will use as a foundation to help us change our bad habits is Colossians 3:1–17. Read and reread this scripture until you are familiar with it. Paul gives many valuable insights in this passage on helping us change our character by changing our habits.

How to Break a Bad Habit in Nine Not-So-Easy Steps

Breaking a bad habit is not easy, but it's worth it. Breaking a habit takes discipline and hard work. With God on our side, we can turn our bad habits into good habits. Here are nine not-so-easy steps toward breaking a bad habit. Pick a habit that you want to break and apply these principles.

Habit Breaker #1: Change Your Stinkin' Thinkin': Colossians 3:1–4

Paul entreats us to *"Set [our] minds on things above, not on earthly things."* To break out of our bad habits, we have to change the way we think. If we have tried to break a habit before but have failed, then we might think that we are powerless to change it. But we aren't powerless. With God's help, we can change anything. We need to start by changing the way we think. We have to throw out any negative thinking and start believing that our lives can be different. Bad thoughts lead to bad actions that lead to bad habits. Begin by changing your stinkin' thinkin'.

Habit Breaker #2: Identify the Culprit: Colossians 3:5–11

Paul puts a name on the sin. He calls it what it is. In this passage, Paul lists sexual immorality, impurity, lust, evil desires and greed (which is idolatry), anger, rage, malice, slander, and filthy language. He identifies the culprit. We have to put a name on the habit that we want to change. Put a name on it. Label it and fill in the blank with the label:

Put to death _____.

Pick one bad habit that you want to work on changing for the next four weeks. Remember that experts say it takes twenty-one days to start or break a habit. So pick a habit and identify it. Write it down. Let the culprit know that there is a new sheriff in town who means business.

Habit Breaker #3: Know the Culprit

After you have identified the habit that you want to change, profile the bad habit by answering the following questions:

- When do I do this?
- Where do I do this?
- How do I do this?
- With whom do I do this?
- What thoughts are behind this habit?
- What actions are behind this habit?

Habit Breaker #4: Plan Your Attack: Colossians 3:8

Decide how you want to go about changing this habit. Draw up the plan and work the plan.

Planning includes:

- Prayer
- Bible study
- Setting your mind for action—meditation
- Setting goals

Habit Breaker #5: Replace the Bad Habit with a Good Habit: Colossians 3:12–14

Paul says, *"Clothe yourselves."* It's time to put on some new clothes. Replace the bad habits with a good or at least a neutral habit. My father smoked for years and years and then one day he quit—cold turkey. He never smoked again. He replaced his cigarettes with toothpicks. At work or at home, he almost always had a toothpick in his mouth. Chewing a toothpick is a neutral habit. He replaced a very bad habit with a neutral one.

In 2 Timothy 2:22, Paul writes, *"Flee the evil desires of youth, and pursue righteousness, faith, love and peace, along with those who call on the Lord out of a pure heart."* Notice what Paul says: *"Flee…and pursue."* When you give up something bad, replace it with something good. When you give up something, it creates a vacuum. If you don't replace a bad habit with something good, then more than likely it will return.

Habit Breaker #6: Share Your Decision with a Friend

When you study the success of twelve-step recovery groups like Alcoholics Anonymous, you see that part of the reason for their success is their mentorship program. Mentorship programs provide accountability. When you need help, someone will be there to help you. Find a trusted friend who will hold you accountable to the changes that you have decided to make.

Habit Breaker #7: Powerfully Affirm Your New Habit: Colossians 3:16

"Let the word of Christ dwell in you richly as you teach and admonish one another with all wisdom, and as you sing psalms, hymns and spiritual songs with gratitude in your hearts to God."

Affirmations are like super-charged nitro. They can propel you to greatness. In Kung Fu, we constantly encourage each other with positive words.

Throughout class, students yell out phrases like:

- "Yes, I can!"
- "Winners never quit. And quitters never win."
- "I will persist until I succeed."
- "What's our goal? Black sash excellence."
- "Who motivates the motivator? The motivator."
- "Keep your eyes on the prize."

We keep these phrases in front of us to make sure that we don't give up. Encouraging each other with positive phrases causes us to push harder. This is what powerful, positive affirmations can do for you as well.

Write down affirmations and keep them close at hand. I have a notebook that I fill with them. Some of the affirmations are scriptures, and some come from personal development books. Some are affirmations that I hear on television or around the Kung Fu Academy. I keep these close so that they will inspire me.

My final encouragement to you concerning affirmations is: Don't be proud; say them out loud. When you say something out loud, you hear it twice. You hear it in your mind, and you hear it with your ears. Plus, if someone else hears you saying it, it will inspire the other person and inspire you to live up to what you just said. So, don't be proud; say it out loud.

Habit Breaker #8: Visualize the Changes

A vivid mental picture is worth a thousand words.[309]
—James E. Loehr, author of *Toughness Training for Life*

Everything around you was created twice. It was first created in the mind: It was visualized. Then it was created in the physical world: It was actualized.

Visualization is a key ingredient in the creation process. Stephen R. Covey writes, "The first creation, vision, is the beginning of the process of reinventing oneself or of an organization reinventing itself. It represents desire, dreams, hopes, goals, and plans."[310]

Visualization doesn't happen without vision. You have to be able to see where you want to go. Your vision will allow you to focus on your destination instead of your obstacles. It will allow you to see where you want to go and show you how to get there.

To be a success, you have to begin by visualizing your success. If you can't see it, then it won't happen. But when you can see it, then you can achieve it. Whatever you focus on in life, you become. If you see yourself as a winner, then you will become a winner. You will achieve what you set your mind to accomplish. I've heard Sifu Karl Romain say, "Anything the mind of man is able to conceive, man is able to achieve."

A study was performed to show the importance of visualization. One group of athletes practiced without any visualization techniques. Another group only used visualization techniques and did not practice. A third group practiced and used visualization techniques. Obviously, the group that practiced and used visualization performed the best and grew the most. But what proved interesting between the other two groups was that the group that only used visualization techniques performed better than the group that practiced but did not use visualization techniques. That is the power of our gift of imagination. That is the power of visualization.

Another study was performed on violin students to see how visualization helped them learn to play music. Brain sensors were used to measure which parts of their brains were stimulated as they learned new pieces of music. The studies demonstrated that the exact same parts of the brain were stimulated when the violin student visualized playing the violin as when the student actually played the violin. To the human brain, visualizing something is as real as physically experiencing it.

To practice visualization takes deliberate action. You have to take the time to focus on what you want to accomplish. You have to stop what you are doing and visualize where you want to go and what you want to be. You have to condition your mind toward visualization.

See yourself as a person worthy of honor. See yourself receiving awards for your humanitarianism and your benefit to society. Look at yourself with respect. If you don't respect yourself, then why should anyone else show you respect? Visualize yourself as the person you want to be. Now go out and live up to that vision.

Habit Breaker #9: Reward Yourself: 2 Timothy 4:6–8

In 2 Timothy 4:6–8, Paul writes to his young intern and lets Timothy know how excited he is at the expectation of receiving his reward in heaven. Paul writes:

> For I am already being poured out like a drink offering, and the time for my departure is near. I have fought the good fight, I have finished the race, I have kept the faith. Now there is in store for me the crown of righteousness, which the Lord, the righteous Judge, will award to me on that day—and not only to me, but also to all who have longed for his appearing.

When you work hard and succeed in breaking a bad habit, reward yourself for a job well done. Buy yourself a gift. Throw yourself a party. Celebrate. Write thank-you notes to people who encouraged you or who held you accountable along the way. Don't forget to thank God. And, don't forget to thank yourself.

Keep this thought in mind as a constant reminder of the importance of developing spiritual habits:

> Sow a thought, reap an action.
> Sow an action, reap a habit.
> Sow a habit, reap a character.
> Sow a character, reap a DESTINY.

Dearest Father,

Without you, I am nothing. I desperately want to be like Jesus. Help me to develop spiritual habits that will make me become more like him. First, I need to let go of some habits that have held me back. Help me to identify these bad habits and give me the power to change them.

In Your Son's Name,
Amen

Bibliography

Abbott, T. K. *A Critical and Exegetical Commentary on the Epistles to the Ephesians and to the Colossians. International Critical Commentary.* Edinburgh: T&T Clark, 1897.

Anders, M. Vol. 8: *Galatians-Colossians. Holman New Testament Commentary;* Holman Reference (348). Nashville: Broadman & Holman Publishers, 1999.

Barclay, William. *The Letters to Philippians, Colossians, and Thessalonians, The Daily Bible Study Series.* Third Edition. Philadelphia: Westminster John Knox Press, 2003.

Barry, Alfred. "The Epistle to the Colossians." In *Ellicott's Commentary on the Whole Bible.* Reprint (8 vols. in 4). Grand Rapids: Zondervan Publishing House, 1959.

Barth, Markus, and Helmut Blanke. Colossians: *A New Translation with Introduction and Commentary. Anchor Bible,* 34B. New York: Doubleday, 1994.

Bruce, F.F. *The Epistles to the Colossians, to Philemon, and to the Ephesians. The New International Commentary.* Grand Rapids: Eerdmans, 1984.

Calvin, John. *The Epistles of Paul the Apostle to the Galatians, Ephesians, Philippians and Colossians.* Grand Rapids: Eerdmans, 1965.

Carson, Herbert M. *The Epistle of Paul to the Colossians and Philemon. The Tyndale New Testament Commentaries.* Grand Rapids: Wm. B. Eerdmans Publishing Co., 1960.

Dunn, James D.G. *The Epistles to the Colossians and to Philemon: A Commentary on the Greek Text. The New International Greek Testament Commentary.* Grand Rapids, MI: William B. Eerdmans Publishing Co., 1996.

Erdman, Charles R. *The Epistles of Paul to the Colossians and to Philemon.* Philadelphia: Westminster Press, 1967.

Garland, David E. *Colossians and Philemon. New International Version Application Commentary.* Grand Rapids: Zondervan, 1998.

Geisler, Norman L. "Colossians." *The Bible Knowledge Commentary: An Exposition of the Scriptures.* J. F.Walvoord, R. B. Zuck, & Dallas Theological Seminary. Wheaton, IL: Victor Books, 1985.

Gorday, Peter, ed. *Colossians, 1–2 Thessalonians, 1–2 Timothy, Titus, Philemon.* Ancient Christian Commentary on Scripture. Downers Grove, IL: InterVarsity, 2000.

Gromacki, Robert G. *Stand Perfect in Wisdom: An Exposition of Colossians and Philemon.* Grand Rapids: Baker Book House, 1981.

Harris, Murray J. *Colossians and Philemon.* Exegetical Guide to the Greek New Testament. Grand Rapids: Eerdmans, 1991.

Hay, David M. *Colossians.* Abington New Testament Commentary. Nashville: Abingdon, 2000.

Hendriksen, William and S.J. Kistemaker. Vol. 6: *Exposition of Colossians and Philemon. New Testament Commentary.* Grand Rapids: Baker Book House, 2001.

Houlden, J. L. *Paul's Letters from Prison. Pelican New Testament Commentaries.* London: SCM, 1977.

Kent, Homer A., Jr. *Treasure of Wisdom.* Grand Rapids: Baker Book House, 1978.

Lightfoot, J. B. *Saint Paul's Epistles to the Colossians and to Philemon.* London: Macmillan, 1897. Reprint, Grand Rapids: Zondervan, 1971.

Lohse, Eduard. *Colossians and Philemon.* Hermeneia. Philadelphia: Fortress, 1971.

Lucas, R. C. *The Message of Colossians and Philemon: Fullness and Freedom. The Bible Speaks Today.* Downers Grove, IL: Inter-Varsity, 1980.

Martin, Ernest D. *Colossians, Philemon. Believers Church Bible Commentary.* Scottdale, PA: Herald Press, 1993.

Martin, Ralph P. *Colossians and Philemon. New Century Bible Commentary.* Grand Rapids: Eerdmans, 1973.

_____. *Ephesians, Colossians, and Philemon. Interpretation Bible Commentary.* Atlanta: John Knox, 1991.

Melick, Richard R. (2001). Vol. 32: *Philippians, Colossians, Philemon. Logos Library System; The New American Commentary* (160–162). Nashville: Broadman & Holman Publishers.

Meyer, H.A.W. *Critical and Exegetical Handbook to the Epistles to the Philippians, Colossians and to Philemon.* Winona Lake, IN: Alpha, 1979.

Moule, C.F.D. *The Epistles of Paul the Apostle to the Colossians and Philemon.* Cambridge: University Press, 1977.

O'Brien, P. *Colossians, Philemon. Word Biblical Commentary.* Waco: Word, 1982.

Peake, A.S. "The Epistle to the Colossians." In *The Expositor's Greek Testament,* vol. 3. Grand Rapids: Wm. B. Eerdmans Publishing Co., 1951.

Schweizer, Eduard. *The Letter to the Colossians: A Commentary.* Minneapolis: Augsburg, 1982.

Simpson, E.K., and Bruce, F.F. *Commentary on the Epistles to the Ephesians and the Colossians. The New International Commentary on the New Testament.* Grand Rapids: Wm. B. Eerdmans Publishing Co., 1957.

Thomas, W.H. Griffith. *Studies in Colossians and Philemon.* Grand Rapids: Baker Book House, 1973.

Thompson, Marianne Meye. *Colossians and Philemon.* The Two Horizons New Testament Commentary. Grand Rapids: Eerdmans, 2005.

Vaughan, Curtis. "Colossians." In *The Expositor's Bible Commentary,* vol. 11. Grand Rapids: Zondervan Publishing House, 1978.

_____. *Colossians: Bible Study Commentary.* Grand Rapids: Zondervan Publishing House, 1973.

Wall, Robert W. *Colossians and Philemon. InterVarsity Press New Testament Commentary.* Downers Grove, IL.: InterVarsity, 1993.

Wiersbe, Warren W. *Be Complete.* Wheaton, IL.: Scripture Press Publications, Victor Books, 1981.

Wilson, R. A *Critical and Exegetical Commentary on Colossians and Philemon. International Critical Commentary.* Edinburgh: T&T Clark, 2005.

Wright, N.T. *The Epistles of Paul to the Colossians and to Philemon. Tyndale New Testament Commentary.* Grand Rapids, MI: InterVarsity Press, 1993.

End Notes

1. K. Aland, M. Black, C.M. Martini, B.M. Metzger, M. Robinson, and A. Wikgren, *The Greek New Testament, Fourth Revised Edition* (with Morphology) (Stuttgart: Deutsche Bibelgesellschaft, 1993, 2006).

2. *The Holy Bible: New International Version* (Grand Rapids: Zondervan, 1984). This edition of the Greek text is used throughout this book.

3. William Barclay, *The Letters to Philippians, Colossians, and Thessalonians, The Daily Bible Study Series,* Third Edition (Philadelphia: Westminster John Knox Press, 2003).

4. Ernest D. Martin, *Colossians, Philemon,* Believers Church Bible Commentary (Scottdale, PA: Herald Press), 18–19.

5. Douglas J. Moo, *The Letters to the Colossians and to Philemon, The Pillar New Testament Commentary* (Grand Rapids: William B. Eerdmans, 2008), 33.

6. Richard R. Melick, *Philippians Colossians, Philemon* (electronic ed.), Logos Library System; *The New American Commentary,* Vol. 32 (Nashville: Broadman & Holman Publishers, 2001), 160–162.

7. Donald Guthrie, *Introduction to the New Testament* (Downers Grove, IL: IVP Academic, 1990).

8. If you are interested in a full discussion on the issues of authorship, then see D.J. Moo's excellent commentary, *The Letters to the Colossians and to Philemon,* The Pillar New Testament Commentary (27) (Grand Rapids: William B. Eerdmans Publishing Company, 2008). Moo concludes his analysis of the authorship of the book with this statement: "For we are not convinced that the arguments against the Pauline authorship of Colossians are finally very convincing. As an authentic letter of Paul (and so recognized by the earliest Christians), Colossians richly deserves its place in the Christian canon" (p. 40).

9. Colossae is spelled both as "Colossae" and "Colosse." I prefer "Colossae" and use this spelling throughout the text of this book. However, in quotes from other authors, you might see "Colosse." For example, the NIV 1984 uses "Colosse."

10. J. B. Lightfoot, *Saint Paul's Epistles to the Colossians and to Philemon* (London: Macmillan, 1897. Reprint, Grand Rapids: Zondervan, 1971), 6.

11. www.google.com/imgres?imgurl=http://oneyearbibleimages.com/colossae.

12. Melick, 163.

13. William Hendriksen and S.J. Kistemaker, Vol. 6: *Exposition of Colossians and Philemon, New Testament Commentary* (Grand Rapids: Baker Book House, 2001), 10.

14. Martin, 20.

15. Ibid., 22.

16. Peter T. O'Brien, Vol 44: *Colossians-Philemon,* Word Biblical Commentary (Dallas: Word, Incorporated, 2002), xxviii.

17. Martin, 23.

18. Moo, 41.

19. Ibid., 42.

20. Ibid., 27.

21. Melick, 162.

22. William Barclay, *The Letters to Philippians, Colossians, and Thessalonians,* The Daily Bible Study Series. Third Edition (Philadelphia: Westminster John Knox Press, 2003).

23. Max Anders uses the stories of Odysseus, Orpheus, and the sirens' song to illustrate the beguiling nature of false doctrine.

24. Melick, 173.

25. Moo, 53.

26. Melick, 180.

27. O'Brien, xxxii.

28. For more information see O'Brien, page xxxiv.

29. F.F. Bruce, *The Epistles to the Colossians, to Philemon, and to the Ephesians,* The New International Commentary (Grand Rapids: Eerdmans, 1984).

30. Moo, 49.

31. Ibid., 70.

32. Ibid., 67.

33. These verses are taken from the New International Version, 1984.

34. Aland et al.

35. This translation is by G. Steve Kinnard. I like to call this the GSKV. I will begin each section by giving my translation of the Greek text.

36. M.D. Dunnam and L.J. Ogilvie, Vol. 31: *Galatians/Ephesian/Philippians/Colossians/ Philemon,* The Preacher's Commentary Series (Nashville, TN: Thomas Nelson Inc., 1982), 327–328.

37. R.G. Bratcher and E.A. Nida, *A Handbook on Paul's Letters to the Colossians and to Philemon, Helps for Translators*; UBS Handbook Series (3–4) (New York: United Bible Societies, 1993).

38. Moo, 75.

39. O'Brien, 2.

40. Martin, 30.

41. C.F.D. Moule, *The Cambridge Greek New Testament: The Epistles to the Colossians and to Philemon* (Cambridge: Cambridge University Press, 1957), 45.

42. Martin, 31.

43. O'Brien, 5.

44. Bratcher and Nida, 6.

45. Ibid., 7.

46. Melick, 193–194.

47. O'Brien, 9.

48. Moo, 83.

49. See James D.G. Dunn, *The Epistles to the Colossians and to Philemon: A Commentary on the Greek Text.* New International Greek Testament Commentary (Grand Rapids: William B. Eerdmans Publishing; Carlisle, UK: Paternoster Press, 1996), 55.

50. Hendriksen and Kistemaker, 46.

51. Melick, 194.

52. Dunn, 56.

53. Hendriksen and Kistemaker, 47.

54 J.F. Walvoord, R.B. Zuck, and Dallas Theological Seminary, "Col 1:5," *The Bible Knowledge Commentary: An Exposition of the Scriptures* (Wheaton, IL: Victor Books, 1985).

55. Bratcher and Nida, 9.

56. Melick, 196.

57. Dunn, 58.

58. Max Anders, Vol. 8: *Galatians–Colossians.* Holman New Testament Commentary; Holman Reference, (Nashville: Broadman & Holman Publishers, 1999), 278.

59. http://www.brainyquote.com/quotes/authors/v/viktor_e_frankl. html#P3e9BiR4oRM813iP.99

60. Hendriksen and Kistemaker, 49.

61. http://www.merriam-webster.com/medical/distraction

62. Ibid.

63. Moo, 83.

64. Ibid.

65. Bratcher and Nida, 12.

66. Anders 279.

67. Dunn, 63.

68. Anders 280.

69. O'Brien, 15.

70. Dunnam and Ogilvie, 331.

71. Hendriksen and Kistemaker, 55.

72 O'Brien 20.

73. Dunnam and Ogilvie, 335.

74. Bratcher and Nida, 15.

75. Melick, 202.

76. Bratcher and Nida, 15.

77. O'Brien, 21.

78. Hendriksen and Kistemaker, 59.

79. Ibid.

80. O'Brien, 26.

81. Anders 293.

82. Hendriksen and Kistemaker, 63.

83. The issue of slavery in Roman culture and in the church will be discussed at the end of Colossians 3.

84. Anders 294–295.

85. Quoted from Hendriksen and Kistemaker, 63.

86. Anders 282.

87. No independent copy of this hymn has been found outside Colossians. The idea that it existed outside of Colossians and was not composed by Paul is a theory.

88. Martin, 30.

89. Anders 282.

90. Dunnam and Ogilvie, 343.

91. See 1 Kings 17:17–24.

92. Moo, 121.

93. Ibid, 123.

94. O'Brien 47.

95. Moo, 125–126.

96. Ibid., 129.

97. O'Brien 53.

98. Moo, 136–137.

99. George Santayana, *Reason in Common Sense,* Volume 1 of *The Life of Reason* (1905). In the public domain.

100. I don't often use the word "wow" in my writing, and you will rarely find an exclamation point in my books. But Colossians 1:22 deserves both a "Wow" and an exclamation point.

101. O'Brien, 68.

102. Words: Charles Wesley, 1739; Music: Thomas Campbell, 1835. In the public domain.

103. Found at http://donbaronsermons.aaapoe.net/cbsermon015.html

104. Moo, 143.

105. Ibid., 144.

106. O'Brien, 69–70.

107. *The Lion King*, screenplay by Irene Mecchi, Jonathan Roberts, and Linda Woolverton, directed by Roger Allers and Rob Minkoff (The Walt Disney Company, 1994).

108. Moo, 148. Moo cites Dunn, 128; Pokorný, 108.

109. Anders, 285.

110. O'Brien, 75.

111. Melick, 238.

112. Hendriksen and Kistemaker, 87.

113. Martin, 90.

114. O'Brien, 79.

115. John 10:10.

116. O'Brien, 82.

117. Martin, 92.

118. O'Brien, 85.

119. Melick, 242.

120. Moo, 157.

121. *The Revised Standard Version* (Oak Harbor, WA: Logos Research Systems, Inc., 1971).

122. Henri J.M. Nouwen, *Can You Drink the Cup?* (Notre Dame Indiana: Ave Marie Press, 1996), 93.

123. A few of my favorites are Richard Foster's *Celebration of Discipline,* Second Edition (San Francisco: Harper Collins, 1988); Terry Wardle, *The Transforming Path: A Christ-Centered Approach to Spiritual Formation* (Siloam Springs, AR: Leafwood Publishers, 2003); and Dallas Willard's *The Spirit of the Disciplines* (San Francisco: Harper & Row, 1988).

124. *The New American Standard Bible* (La Habra, CA: The Lockman Foundation, 1960, 1962, 1963, 1968, 1971,1972,1973,1975, 1977,1995).

125. Dallas Willard, "The Gospel of the Kingdom and Spiritual Formation" in *The Kingdom Life: A Practical Theology of Discipleship and Spiritual Formation,* General Editor Alan Andrews (Colorado Springs, CO: NavPress, 2010).

126. Keith Meyer, "Whole Life Transformation" in *The Kingdom Life: A Practical Theology of Discipleship and Spiritual Formation,* General Editor Alan Andrews (Colorado Springs, CO: NavPress, 2010).

127. Moo, 161.

128. O'Brien, 88.

129. Hendriksen and Kistemaker, 92.

130. Melick, 242.

131. Hendriksen and Kistemaker, 92.

132. Ibid., 93.

133. Martin, 94.

134. Dunn, 127.

135. Hendriksen and Kistemaker, 94.

136. Ibid., 104.

137. Moo, 163.

138. Anders, 301–302.

139. Hendriksen and Kistemaker, 102.

140. Melick, 242.

141. Martin, 96.

142. Moo, 65.

143. Dunn, 130.

144. Moo, 67.

145. Ibid., 69.

146. Ibid., 70.

147. When someone from Sawdust, Tennessee passed away, the local radio broadcaster on WKRM would say, "After a long illness, Mr. So-and-So died last night, and he will be buried tomorrow in Sawdust."

148. Moo, 72; ESV, *English Standard Version;* NASB, *New American Standard Bible* (rev. ed.).

149. Dunn, 134.

150. O'Brien, 99.

151. Anders, 286.

152. Ibid., 300.

153. Dunn, 138.

154. Moo, 77–178.

155. O'Brien, 104–105.

156. Moo, 77–178.

157. Anders, 304.

158. Not for nothing, but if you haven't seen the movie *Gandhi*, starring Ben Kingsley, then you are missing out on one of the greatest movies ever made.

159. Hendriksen and Kistemaker, 107.

160. Dunn, 142.

161. Moo, 81.

162. Melick, 248.

163. Ibid., 250–251.

164. Anders, 304–305.

165. Moo, 85.

166. Ibid., 87.

167. Hendriksen and Kistemaker, 109.

168. Martin, 109–110.

169. Melick, 255.

170. Hendriksen and Kistemaker, 111.

171. Melick, 255.

172. Anders, 315–317.

173. Moo, 87.

174. Hendriksen and Kistemaker, 114–115.

175. Dunnam and Ogilvie, 373.

176. Melick, 259.

177. Ibid., 260.

178. Moo, 202.

179. Ibid.

180. Hendriksen and Kistemaker, 117.

181. Martin, 125. The bold for emphasis is from Martin.

182. Hendriksen and Kistemaker, 120.

183. Nouwen, 27.

184. Ibid.

185. Martin, 117.

186. Hendriksen and Kistemaker, 113.

187. Anders, 308.

188. Moo, 223.

189. Anders, 309.

190. Melick, 271.

191. Moo, 227.

192. Hendriksen and Kistemaker, 128.

193. Melick, 273.

194. Moo, 234.

195. Hendriksen and Kistemaker, 131.

196. Moo, 237.

197. The tools of asceticism have value when practiced for the right reason and in the proper manner. We know that Jesus practiced fasting. When practiced in the right way, fasting can help us draw near to God and purify our hearts.

198. Melick, 279.

199. Anders, 310–311.

200. Ibid., 325.

201. From Anders, 324.

202. Anders, 326.

203. Moo, 244.

204. Martin, 133.

205. Ibid., 139.

206. Ibid., 140.

207. I co-authored a book with Sifu Romain entitled *The Shaolin Athlete*.

208. Anders, 326.

209. Moo, 246.

210. Martin, 138.

211. As found in Martin, 142.

212. Moo, 249.

213. Anders, 327–328.

214. Melick, 285.

215. Ibid., 285.

216. Anders, 328.

217. Martin, 168–169.

218. W.F. Arndt, F.W. Danker, and W. Bauer, *A Greek-English Lexicon of the New Testament and Other Early Christian Literature,* 3rd ed. (Chicago: University of Chicago Press, 2000), 34.

219. Hendriksen and Kistemaker, 146.

220. Arndt et al., 824.

221. Christian perfectionism is the belief that the Christian can mature to the point where he or she lives a sinless (perfect) life. The reformed theology of John Calvin teaches this doctrine. There are many varieties of it. One variation says that we become perfect, not because we are sinless, but because Christ makes us perfect. To me, that is a very different position

from that of the person who says a person can live a sinless life. Paul was not a Christian perfectionist in the first sense. But in the second sense, he did believe that we are made perfect (complete/mature) in Christ.

222. Moo, 264.

223. Arndt et al., 461.

224. Ibid., 29.

225. Dunnam and Ogilvie, 375.

226. Moo, 266.

227. Martir, 152.

228. Melick, 295.

229. Martir, 153.

230. Theodore H. Robinson, *Prophecy and the Prophets in Ancient Israel* (New York: Charles Scribner's Sons, 1923), 104.

231. Moo, 275.

232. Barclay, 188.

233. Melick, 299.

234. Martir, 157.

235. Arndt et al., 612.

236. Martir, 158.

237. Arndt et al., 78.

238. Dunnam and Ogilvie, 380.

239. Melick, 300.

240. Arndt et al., 1078.

241. Dunnam and Ogilvie, 380.

242. Moo, 280.

243. Ibid., 283.

244. Arndt et al., 183.

245. Moo, 284.

246. Hendriksen and Kistemaker, 160.

247. Melick, 303.

248. Ibid., 304.

249. Moo, 289.

250. Arndt et al., 1027.

251. James 5:17.

252. Melick, 304.

253. Hendriksen and Kistemaker, 166–168.

254. Martir, 183.

255. Dunnam and Ogilvie, 386.

256. *New English Bible* (Oxford Univer. Press, Cambridge University Press, 1961, 1970).

257. *New Revised Standard Version* (Iowa Falls, IA: World Bible Publishers, 1997)

258. Melick, 311.

259. Ibid., 312.

260. Moo, 302–303.

261. Melick, 313.

262. Including my translation.

263. Dunn 249.

264. Melick, 314.

265. Moo, 306.

266. John and Karen Louis, *Good Enough Parenting* (Singapore: Louis Counselling & Training Services Pte. Ltd., [n.d.]).

267. Ibid., 46.

268. Ibid., 43.

269. Melick, 316.

270. Ibid., 315–316.

271. Dunn, 246.

272. Martin, 185.

273. Dunn, 255.

274. Martin, 187.

275. Dunn, 257.

276. Hendriksen and Kistemaker, 175.

277. Melick, 319.

278. Moo, 316.

279. Martin, 194.

280. Melick, 320.

281. Arndt et al., 881.

282. O'Brien, 237.

283. C. S. Lewis, *The Joyful Christian,* (New York: Macmillan Publishing Co., 1977), 88–89.

284. Dunn, 262.

285. O'Brien, 236.

286. Arndt et al., 1048.

287. O'Brien, 241.

288. Ibid., 241.

289. Dunn, , 266.

290. Martin, 200.

291. See O'Brien, 241, for a more detailed discussion of this point.

292. Dunn, 272.

293. 2 Timothy 4:11

294. Moo, 339.

295. Martin, 213.

296. Dunn, 278.

297. Ibid., 281.

298. Arndt et al., 852.

299. Anders, 351.

300. O'Brien, 256–257.

301. Martin, 216.

302. Dunn, 286.

303. Martin, 219–220.

304. "It's the Real Thing" Coca-Cola jingle by Bill Backer, 1969.

305. "I'd Like to Teach the World to Sing (In Perfect Harmony)," performed by The Hillside Singers and by The Seekers, was based on the Coca-Cola jingle, "Buy the World a Coke" by Bill Backer, Billy Davis, Roger Cook, and Roger Greenaway, 1971.

306. Martin, 227–228.

307. Hendriksen and Kistemaker, 5.

308. Stephen R. Covey, *The 7 Habits of Highly Effective People* (New York: Free Press, 1989), 61.

309. James E. Loehr, *Toughness Training For Life* (New York: Plume, 1993), 193.

310. Stephen R. Covey, *The 8th Habit: From Effectiveness to Greatness* (New York: Free Press, 2004), 70.

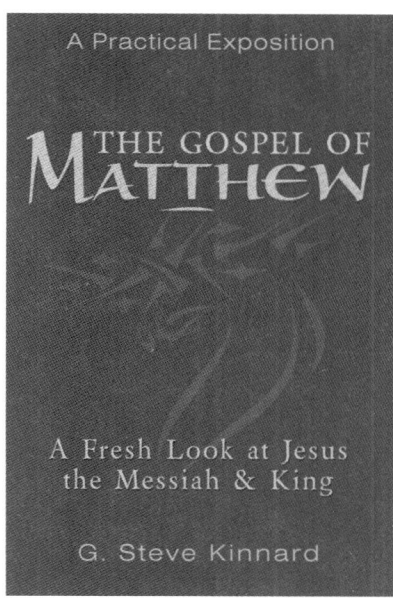

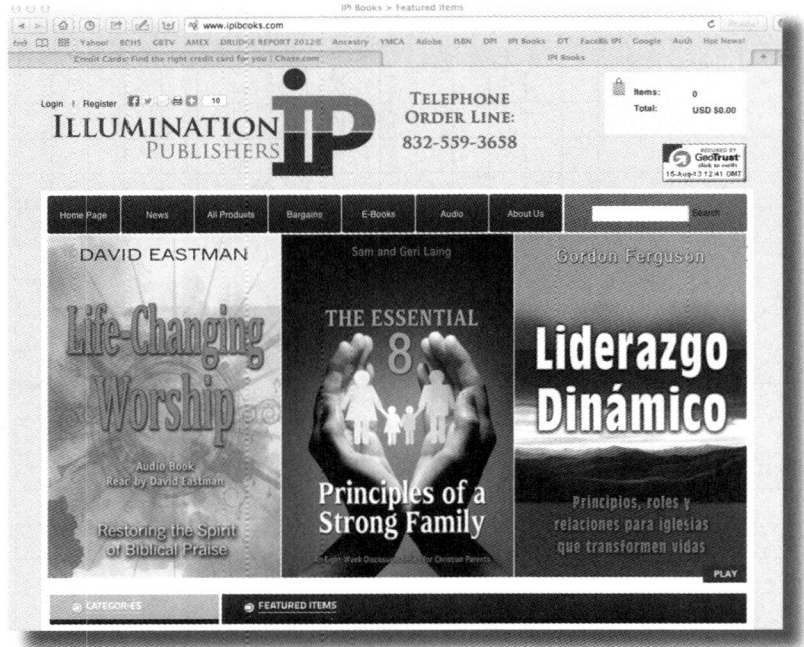

www.ipibooks.com